Cinderella Boys

Cinderella Boys

The Forgotten RAF Force that
Won the Battle of the Atlantic

LEO McKINSTRY

JOHN MURRAY

First published in Great Britain in 2023 by John Murray (Publishers)
An Hachette UK company

I

Copyright © Leo McKinstry 2023

A CIP catalogue record for this title is available from the British Library

Hardback ISBN 978-1-529-31936-1
Trade Paperback ISBN 978-1-529-31934-7
eBook ISBN 978-1-529-31938-5

Typeset in Bembo MT by Hewer Text UK Ltd, Edinburgh
Printed and bound in Great Britain by Clays Ltd, Elcograf S.p.A.

John Murray policy is to use papers that are natural, renewable and recyclable products and
made from wood grown in sustainable forests. The logging and manufacturing processes
are expected to conform to the environmental regulations of the country of origin.

John Murray (Publishers)
Carmelite House
50 Victoria Embankment
London EC4Y oDZ

www.johnmurraypress.co.uk

This book is dedicated to my dear brother Jason,
despite his antipathy to most things maritime

Contents

Introduction: Valour

BENEATH THE CLEAR blue sky, the Mediterranean was calm as the twin-engined RAF Hudson began the search for its prey, flying steadily at an altitude of 7,000 feet. The pilot was the highly experienced New Zealander Mike Ensor, whose exceptional eyesight was matched by an intrepid spirit and aerobatic skill. Now on his sixty-sixth operation with 500 Squadron, he had taken off that day, 15 November 1942, from Gibraltar to make an anti-submarine sweep off the Algerian coast. The mission could hardly have been a more vital one, for the Germans were frantically sending naval reinforcements to the area in response to the Allied landings a week earlier, designed to drive the Axis Powers out of Africa.

Suddenly a member of Ensor's crew spotted a surfaced U-boat to the north of the plane. At once he swung the Hudson down in its direction, and the submarine soon came into his line of vision about 15 miles away, 'fully surfaced and leaving a huge white wake', as Ensor recalled.[1] He had to go on the attack immediately because the U-boat could dive within forty seconds of sighting the Hudson, which meant that Ensor had only a few minutes to get within range of his target. Coming down swiftly to sea level, he kept his eye on the enemy as he prepared to drop his depth charges. Then, in order to provide a stable platform for the assault, he drastically reduced his speed, a process helped by opening the bomb doors, which acted as air brakes. Now flying at just 150 knots and at a height of 50 feet, he focused intently on the U-boat's foredeck. 'I take a deep breath and, as with a sporting rifle, wait for my reflexes, trained by practice, to make me press the release button and let go four 250-pound Torpex high explosive depth charges in a row spaced 25 feet apart.'[2]

But immediately after he had pressed the button, Ensor sensed that something had gone badly wrong.

> There's a great whoomph and a feeling of being compressed . . . For a moment, I've no outside vision – but my instinct is to pull the nose up. The control wheel falls back uselessly into my lap – which is covered with bits of Perspex from the shattered cockpit windows.[3]

Fearful that the Hudson was about to crash, Ensor in his desperation rammed the throttles fully open and to his exhausted relief the plane began to climb. But he now faced a new problem: the rudders, ailerons and elevators had been badly damaged, with the result that the stricken Hudson was difficult to manoeuvre. The crisis soon passed, however, once Ensor hit on the creative idea to use two of the crew as a kind of human ballast, moving them around the flight deck area to give him better control. So great was the noise inside the plane, because of the smashed cockpit windows and the engines roaring at maximum revolutions, that he had to give his instructions in hand signals, but the makeshift system worked.

Even better news followed when the gunner in the rear turret told Ensor that he had seen the U-boat blow up, leaving 'bits everywhere'.[4] Yet Ensor could not relax for a moment. The next challenge for him and his crew was how to exit the Hudson while still over the sea. Not only was the plane too battered to land but it had also begun to lose height and its overworked engines could fail at any moment. Fortunately, Ensor had spotted a Royal Navy sloop 12 miles off the African coast, which improved their chances of being rescued once they bailed out, so when the Hudson was at 1,500 feet he signalled for the men to gather by the escape door. The four of them then jumped in turns from the aircraft, which soon went into a steep diving arc before it crashed into the sea. Just as he had hoped, Ensor and the rear gunner were picked up by the Navy, but tragically the other two did not survive. One suffered a fatal injury when his head struck the Hudson's fuselage as he exited the aircraft; the second plunged to his death when his parachute failed to open.

Although this remarkable incident could not be definitively explained, in Ensor's view, the devastation to his Hudson had been caused by the explosion of depth charges underneath his plane. With the attack made at such a low level, the blast from the 250-pound Torpex bombs, perhaps detonating prematurely due to a faulty fuse, would have been sufficient both to sink the U-boat and wreck the RAF aircraft. Whatever occurred, Ensor, who subsequently won the Distinguished Service Order (DSO) for his valour in the episode, showed astounding qualities of judgement, resourcefulness and leadership. Indeed, the aviation historian Dr Alfred Price wrote that his 'display of airmanship and cool-headedness can have few equals in the history of flying'.[5]

Courage such as Ensor's was central to the story of Coastal Command, which during the Second World War had the crucial tasks of protecting the Allies' sea routes, especially in the Atlantic, and weakening the Axis's shipping capacity. As a maritime nation at the heart of a vast empire, Britain's very survival depended on the maintenance of her global trade. It was a daunting duty, given the strength of the Reich, the firepower of the U-boats, the dangers of low-level flying and the harshness of environments as inhospitable as Iceland and the Outer Hebrides. Sir John Slessor, the senior RAF strategist who took charge of Coastal Command in February 1943, described how his men had to work

> hundreds of miles out in the Bay of Biscay or on the convoy routes, fighting the elements as much as the enemy, but when the tense moment came, going in undaunted at point blank range against heavy fire, knowing full well that if they were shot down into the cruel sea, their chances of survival were slender.[6]

The struggle required diligence, patience and fortitude, for the men of Coastal Command undertook long operational tours that could last up to 800 hours for crews of four-engined planes. One Wellington airman, Peter Beswick, recalled that 'virtually all the hours of your flight were over the sea. We operated as single aircraft all the time and it was pretty tiring. You were always looking down at the North Atlantic, which you knew would be bloody cold if you went down into it.'[7] The sense of isolation was also captured by Wing Commander Patrick Gibbs, who wrote of 'the lonely sea stretching all around to

3

the horizons without sight of land'.[8] Graham Harrison, a gunner in a Wellington with 612 Squadron, referred to the 'howling purgatory' of the rear turret, with the 'elevator and rudder cables jerking nakedly along the fuselage side' and a chemical toilet so primitive that 'it was a point of honour never to move the bowels in flight'.[9] Pilot I. F. B. Walters, who flew Short Sunderland flying boats from 1940, stated: 'the thing that shook me most was the risks we took with the elements. We operated from advanced bases like the Shetlands and Ireland, with very few modern aids, in weather which makes me think it was a miracle that made us survive.'[10]

Not all did survive. During the war 8,874 members of Coastal Command lost their lives and another 141 were missing in action. Peter Burden, a navigator with 206 Squadron, recalled in his unpublished memoir how his occupation made him

> very hard. I had, in under three years, become used to my colleagues being killed. Or rather they were not killed, but 'went for a Burton'. Their aircraft did not have a crash but 'had a prang'. We did not say our work was dangerous, only that 'there was very little future in it'. In Coastal Command many of our casualties were when an aircraft simply failed to return from an operation and the crew just disappeared. The sea was as cruel to airmen as it was to mariners.[11]

Among those who lost their lives was Lloyd Trigg, a pilot in 200 Squadron and another tough New Zealander, who on 11 August 1943 undertook a patrol off the West African coast from his base at Yundum, near Bathurst in the Gambia, now Banjul International Airport. It was to be his first operational sortie in a B-24 Liberator, the mighty four-engined American bomber that had recently replaced the Hudson at 200 Squadron and was transforming the capabilities of Coastal Command with its tremendous range. After eight hours' uneventful flying in the huge but unfamiliar aircraft, Trigg's crew sighted a U-boat on the surface. Just as he nosed the Liberator into position for a diving attack, the German vessel opened up with sustained anti-aircraft fire after one of its lookouts had seen the RAF bomber's approach. This was a decisive period in the maritime war when the U-boats had been instructed by the Kriegsmarine's high command to fight back on the surface against British aerial attacks instead of diving, an order buttressed by a significant increase in anti-aircraft guns. But even in the face of this barrage, which set his plane ablaze, Trigg managed to make two runs on the target, dropping some of his depth charges on either side of the vessel. By the time he turned away for the second time, the rear of the Liberator was engulfed in flames. At this point Trigg could have broken off the attack and made a forced landing in the sea, but he did not hesitate to come in again for a third run, flying at just 50 feet over the U-boat as shells hit the underside of the burning Liberator. Now doomed, the aircraft managed to release the remainder of the depth charges before it staggered a short further distance in the air, then crashed into the ocean. Trigg and all his crew perished beneath the waves. At the same time, having reached the requisite depth, the charges exploded around the German submarine with devastating effect. As the U-boat sank, a few of its crew, including the captain, Klemens Schamong, managed to escape and make it to the Liberator's rubber dinghy, which had broken free from the wreckage and was floating nearby. The next day they were picked up by a Royal Navy corvette sent to the scene after the dinghy was spotted by an RAF plane, which had presumed it contained survivors from the Liberator. The rescue, even if it was based on a misapprehension, had one posthumous benefit. Having taken Captain Schamong into captivity, the British authorities were so impressed by his testimony about the attack that they awarded Trigg the Victoria Cross (VC), the only time in history that the medal was given solely on the evidence of an enemy combatant. In his citation Schamong stated that Trigg's exploit had been one of 'grim determination and high courage',[12] while in a letter written in 1961 he said that Trigg 'must have been a very brave man. I think that he could have saved his life. That he did not do so in spite of his plane already being mortally wounded, and in spite of our well-aimed fire, has my highest admiration.'[13]

Yet for all the extraordinary, selfless heroism of figures like Ensor and Trigg, direct engagements with the enemy were sporadic rather than regular in the saga of Coastal Command. The organization's war was mainly one of attrition. There were no titanic aerial clashes like Fighter Command fought in the Battle of Britain, no massed frontal incursions like Bomber Command's raids on Hamburg or Dresden.

For much of the time, the work of Coastal Command was solitary and monotonous. Frustration and fatigue were prime characteristics. The fight was sometimes more against sleep than the enemy.

> For most people, the Battle of the Atlantic meant getting up at some ghastly hour, going out in the pouring rain, waiting for your aircraft to be made serviceable, flying out into the Atlantic in foul weather, and coming back twelve hours later to somewhere like Ballykelly, with your heart in your mouth . . .

So remembered Wilfrid Oulton, who served in Coastal Command with distinction throughout the war.[14] Frank Tudor, who before the war had been a butcher's assistant in Birkenhead, said of his sorties over the Bay of Biscay as a wireless operator and gunner:

> On occasions, we took off at two or three in the morning in the dark. We would sometimes have to fly 200 or 300 feet above the waves, which was hard going for the pilot. There was nothing to see, flying low over the water, looking for U-boats. Searching, searching, searching. All the time on these searches we saw only one boat, which we attacked with depth charges, but I could not say we sank it.[15]

It was partly the enervating nature of these routines that meant, despite the importance of its role, Coastal Command neither thrilled the wartime British public nor received the credit it deserved for its role in the ultimate victory. Hector Bolitho, the RAF intelligence officer who edited the in-house journal *Coastal Command Review*, wrote in his diary for May 1944 that the branch 'has done its rather dull job without much recognition or appreciation. There has been no romance in the lonely vigils over the Atlantic, nothing to startle the public imagination.'[16] The Command was widely seen as less exciting than Fighter Command, less pivotal than Bomber Command to the war against Germany, an attitude that shines through the memoir of Polish pilot Josef F. Jaworzyn who flew with 304 Squadron but often thought of how to 'escape the clutches of Coastal Command' and move to fighters. Recounting his first operational flight in 1942 in a Wellington, he wrote,

Stuck in the middle of the Bay of Biscay on a cloudless day, broiling in the sun, and so far in five hours all we had done was change courses and hear who was getting shot down and where. With an imagination like mine there was too much time to think in this kind of flying. I lit an umpteenth cigarette, poured another cup of coffee.[17]

One pilot who succeeded in transferring from Coastal to Fighter Command was Squadron Leader Joe Bodien. In a letter to his sister in November 1940, he set out his attitude:

There have been several things happen in the last two years that make it imperative I get right at those Huns. It's not hate, but a combination of little incidents that have affected me. Coastal Command was OK at times but the fights were too few and far between. I cannot explain why but I must be on fighters and that's just where it ends.[18]

Until the later part of the war, the sense of disdain towards Coastal Command was mirrored at the highest ranks in government and the Air Ministry. A culture of neglect and indifference prevailed, which meant that it was known by some senior officers and politicians as the 'Cinderella Service'. That term, reflecting the belief that the Command was denied the necessary aircraft, equipment and personnel for its job, was first used by the Admiralty in November 1940 during a fierce debate within the government over the direction of air strategy. Ever since its creation in 1918 under Hugh Trenchard, the RAF had regarded bombing as its central purpose, indeed, the very justification for its existence. It was an outlook largely shared by Churchill, who told Cabinet colleagues that 'the bomber offensive should have the first place in our war effort'.[19] This disregard of Coastal Command's needs created deep friction within the RAF, particularly from the organization's chiefs in the opening years of the war.

Just as vociferous was the Admiralty, which before the war had shown little interest in aircraft as a weapon against shipping or the submarine. But the lethal effectiveness of the Kriegsmarine's U-boat wolf packs, along with the Reich's control of most of the waters around northern Europe after the fall of France, quickly changed that. Naval chiefs soon saw that air co-operation was a key element of Britain's maritime defences and were exasperated that the Air Ministry did not appear to accept this.

The indignation of the Admiralty over the RAF's policy on Coastal Command was seen at its fiercest in two political clashes that convulsed the government during the darkest years of the conflict, when Britain's fate still hung in the balance. Both involved fractious ministers, disputatious service chiefs and angry Cabinet arguments, with Churchill himself playing a leading but not always constructive part. One arose in late 1940 over operational control of the Command between the RAF and the Royal Navy. Even after an awkward settlement was reached, discord continued in a long, intense conflict over strategic priorities. Known as the Battle of the Air, the dispute reached its combustible peak in the most difficult months of the Atlantic struggle in late 1942 and early 1943.

The Battle of the Air raged across a number of flashpoints, including the provision of airborne radar, the bombing of the western French ports, the development of weaponry, the use of intelligence and the serviceability of Coastal Command's squadrons. By far the most explosive issue was the supply of very long-range aircraft, particularly the American B-24 Liberator, which had the potential to transform the Battle of the Atlantic by dramatically widening the radius of anti-submarine warfare and closing the so-called gap in the northern part of the ocean where the U-boats could operate with impunity beyond the reach of Allied aircraft. Yet Coastal Command and the Admiralty had to engage in an often vexed campaign to receive the Liberators in sufficient numbers. Writing of the high-level debates within the government, Sir Philip Joubert de la Ferté, the Command's second wartime chief, said, 'A few crumbs would be thrown to Coastal. It is almost incredible that it took months of arguments and discussion to allocate the 27 very long range aircraft for the U-boat war.'[20]

Even on this limited scale, the enhancement of Coastal Command's capabilities was keenly felt by the U-boat fleet led by the resolute Admiral Karl Dönitz, who had once said that 'the aeroplane can no more eliminate the submarine than the crow can fight the mole'.[21] Coastal Command forced him to rethink those words, especially when its new aircraft featured advanced technology, camouflage and experienced crews. In his diary for 24 June 1942, Dönitz recorded that such aircraft were now a danger, 'not only to the isolated U-boats surprised and attacked, but also to the whole method of conducting submarine warfare, which is based on mobility and operations on the surface'.[22]

In fact, by 1943 Coastal Command was fast becoming a formidable branch of the RAF. No longer an overstretched, defensive organization, it had gone on the attack. As well as the U-boats, its widening range of targets included enemy merchant shipping, coastal installations, German naval vessels and the Luftwaffe. For the first time in the war, it had the weapons to do its job effectively, from aircraft like the pugnacious Bristol Beaufighter and the versatile De Havilland Mosquito to advanced arms like rocket projectiles and heavy cannon. As the tide turned, morale was boosted. 'We all seemed to feel that now we were, at last, after many monotonous flying hours, doing something worthwhile,' wrote Jack Colman, who flew patrols over the Atlantic in 120 Squadron.[23]

With Coastal Command in the ascendancy, even home waters were not safe for the Germans. Douglas Young, a navigator with 489 Squadron, which was part of an elite, well-equipped strike force, recalled an assault by three Beaufighter squadrons on a large enemy convoy near Heligoland in July 1944. As the German anti-aircraft fire opened up, 'down we went and our four cannons burst into life with a shattering roar above the noise of our engines'. Young's Beaufighter scored a direct hit on a German vessel, which 'seemed almost to leap out of the water as we pulled out of our dive only feet above the now smoking decks. Clouds of steam and smoke, as well as streams of yellow flashes cascaded about us as we swept on just above the waves.' The Coastal Command planes left behind a spectacular scene of wreckage as they began their journey home. 'In the space of perhaps three or four minutes absolute havoc had been inflicted from the skies on that convoy. Almost every ship was belching thick clouds of oily smoke and some were already listing heavily and seemed to be turning in helpless circles.' The next day the press reported that the 'biggest German convoy of the war' had been 'smashed' by the RAF. '40 ships put to sea: not one escaped'.[24]

In February 1941 Churchill wrote to his old friend Air Secretary Sir Archie Sinclair, who was also leader of the Liberal Party,

> Anything that can help Coastal Command will be supported by me. I am of the opinion that the service has been Cinderella through the years. So if I can back you up in playing the role of The Prince, to which you are eminently suited, you will have all the shoes I can send you.[25]

The prime minister did not always live up to those words, but eventually Cinderella made it to the ball – and gave a decisive performance.

I

Reconnaissance

THERE WAS NO 'Phoney War' for Coastal Command. While stalemate prevailed for months in western Europe following Germany's invasion of Poland on 1 September 1939, the RAF's maritime wing was in action almost from the opening of the conflict. Its endeavours were given a sense of urgency by the predations of the German U-boat force led by Karl Dönitz, who fervently believed that the submarine would be the key to the Reich's victory. 'I am convinced that it is the means of inflicting decisive damage on England at her weakest point,' he wrote.[1] This outlook prompted him, just hours after Britain's declaration of war on 3 September 1939, to issue orders for his U-boats to attack Allied shipping. His edict had an immediate impact. That very evening a U-boat captained by Julius Lemp fired two torpedoes at a ship sailing off the west of Scotland, one of which exploded in her engine room and sank her. Lemp later claimed that he thought the vessel was an armed merchant cruiser or a troopship, but in fact she was the liner *Athenia* taking civilians, including Jewish refugees and evacuated children, to Canada. In the devastation of the attack ninety-eight passengers and nineteen members of the crew were killed.

The Kriegsmarine had provided a dramatic early illustration of the ruthlessness with which they would conduct the war. During September the German U-boats sank forty-eight ships, another thirty-three in October, twenty-seven in November and thirty-nine in December, bringing the total Allied merchant losses in 1939 to 509,321 tons: the toll would have been even higher if Dönitz had possessed the size of submarine armada that he had continually but forlornly demanded during the late 1930s from the Reich's high command. To his regret, he had only fifty-seven U-boats in commission at the outbreak of war, a number far short of his vision of a 300-strong fleet. Nevertheless, due in part to his dynamic leadership, it was a well-trained, highly competent force that at once put Britain on the defensive.

Coastal Command's response was energetic and determined but ineffective, as typified by Mike Ensor's encounter off the Algerian coast. Just two days after the declaration of war, Pilot Officer George Yorke of 233 Squadron, based at Leuchars in Fife, was carrying out a reconnaissance patrol over the North Sea in his Avro Anson when he thought he sighted a U-boat on the surface of the water. Flying towards his target, he released two 100-pound anti-submarine bombs and eight 20-pound Cooper bombs (the primary weapon of the Royal Flying Corps in the First World War). But the chief impact of the bombs' explosions was to riddle the underside of Yorke's plane with shrapnel, puncturing the fuel tanks. As a result they ran dry on the Anson's journey back to Leuchars, so Yorke and his crew were forced to ditch in the sea. The men survived, but on their arrival back at the station they were told that their self-destructive attack had been made not against the enemy but against HMS *Seahorse*, a Royal Navy S-class submarine, which had suffered minor damage that meant it had to return to port for repairs. Equally fruitless was an attack the same day by an Anson of 206 Squadron on a U-boat off the Dutch coast, while 5 September also saw Coastal Command's first aerial combat of the war, which ended in another Anson of 206 Squadron being shot down.

In fact, Coastal Command did not sink a single U-boat in 1939. Nor were anti-shipping operations much more successful during these early months, prompting the commander-in-chief, Sir Frederick Bowhill, to complain about 'the lack of a powerful striking force'.[2] But there was certainly no absence of diligence. In September Coastal Command spent almost 2,400 hours flying in support of convoys, 3,300 on reconnaissance and another 1,600 on anti-submarine patrols, figures that led Air Secretary Sir Kingsley Wood to tell the House of Commons that the activities of the service 'have been unremitting and strenuous in the extreme from the first day of the war'. With a flourish, the minister added, by its very nature the work is silent and normally unspectacular. It demands continuous flying over the sea in all weathers. The magnitude of the effort of Coastal Command may be judged by the fact that during the first four weeks of war, the Command flew on reconnaissance, anti-submarine and convoy patrols a distance of approximately one million miles and provided escorts for over 100 convoys.[3]

Eager to cheer on the war effort, the press took up the theme of Coastal Command's indefatigability. In an article about the Command's vast Sunderland flying boats, *Sunday Times* correspondent Virginia Coles wrote excitedly of how, 'from an English coast in the early dawn', these planes 'slip across the water and rise into the air like great flying whales, as they leave to scour the Atlantic for hundreds of miles in search of German submarines.' Coastal Command, she continued, 'is performing one of the most dramatic and daring services of the war', acting as 'watchdogs for the fleet' and keeping 'the Empire's trade routes open'.[4] In the same vein, *The Times* reported in early December that

> the shore-based aircraft of the Royal Air Force are now proving themselves capable of throwing out a defensive screen over the sea far from the coasts of Britain, and of maintaining constant daylight supervision over the movements of shipping in large tracts of the North Sea and the Atlantic Ocean.[5]

Coastal Command had neither the aircraft nor the armaments to take on the Kriegsmarine successfully or provide strong aerial defences. Too many planes were obsolete, with inadequate equipment, limited range and meagre firepower. At the start of the war the Command had just 236 planes, including 12 Vickers Wildebeests, 12 Saunders-Roe Londons and 6 Supermarine Stranraers, all of them hopelessly outdated biplanes.[6] The Wildebeest, which had entered service in 1928, was a single-engined torpedo bomber that had a radius of just 180 miles and a top speed of only 150 mph. 'To all intents and purposes it was a completely useless plane,' wrote Sir Philip Joubert de la Ferté, who had two difficult spells as commander before and during the war.[7] The unsuitability of the Wildebeest for its main purpose was exacerbated by the absence of any fighter cover in Coastal Command for its dangerous torpedo missions. More advanced were the 164 rugged Avro Anson monoplanes, which made up the backbone of Coastal Command. Having entered service in 1936, they were liked by crews because they were comfortable, steady and had few vices; 'no one was ever sick in them,' reflected Arthur Beech, a navigator with 42 Squadron.[8] Yet they were also slow, had a limited range, unable even to reach Norway, and their bomb load was 'pitifully small', to quote the liaison officer Captain Dudley Peyton-Ward.[9] Even their most modern feature, the retractable undercarriage, was cumbersome, for it could only be raised or lowered manually by winding a large handle. 'It was all a bit Heath Robinson,' recalled rear gunner Edward Nichols.[10]

Fortunately, there was a far higher level of performance from two other planes that had started to arrive in Coastal Command before the war: the American Lockheed Hudson and the Short Sunderland. Interestingly, both were military versions of successful civil airliners. The twin-engined, highly versatile all-metal Hudson, the first of a succession of impressive American aircraft in Coastal Command, was developed from the pioneering Lockheed Electra, the plane that flew Neville Chamberlain from Munich to Heston airport after the notorious Munich conference in 1938. Similarly, the huge four-engined Sunderland was derived from the luxurious Empire flying boat that served the far-flung destinations for Imperial Airways in the late 1930s.

Still, by September 1939 there were only eighteen Hudsons in Coastal Command, a reflection of the fact that the RAF's contract for 200 of the type had only been signed with Lockheed in June 1938 at a cost of £17,000 each. Described by pilot navigator Hugh Eccles as 'a grand aeroplane, really quite sophisticated', the Hudson became a mainstay of early reconnaissance and anti-submarine patrols, able to carry 1,000 pounds of bombs to a range of 1,000 nautical miles.[11] 'For a comparatively big and heavy aircraft, it is very manoeuvrable,' said the *Coastal Command Review*.[12] 'The wingspan was only nine feet more than the Anson but it could manage three and a half times more power,' recalled Jack Colman, who also highlighted one dangerous weakness. 'She had a reputation of being a bit of a bastard because the

high wing loading meant she had a vicious stall, some nasty characteristics at slow speeds and she would ground loop if you did not
watch it.'[13]

There were just two squadrons of Sunderlands, made up of twelve
aircraft in total, in service with Coastal Command at the start of the
war, but they soon proved themselves to be of a high calibre. Until
the advent of the Liberator, the type was the most capable anti-
submarine aircraft in the RAF due to its ability to carry up to two
thousand pounds of bombs or depth charges, its vast fuel capacity that
enabled it to fly for fourteen hours, its reliable Bristol Pegasus radial
engines and its bristling armament, including guns in the front turret,
the mid-upper turret, the tail and, in some makes, both sides of the
fuselage, hence its nickname of the Flying Porcupine. What so often
impressed observers was the Sunderland's size, with its height of 32
feet and its wingspan of 113 feet. As befitted a vehicle with origins as
a long-distance airliner and with a unit cost of £80,000, it was probably the most well-appointed plane in the RAF. Spread over two
decks, it had six bunk beds, a galley kitchen, a porcelain flush toilet,
a machine shop for minor in-flight repairs and spacious compart-
ments for a crew of eleven. Harry Prout, who joined the RAF in
1940 as an engineer, eulogized every aspect of the plane, even its
Pegasus power plants:

> Everyone loved the engine, the old 'Peggy'. When the plane took off,
> they used to sing a beautiful note. It was a lovely plane to fly in. I once
> flew one when the skipper said I could have a go. It was easy. The
> plane could almost fly itself. I loved the Sunderland. You went on
> board and felt at home. Because it carried quite a few crew, you were
> always in company.

Operating as a flying boat, however, could sometimes be a problem.
'If you landed a Sunderland heavily on the water, it could bounce like
a golf ball,' recalled Prout, while in 'really stormy' conditions 'you
could lose a float, no trouble at all'.[14] But there was a bigger difficulty
with the Sunderland which reflected the priorities of the government. Despite the plane's obvious qualities, production was confined
to just five a month in the early part of the war because the supremacy

of the strategic offensive against Germany meant that Shorts the manufacturer had to concentrate on the output of the four-engined Stirling bomber, which, in contrast to the flying boat, turned out to be a dismal failure.

Yet the quality of neither the Hudson nor the Sunderland could disguise the wider aircraft shortages. At one stage Sir Frederick Bowhill was so desperate that, in an attempt to deter German raiders and U-boats from British waters, he even resorted to the use of unarmed biplane Tiger Moth trainers on so-called 'scarecrow patrols', organized in six flights around the British Isles. The logic of the move could not be faulted, as Squadron Leader Tom Dudley Gordon wrote,

> To the fish, no doubt any bird looks like a cormorant and to the U-boat, any aircraft spelt danger. So Tiger Moths were pressed into service. These two-seater trainers went into operations with a grand spirit – and nothing else. Sometimes the pilots carried revolvers, more as a gesture than a weapon. But they had no bombs or machine guns.[15]

Nor did the newer planes compensate for Coastal Command's technical deficiencies. Navigation aids were poor, altimeters unreliable and radio sets rudimentary. George Bain, a wireless operator with 200 Squadron, recalled how, even on the Hudson, 'the very basic' radio receiver worked on a high-tension, 120-volts battery and a one-and-a-half volts accumulator which could be charged after each flight. The way to get Morse signals, he remembered, was to 'wet your finger and tap the ball bearing on top of the receiver and you'd hear it bleep'. Meanwhile, 'the transmitter was a huge, boxlike thing. When you switched it on, the valves would glow and illuminate the whole cockpit.'[16] Nor was the first version of air-to-surface-vessel (ASV) radar, which went into production in 1939, satisfactory, particularly against U-boats, as Squadron Leader Tony Spooner reflected,

> ASV was a very elementary form of airborne radar and it lacked the sensitivity and definition to pick up a submarine. It might find a U-boat in dead calm water but not in the Atlantic rollers. Also we

were not told how to use it because it was top secret. None of us had done a course in radar or ASV or had even been told its principles. We had to work it out for ourselves and I am sure we were not applying it correctly.[17]

Peter Burden of 206 Squadron agreed, 'The first ASV equipment was soon shown to be pretty primitive and was not nearly as reliable or easy to use as later models.'[18]

Perhaps even more serious was the impotence of Coastal Command's armoury. The standard Mark III anti-submarine (AS) bomb, weighing just 100 pounds, was a feeble weapon. In one telling friendly fire incident on 3 December 1939, an Anson of 206 Squadron erroneously attacked the British submarine HMS *Snapper*, scoring a direct hit on its conning tower with a 100-pound bomb, but the only damage inflicted was four broken electric light bulbs and some shattered crockery in the wardroom. The 250-pounder was slightly better, in that it could crack the pressure hull of a U-boat if it exploded within six feet, but it could not be carried by the Anson. Depth charges were potentially more effective, but the unmodified 250-pound naval version could not be used as an air weapon because of its tendency to break up when dropped from a height, while only the Sunderland would be able to carry the 450-pound charge, which was under development for aerial use. Similarly, the rifle-calibre .303 Browning guns used throughout Coastal Command could not penetrate the metal structures of enemy ships or submarines. 'All we could do was harass and frighten,' wrote Peyton-Ward.[19] Altogether, Coastal Command was in a sorry state in September 1939. In the words of historian Correlli Barnett, the service 'was a seabird weak on the wing, short of sight and weak of beak'.[20]

The meagre resources partly explain why Coastal Command's role was so restricted when the war began. Anti-shipping and submarine warfare were secondary duties behind its primary task of carrying out maritime reconnaissance, particularly over the North Sea where it was feared the Kriegsmarine would operate on a large scale or break out into the Atlantic. In his post-war despatch about his time in charge, Bowhill wrote with some bitterness,

My operational strength did not in any way provide a suitable striking force and the role of my command was thus largely limited to recon- naissance in the early stages, and this in many ways had to be strictly limited owing to the shortage of aircraft.[21]

Those limitations were illustrated in the simplistic and largely fruitless operations of the North Sea line patrols, where the Command's planes just followed basic parallel tracks to a set range. The concentration on reconnaissance, which in turn was fed by the institutional neglect of Coastal Command, reflected the pre-war lack of faith, within both the Air Ministry and to a lesser extent the Admiralty, in air power as a decisive factor in a maritime conflict. In one sense, this attitude was extraordinary because it ignored the lesson of the First World War where aircraft, despite being in their technological infancy, were invaluable for the Allies at sea in providing cover and serving as a deterrent. Remarkably, of the 16,000 ships that sailed in ocean convoys and the 68,000 that sailed in coastal and shorter sea convoys, just five were lost where aerial escorts had been present, even though the planes had no weapons and could effectively only act as submarine spotters. That had been enough to make the U-boats abandon British coastal waters and move further west, beyond the reach of Allied naval aircraft. Encouraged by this success, the Royal Navy wanted to use adapted long-range bombers for more extensive anti-submarine operations towards the end of the war, but in a harbinger of things to come during the Second World War, the newly created Royal Air Force, under the bullish Hugh Trenchard, sought to retain all such aircraft for the sole purpose of bombing the enemy on land.

By the late 1930s, however, the Admiralty was much less concerned about the U-boats. This was mainly because of its belief that its ASDIC device (the acronym is derived from a combination of 'sonic' and the Admiralty's Anti-Submarine Division), which had been developed after the First World War and which used sound waves to detect objects underwater, had effectively eliminated the threat. The optimism inspired by ASDIC was buttressed by a number of interna- tional treaties, including the London Naval Protocol of 1936, which formally outlawed unrestricted submarine warfare – Nazi Germany, ironically, was among the signatories to the agreement. The following year the British Naval Staff was moved to comment that 'the submarine will never again be able to present us with the problem that we were faced with in 1917'.[22] Joubert de la Ferté, Coastal Command's chief in the middle of this decade, later commented how

> it was quite fantastic that, in the light of the experiences of the 1914–1918 war, no attention was paid to the problem of attacking submarines from the air as part of our trade protection measures. It seemed at this time the Admiralty believed that U-boats no longer presented a danger to our national existence. The Air Ministry did not disagree.[23]

Indeed, such profound complacency suited the Air Staff, who were still wedded to the Trenchard doctrine of the bombing offensive. To most of them, maritime aviation was a matter of irrelevance compared to building up Bomber Command, which swallowed almost 60 per cent of the government's huge RAF expansion programme. This mentality was clearly revealed in December 1936 by a statement from Arthur Harris, then the Air Staff's deputy director of plans, later to be head of Bomber Command: 'It would be unnecessary to keep any ponderable number of aircraft either employed in or standing by for reconnaissance operations in connection with a trade defence war that might not happen.'[24]

The combined outlook of the Air Ministry and the Admiralty meant that Coastal Command was starved of investment and support. One of the reasons why the Anson had been preferred to more effective flying boats was that the Air Staff said the latter were too expensive to maintain compared to similar land-based aircraft. The same parsimony lay behind the refusal to equip Coastal Command with a dive bomber even though anti-shipping trials conducted since 1929 had shown that dive bombing was the surest way to sink a moving vessel at sea, as naval experiences in the Second World War were to prove. Ignoring the evidence from successful experiments, the Air Staff opportunistically argued that attacks on surface enemy forces were best carried out by high-altitude bombing, a claim that justified the continued priority for heavy bombers. As the military historian Professor John Buckley has pointed out, even the worthless Vickers Wildebeest 'only survived' because it 'could double up' as a general-purpose bomber and therefore could be theoretically used as part of a strategic campaign.[25]

The neglect of Coastal Command in the build up to war was in tune with the history of maritime air power in Britain, stretching back to the creation of the independent Royal Air Force in 1918 through a merger of the Royal Flying Corps and the Royal Naval Air Service. Only with reluctance did the Admiralty accept the move, which involved the transfer of almost 3,000 aircraft and 67,000 personnel to the new force. It was the start of more than two decades of friction and uneasy co-operation between the two services. Once the First World War was won, the first task of the new RAF was to preside over a massive contraction in its resources. As part of this process, the RAF's organization in 1919 was shrunk to just three commands; two of them were geographical, Northern and Southern, soon to be amalgamated under the title Inland Area, and one was functional, named Coastal Area, which took over the former RNAS infrastructure. There was not much of this; by March 1920 Coastal Area had just three squadrons while its duties were vague, loosely based on the protection of shipping, co-operation with the Navy and reconnaissance. In the climate of post-war austerity, modernization and expansion were painfully slow, and not helped by continued agitation from the Admiralty for the return of some of its aerial assets, though when the Fleet Air Arm was established in 1924 for the embryonic carrier-based force, it was placed by the government under RAF control.

Despite the creation of the Fleet Air Arm, throughout the remainder of the 1920s Coastal Area continued to struggle. By 1925 it was reduced to just eleven front-line aircraft and eighteen training planes. The beginning of the 1930s, characterized by economic crisis and demands for international disarmament, was just as difficult. Sir Arthur Longmore, who had taken command of Coastal Area in 1934, fought a continual battle to preserve his depleted force. But from that year there was a major change in government air policy, precipitated by the rise of Hitler. Wishful thinking about permanent peace gave way to greater realism about the need for strengthened armed forces, especially the RAF, through a series of ambitious schemes for growth. Not much of the additional new air funding reached Coastal Area, but the expansionist environment led in 1936 to the wholesale reform of the RAF's organization, with the creation of four new commands to replace the previous structure.

In contrast to the advent of Fighter, Bomber and Training commands, the formation of Coastal Command was the least radical step, for it involved little more than an alteration in its name from Coastal Area. Its headquarters remained at Lee-on-the-Solent in Hampshire and the commanding officer, the gregarious Australian-born Longmore, stayed in charge. But the wider RAF reorganization was hailed as the sign of a more dynamic approach. The *Daily Mail* predicted that the changes would bring 'greater speed and efficiency', adding that 'the effect of the new system will be to give the commanders-in-chief more time for the strategical, operational and training aspects of their commands'.[26] The *Daily Telegraph* argued that the new organization would help the RAF move on to a wartime footing by improvements to liaison, training and discipline, while the paper also praised the 'brilliant careers' of the four commanders, including Longmore, who was 'one of the first four Naval officers permitted by the Admiralty to learn to fly in 1911', later becoming the commandant of the RAF college at Cranwell.[27]

Longmore did not last long. Within a few weeks he had been appointed the head of the Imperial Defence College and was replaced in September 1936 by Sir Philip Joubert de la Ferté, an experienced senior officer of French heritage who had served with distinction in the First World War. Articulate and thoughtful, Joubert was immediately confronted by the reality of the small force under his command, consisting of just eight squadrons, with little prospect of significant reinforcements. The feeling in the government, he wrote, was that the British naval forces 'were so superior to those of Germany that no great importance need be attached to the supply of aircraft for air/sea operations'.[28] Joubert swiftly made one useful change to the machinery at his headquarters, however, when he set up a combined operations room to improve liaison with the Royal Navy. The move was to have a lasting impact on the work of Coastal Command during the war, when close co-operation proved vital.

But it was a much bigger, more immediate aspect of relations with the Navy which dominated the remainder of Joubert's brief, first spell in charge. In the wake of the RAF's reorganization, the Admiralty had renewed its campaign to take over maritime aviation, including not just the Fleet Air Arm but also all Coastal Command's assets. Inevitably, the RAF resisted this, so in time-honoured fashion the government set up a committee under Sir Thomas Inskip, the new defence co-ordination minister, to find a solution. A Protestant lawyer with a fine legal mind unencumbered by any experience of military or naval matters, Sir Thomas had already outraged the Air Staff by his willingness to challenge the Trenchard doctrine through his emphasis on the need for strong fighter defences. Now he came up with a compromise whereby Coastal Command would remain part of the RAF but the Fleet Air Arm would be transferred to Admiralty control. Announcing the policy in the Commons in July 1937, Prime Minister Neville Chamberlain declared that the plan represented 'a final and satisfactory settlement of a prolonged controversy which it is in the public interest to close'. But the Labour leader Clement Attlee was doubtful about this, warning that 'internecine warfare' could continue. 'If it has not been settled, it is no use pretending that it has,' he said, words that were to be borne out within little more than four years.[29]

The Inskip award, as it became known, was another blow to Coastal Command's prestige and cohesion of purpose. Soon afterwards, Joubert left to take charge of the RAF in India. He was succeeded by Sir Frederick Bowhill, an officer with natural authority, who had begun his career in the merchant navy, won the DSO in 1918 while serving with the RNAS in East Africa, and had subsequently held a string of senior positions in the RAF, most notably as the Air Staff's head of personnel. Nicknamed Ginger because of his thinning red hair and weather-beaten face, he was a figure of resourcefulness and toughness, virtues that he displayed in one incident during his naval days when he amputated a wounded seaman's leg with a butcher's knife by the light of a hurricane lamp during a storm. According to his biographer, 'his tremendous beetling eyebrows gave him a rather ferocious appearance, but behind this façade he was kindly and had a keen sense of humour'.[30] Admiration for him was not universal within the Air Force, where some saw him as a poor administrator. Sir Wilfrid Freeman, the outstanding vice chief of the

Air Staff during the war, told Air Secretary Sinclair that Bowhill was personally to blame for many of the failings in Coastal Command. 'With all his good qualities as a leader and co-operator, he is too old and is no great organizer.'[31]

For all such criticism, Bowhill at once made his mark on Coastal Command. One of his first acts was to move its headquarters from Lee-on-the-Solent to Eastbury Park near Watford, a grand mid-nineteenth-century house constructed in the Scottish Baronial style. During its chequered history before its sale to the RAF, it had variously been a private residence, a girls' boarding school and a country club with a dubious reputation and a clandestine membership that was said to include the Prince of Wales, later the Duke of Windsor. Camouflaged by trees in Eastbury's grounds, a wooden building was erected to accommodate the Combined Operations team, complete with a huge map on one wall that showed the location of aircraft and ships in British coastal waters.

From Eastbury Park, Bowhill presided over an organization that had around 10,000 personnel and was divided into four groups: No. 15 in the south-west with its headquarters in Plymouth and covering the Western Approaches; No. 16 with its headquarters at Chatham, covering the eastern part of the English Channel and the southern part of the North Sea; No. 17, based in Gosport and responsible for training; and No. 18, with its headquarters at Rosyth and covering the rest of the North Sea and waters around Scotland. Each of the group headquarters had been set up in an area with a strong naval presence to facilitate liaison between senior officers in the two services, prompting Bowhill to claim that 'the closest collaboration was maintained'.[32] The tone for this collaboration was set by Dudley Peyton-Ward, whose instinctive understanding of German naval tactics was matched by his phenomenal work ethic. A former submariner who had been compelled to leave active service because of severe arthritis, he never allowed his painful condition to undermine his indefatigability.

Yet collaboration and practicable management were not enough, as Bowhill knew. 'Throughout the period of my command, I made repeated representations to the Air Ministry for an increase of aircraft, not only for reconnaissance but also for long-range fighter and long-range torpedo aircraft,' he wrote in his post-war despatch.[33] Once the war started, the shortcomings of his force became stark. What made Coastal Command's predicament all the greater at the end of 1939 was that the service would soon face far greater tests than anything experienced in the first months of conflict.

2

Retreat

THE WINTER OF 1939/40 was the most bitter in living memory. As arctic weather gripped Britain in December and January, plunging temperatures were accompanied by heavy snowfalls and storms. Much of the Thames, the Grand Union Canal and the sea off the south coast froze over. Telephone wires snapped under the weight of ice; roads turned into skating rinks. It was not until mid-February that a thaw finally set in. Yet even in this meteorological adversity, Coastal Command stuck to its duty. In a review for the Air Ministry of his force's work in January, Bowhill stated,

> This month has been remarkable for the persistence of severe winter conditions, with the prevalence of frost and snow over most of the British Isles. This has made working conditions very difficult at times, from the point of view of both operating and maintaining aircraft. Nevertheless, flying times for the month are up to average and prove the ability and determination of all ranks and trades to overcome climatic difficulties and maintain our air patrols, which have become an essential part of the protection of trade in home waters.[1]

The steadfastness of the Coastal Command squadrons was also emphasized by the press. After a visit to one station, Charles Graves of the *Daily Mail* wrote of how impressed he was by the 'ardours and endurances' of the Command, 'where many of the personnel don't see England by daylight for a week at a time, going out as they do at dawn and coming back at dusk'. Even with these long hours, Graves explained that the enemy was only occasionally seen in the sky: 'the shooting down of a Hun seems to be as rare, but no more than getting a rhinoceros'.[2] In an article of 24 January 1940 headlined 'Britain's Air

Coastguard Keeps Vigil Far Out to Sea', the *Daily Telegraph*'s correspondent James Wentworth Day wrote of how Coastal Command's exploits 'are adding an Elizabethan page to the book of English history'. Its planes, he continued, 'have flown the equivalent of 220 times round the world – a distance of 5 million miles . . . Their endless chain patrol of the sea goes on day after day through snow, ice, tempest and sunshine'. He ended with the prophecy that 'before long, Coastal Command will burgeon as a complete Air Force on its own with its own fighter and bomber units'.

But this was a distant fantasy. In early 1940 Bowhill's command was still mired in a dearth of modern aircraft and equipment, symbolized by the continuing use of the Tiger Moth 'scarecrow' patrols. Planes which would have been valuable in an anti-shipping role, like the Armstrong Whitworth Whitley or the Vickers Wellington, were monopolized by Bomber Command. Several of the new types that had been promised turned out to be disappointments. The twin-engined, high-wing Saunders-Roe Lerwick flying boat, seen as a replacement for the Stranraer and the London, was immediately revealed to be a menace to its own crews because of its flawed design. Entering service in early 1940 as a reconnaissance, convoy protection and anti-submarine plane after an agonizing development programme that failed to resolve its inherent problems, it had a vicious stall, faulty hydraulics and a tendency to lose its floats. After a worrying number of accidents, it was withdrawn. The same fate was suffered by the Blackburn Botha, introduced in December 1939 as a twin-engined reconnaissance and torpedo bomber. The Air Ministry had been so impressed by the initial concept in 1936 that 442 had been ordered even before the maiden flight, but the Botha proved to be a disaster, with a poor lateral stability and highly restricted views for the crew because of the position of its underpowered engines. 'I don't know how it ever got into service. It was a relief when we changed back to Ansons,' recalled Hugh Beresford of 608 Squadron.[3] The high early hopes invested in the Bristol Beaufort as a torpedo bomber replacement for the discredited Vickers Wildebeest were also dashed, as teething difficulties plagued the new plane when it went into service with 22 Squadron in January 1940. Crews were particularly concerned about the reliability of its Taurus engines, which were prone to overheating or cutting out when the throttle was rapidly applied, while they also found that it needed a long bombing run, leaving them vulnerable to anti-aircraft fire. 'They proved far more difficult to handle than the docile Ansons,' remembered Roy Conyers Nesbit, who flew the Beaufort in 217 Squadron.[4] So serious were the failings that the Beaufort did not even undertake its first torpedo operation until September. Although the plane underwent significant improvements, it was never satisfactory. During the war, more were lost to accidents and mechanical failures than to enemy action.

The supply of depth charges remained inadequate, just as progress to install ASV radar was slow because of a shortage of sets; nor did the Mark I ASV live up to expectations as a hunting aid. In fact, the maritime war was turning out differently to the predictions of the strategists. Germany's surface fleet had been much less active than had been feared, in contrast to Dönitz's U-boats, whose deadly attacks shattered the complacent theory that the Royal Navy's use of ASDIC would counter their threat. In fact, ASDIC proved to be of only limited effectiveness, partly because it was useless against a surfaced submarine, and partly because, in the absence of forward-throwing technology, any British vessel on the attack against a submerged one had to pass over the U-boat to drop its depth charges astern, a requirement that rendered ASDIC temporarily deaf at the vital moment of combat when the enemy could simply dive or turn to escape destruction. Far from being neutralized, the U-boats continued to inflict a colossal toll. By May 1940 the Allies had lost 2,250,000 tons of shipping, half of this total to German submarines despite Dönitz's limited numbers. The British government and service chiefs had begun to realize that not only would they have to change the Royal Navy's approach, but they would also have to rebalance Coastal Command's role, with less emphasis on reconnaissance and more on anti-submarine warfare.

These faults undermined official rhetoric about the performance of the Command. In early March 1940 Air Secretary Kingsley Wood told the Commons that even in the abysmal recent weather, 'not a day passed without finding the aircraft of Coastal Command at their ceaseless task: sighting and bombing submarines; escorting convoys;

shooting down or driving off enemy aircraft; destroying mines and accompanying leave ships safely into port'. In the same reassuring tones, Wood further claimed that the Command enjoyed 'the closest co-operation' not only with the Admiralty but also with 'Fighter and Bomber Commands'. Hugh Dalton, the well-connected opposition front bencher, was not convinced. He informed MPs how he had heard that 'things are not as good as they might be. It is said that Bomber Command is sometimes rather insensitive to suggestions that some bombers might be used' by Coastal. Warning against 'petty' compartmentalization, Dalton said that the RAF 'ought to be a flexible instrument, with no stiffness between the Commands'.[5]

Amid the problems, however, there were some causes for optimism. Hudsons were arriving in greater numbers, prompting the Air Ministry to increase its original order with Lockheed to 351 planes. To boost trade protection, four squadrons of twin-engined Bristol Blenheims were also borrowed from Fighter Command, the first of them, No. 254, going into action in February 1940. A highly versatile aircraft which was used in a range of roles during the war, the Blenheim had been a pioneer when it entered service in 1937 with its high speed, all-metal construction, retractable undercarriage and power-operated gun turrets, though it was heading for obsolescence by the start of the war due to rapid advances in aeronautical engineering. Nevertheless, it was a useful addition to Coastal Command, as former navigator Geoffrey Garside, who flew with 236 Squadron early in the war, recalled:

> It was a marvellous machine, with guns in its turret and wings. From a navigator's point of view, I could see way ahead, sitting just behind the pilot but still in the nose. We had the job of escorting flying boats, which was a funny experience as they were much slower, so we had to zigzag above them to keep with them, otherwise we should have left them far behind.[6]

The spirit of innovation was also strong in parts of the Command, as an unorthodox use of one of its units reveals. From the start of the war, the Germans had placed magnetic mines in the approaches to British harbours, causing severe damage to shipping. By the end of

1939 seventy-nine vessels had been lost in this way, weighing 163,000 gross tons. The Royal Navy was desperate for an answer because the task of clearing them was beyond traditional minesweepers and it would take months to develop shipborne degaussing equipment. But British research scientists had a swift and ingenious solution, inspired by a deep understanding of magnetic power. On their instructions, a Vickers Wellington bomber was fitted underneath its airframe with a huge ring, 48 feet in diameter and made of balsa wood. In this ring were strips of aluminium that emitted electrical impulses when charged by an electrical current, which in turn was supplied by a Ford motorcar's V8 engine driving a generator. Early tests with the experimental Wellington on a disarmed magnetic mine showed that the theory worked. By the beginning of 1940 fifteen of the modified planes had been built by Vickers, who used the deliberately misleading title of Directional Wireless Installation (DWI) Wellingtons. They were assigned to the General Reconnaissance Unit of Coastal Command's No. 16 Group, based at the Kent airfield of Manston. Within four days of their arrival they had their first success when on 9 January 1940 a DWI Wellington fully blew up a mine in the Thames Estuary. On 14 January they detonated another, but that achievement almost resulted in disaster because the plane was flying too low, as the author and former naval intelligence officer Carl O. Schuster recounted: 'The Wellington was propelled upwards about 40 feet by the blast, its hatches were blown off and the accelerometer recorded ten Gs of force on the airframe. In a testament to the bomber's robustness, no structural damage was inflicted beyond the loss of the hatches.'[7] With experience, the crews learnt that 60 feet and 130 mph were the optimum height and speed for detonation. It was demanding, dangerous work, not just because of the risks from exploding mines but also because the planes were unarmed, their guns having been removed to accommodate the weight of the incongruous ring. Moreover, the fumes from the generator could induce violent nausea. The early success of the DWIs in clearing British ports led Coastal Command to form a second unit of them in April 1940, and by the summer the danger had passed, the Royal Navy having developed practical degaussing gear for ships. But the Command's DWIs were not redundant. Several were sent to Egypt to protect the Suez Canal and coastal waters in the Mediterranean as the North African campaign intensified.

There were other successes in early 1940 which highlighted the potential of Bowhill's force. On 30 January Coastal Command claimed its first kill of the anti-submarine war when a Sunderland of 228 Squadron, piloted by Flight Lieutenant Edward Brooks, used its bombs and machine-gun fire to attack U-boat U-55, which had just been damaged by depth charges dropped by a Royal Navy destroyer. Unable to dive or escape, the submarine was then hammered by another Allied ship guided to the area by Brooks's Sunderland. Mortally stricken, the U-boat was scuttled by its crew off the coast of the Scilly Isles, with the survivors picked up by the Navy. An official assessment committee subsequently gave part of the credit for the sinking to 228 Squadron though the incident was further proof of how ineffectual Coastal Command's bombs were, for, despite Brooks's assault, it took the Navy to finish off U-55. There were further sightings and attacks in February, one of which saw a Hudson come under fierce anti-aircraft fire when it tried to bomb three German destroyers sighted during a patrol of the eastern North Sea. In a report to Chamberlain's War Cabinet, the Air Staff explained that, after the Hudson's bombs had missed their targets,

eight Messerschmitt 109s had then appeared on the scene. These had registered hits on the tail unit, turret and wireless cabin of the Hudson and had made the port rudder control unserviceable, but had refused to come within striking range of the rear turret of our aircraft. Taking advantage of the clouds, the Hudson then completed its patrol.[8]

At the end of March Bowhill felt able to boast that 'the hours spent on convoy duties reached a record figure', with 'air escorts found for 265 convoys, involving the protection of nearly 4,000 ships'. During the month, he further noted, 'ten submarines were sighted, and of these eight were attacked', though there was no evidence any were sunk. Bowhill also reported that, in five aerial clashes with the Luftwaffe in March, 'it is almost certain that one failed to get back to base and in four of the other combats damage was undoubtedly inflicted on the enemy'.[9]

Of far greater significance for the course of the war was Coastal Command's involvement in an episode that took place in the North Sea on 16 February 1940, after intelligence had reached the Admiralty that the *Altmark*, a German supply ship, was sailing near Norway with 299 Allied prisoners of war on board. The War Cabinet, normally so hesitant seizing the initiative, decided that action must be taken to rescue the men, even though such a move would violate Norwegian neutrality. Three Hudsons from 220 Squadron, based at Bircham Newton in Norfolk, were therefore sent across the North Sea to look for the *Altmark* along Norway's coast. Bruce Forbes, one of the pilots, later told the press that he had been 'roused at 6 a.m. and in the Operations Room was told that a very special job was in hand'. The briefing officer informed the crews that the *Altmark*, when last seen, had been painted black with white upperworks and a large single funnel aft. Visibility was poor when the Hudsons set off, but the weather swiftly improved as they approached Norway, whose snow-covered mountains could be seen from more than 30 miles away.

> Flying well outside territorial waters, I examined every mile with binoculars. Then, 15 miles ahead I saw a smudge of smoke. A minute later a ship with black hull and cream upperworks was steaming directly towards us. My heart sank when I recognized from her lines that she could not be our quarry. Fifteen seconds later I spotted something else, a grey ship with a funnel aft.

Immediately, the three planes swept down. 'As we dived, my eyes were riveted on the stern searching for a name. I saw letters about a foot high. I could not suppress a whoop of joy when I saw they read "Altmark",' reported Forbes.[10] The sighting was reported to the Navy, and in the early afternoon HMS *Cossack* followed the *Altmark* into a fjord, where she tried to take refuge but ran aground. That evening, the *Cossack* sent a boarding party onto the *Altmark*. After some hand-to-hand combat, the British sailors overwhelmed the Germans, freed the prisoners and took them on to the *Cossack*, whose homeward voyage was escorted by the Hudsons.

The *Altmark* incident provided a tremendous boost to the morale of both the Royal Navy and Coastal Command. But it also led to a dramatic escalation in the war between Britain and Germany as both sides became increasingly hostile towards the restraints of Norwegian neutrality. For their part, the British now drew up plans to mine Norway's territorial waters in order to halt the passage of iron ore, essential to the Nazi war effort, from Sweden to the German ports. For his part, Hitler had been made all the more suspicious about Allied designs on Scandinavia and stepped up his plans for a pre-emptive invasion of Denmark and Norway. The fires were about to be lit for a new stage in the conflict which would soon engulf most of Europe.

An insight into British thinking can be found in a 'most secret' memorandum of 4 April sent to Bowhill by the deputy chief of the Air Staff Sir Richard Peirse, soon to become the head of Bomber Command. Having outlined 'Operation Wilfred', the plan to mine Norway's waters which was due to commence on 9 April, Sir Richard said, with a worrying degree of complacency, that in response the Germans 'may take no military action in Scandinavia, at least at the outset'. If they did, he argued, they would probably launch a large-scale aerial bombardment of the British fleet in the North Sea, establish air and naval bases in southern Norway and perhaps occupy southern Sweden. In turn, this would be met by a British counter-offensive through landings at key ports, intensification of air cover and mining of traffic on the Rhine.[11] But it was Hitler who advanced first before any mines had been laid. On 8 April the crew of a Sunderland from 204 Squadron, on patrol over the Norwegian coast, spotted the mammoth German battleship *Scharnhorst*, accompanied by two cruisers and two destroyers. At once, the German flotilla saw the Sunderland and opened up with a barrage of anti-aircraft fire, holing two of its fuel tanks. The damaged plane was able to report the sighting and just make it back to base after the loss of 300 gallons of fuel. Over the next twenty-four hours other Coastal Command reconnaissance aircraft were despatched to Norway where they witnessed a huge increase in German naval activity. The Reich's assault on Scandinavia had begun.

The Norway campaign should have been the ideal arena for Bowhill's Command and the Fleet Air Arm to show their capabilities, particularly in reconnaissance, strikes against enemy shipping and attacks on occupied ports and coastal air bases. But, no matter how doggedly the personnel served, the fight in Scandinavia again exposed their weaknesses as the Germans quickly gained mastery of the air and control of the land. Even in the official Air Ministry account, intelligence officer Hector Bolitho wrote, 'the numbers of aircraft at the disposal of both services were too small; the distances they had to fly too great'.[12] For Coastal Command, the burden of challenging the Germans fell to the Hudsons and Blenheims, but the journey of between 300 and 400 miles to Norway meant the planes only had a short time over the combat area. Nor were the Blenheims a match for the Luftwaffe's marauding Messerschmitt 109s, while the engine troubles with the Beaufort meant that Coastal Command still had no meaningful torpedo force.

One incident on 17 April, a little more than a week after the start of the German invasion, typified the problems. A Hudson of 233 Squadron had been given the task of acting as a gun spotter for the Royal Navy heavy cruiser HMS *Suffolk*, which was attempting to shell Stavanger airfield in south-western Norway, but the mission went badly wrong, as historian Chris Ashworth, a Coastal Command veteran himself, recounted:

> Due to communications difficulties and inexperience, the co-operation was a dismal failure . . . and most of the 202 eight-inch shells expended undoubtedly missed the target. To compound a catalogue of errors the ship was then ordered to intercept a number of German destroyers as she withdrew and was therefore not where her planned escort of Blenheim fighters expected her to be at the rendezvous time. Unescorted, the Suffolk was subjected to fierce attack by the Luftwaffe.[13]

In similar vein, an experiment on 15 April in using the Beaufort as a mine-layer was an initial disappointment because of poor weather and a shortage of aircraft, with the result that Bowhill had to ask 815 Squadron of the Fleet Air Arm to assist with these early, unproductive mine-laying operations.

The first Allied aircraft shot down during the Norway campaign gave rise to one of the most extraordinary tales of survival during the war. On 9 April, at the start of the German invasion, a Short Sunderland of 210 Squadron left its base in Invergordon, Scotland, to fly on a reconnaissance mission to Norway. When the plane reached the Oslo fjord it immediately came under fire from a couple of twin-engined Messerschmitt 110s. Staggering through the sky at 3,000 feet, the Sunderland exploded in mid-air over the mountain village of Sylling. As the plane was ripped apart by the blast, nine of its ten-man crew were killed. But the wireless operator, Welshman Ogwyn George, was thrown from the flaming wreckage and began the plunge towards the earth. Given that he was badly injured and without a parachute, death seemed inevitable. By a miracle, however, his fall was broken by thick pine trees before he landed in deep snow. Almost as incredibly, the combat had been witnessed by a local woodsman, Johan Brathen, who began the long, exhausting climb up the mountainside to look for any survivors. On his first search he failed to find George, who had painfully managed to struggle a short way before collapsing. Yet Brathen refused to give up. Later that night he returned to the task having come across an animal track that followed a trail of George's blood. By now George, drifting in and out of consciousness, thought his end was close and, with what seemed his final breath, shouted out, 'Lord if you want me, take me!'[14] His cry was heard by Brathen, who managed to bring him to a local hospital. George had suffered frostbite and severe burns, but, with medical help, he recovered sufficiently to be sent to a prisoner of war camp, where he spent the next five years. In a heart-warming moment in 1972, he travelled to Norway, appeared on television there and met Brathen, the man who had saved his life.

Within weeks of the German invasion the British position was hopeless. Troops who had only just landed at Åndalsnes and Namsos were told to prepare for evacuation. A military presence was retained at the northern port of Narvik, more as a forlorn gesture of defiance than as a realistic base for a counter-attack. Coastal Command's task changed from bolstering resistance to covering retreat, with little improvement in results. That air of futility was captured in a report to the War Cabinet of 8 May about action on the day before, when six Beauforts had tried to attack a German cruiser said to be anchored off Norderney in the East Frisian Islands. 'Only one aircraft had located the target. No hit was claimed. One Beaufort had been attacked by a Messerschmitt Bf 109 and hit, the resulting damage causing it to crash on landing. One Beaufort was missing. Subsequent reconnaissance of the area had failed to sight the cruiser.'[15] An attempted attack on several German ships, including the renowned *Scharnhorst*, on 10 June at Trondheim harbour caused little damage for the loss of two Hudsons. Equally ineffectual was a subsequent attack two days later on the *Scharnhorst* by six Hudsons and nine Beauforts, which were loaded with bombs because the continuing technical problems meant that torpedo training had still not begun. The huge battleship was unscathed again as all the bombs missed their target, while four Beauforts were shot down by Me 109s and every Hudson was damaged by heavy flak. In his monthly summary on 11 June, Bowhill said that the German triumph in Norway 'had a profound effect on the role of this Command and on the tactical employment of my squadrons'. His force's task, he went on, had 'been made much harder and increased risks and greater odds have to be faced in maintaining our reconnaissance over the North Sea'.[16]

Defeat in Norway also had a profound effect on the political scene. After a sweeping rebellion by back-bench Tory MPs against the government on 8 May at the end of the Commons debate on the doomed campaign, Chamberlain resigned as prime minister and was replaced by Winston Churchill at the head of an all-party coalition. The creation of a national government had major consequences for the oversight of Coastal Command. Sir Kingsley Wood was succeeded as air secretary by Sir Archibald Sinclair, the Liberal leader who was a close friend of Churchill; their bond was cemented not just by politics, for Churchill had been a Liberal MP for twenty years until 1924, but also by their joint service with the Royal Scots Fusiliers in the trenches during the First World War. To his admirers, Sinclair was articulate, well organized and debonair. To his detractors, he was little more than the smooth-tongued mouthpiece of Churchill or the Air Staff. Churchill's successor as the new First Lord of the Admiralty was the Sheffield Labour MP and leader of the Co-Operative movement Albert (A. V.) Alexander, once described by the Fabian socialist Beatrice Webb as 'a vigorous and masterful personality, with a good physique, alert mind and straightforward manner, but without charm or brilliance'.[17] Like Sinclair, he was respected for his loyalty and patriotism but to critics he was too much the creature of his service chiefs. Apart from these two men, who each served in his post until the end of the European war, a far more controversial appointment was that of the maverick Canadian press tycoon Lord Beaverbrook as minister for aircraft production, bringing both dynamism and friction to the heart of the Cabinet.

The new government immediately had to deal with the titanic crisis sparked by Germany's invasion of western Europe on 10 May, which soon overwhelmed the Low Countries and plunged Britain's closest ally France into a desperate battle for survival. After the setbacks in Norway, the new theatre further strained the limited resources of Coastal Command. As before, the crews fought gallantly despite the daunting circumstances from the outset. Beauforts of 22 Squadron bombed Rotterdam airport in an unsuccessful attempt to prevent its use by the Germans, while 220 and 235 squadrons bombed oil storage depots in Bremen and Hamburg. Ansons were in action patrolling the coast, escorting Allied ships and attacking German fast-attack E-boats with some success; on 24 May off the Netherlands, an Anson blew up one E-boat and raked two others with machine-gun fire.[18] According to official figures, during the first twenty days of operations in the West, Coastal Command flew ninety-four daylight patrols over Holland, Belgium and northern France.

Activity intensified enormously at the end of May when much of the British Expeditionary Force, beaten again by the Wehrmacht, retreated to Dunkirk, from where an epic evacuation, code-named Operation Dynamo, began. Working closely with Fighter Command, the aircraft of Bowhill's force protected the vast naval flotilla in the waters of the English Channel as best they could, despite complaints from the retreating British Army about the absence of the RAF. In the four days from 31 May, 16 Group of Coastal Command flew 327 sorties. Examples of heroism in the skies abounded. On 1 June one Anson of 500 Squadron, flown by Pilot Officer Philip Peters, shot down two Me 109s and disabled two others over Dunkirk, an achievement for which he was awarded the Distinguished Flying Cross (DFC). The citation stated that Peters, menaced by nine Messerschmitts, had 'immediately turned to the attack and so skilfully manoeuvred his aircraft that he and both the air gunner and the navigator were enabled to concentrate their fire on the enemy'.[19] Peters's plane was part of a formation of three Ansons on the search for E-boats. Jack Watehous, the wireless operator in the leading aircraft, left a vivid account in an interview about his own experience of coming under fire when flying at just 50–80 feet.

> The cabin was full of explosive bullets. I instantly started to send an SOS, still sitting at the desk . . . There were three attacks on us during which our gunner was critically injured. After I sent the SOS, I went back to man the gun on the left-hand side but as I approached, our pilot did a sharp turn and I was thrown onto the floor right near the air gunner's entrance. And when I picked myself up I could see he had collapsed in his turret.

The plane was badly damaged and leaking fuel but the pilot managed to nurse it back to Manston. 'As we landed, both engines packed up, one almost immediately after the other. We just plonked down and the undercarriage came down but the wheels were shattered with bullets so we stopped dead,' recalled Watehous. Soon afterwards the ambulance arrived, but the gunner succumbed to his wounds two days later in hospital.[20]

Another account of Coastal Command's fight over Dunkirk came from Alastair Panton, a Blenheim pilot in 53 Squadron, which was given the task of bombing German field batteries and gun positions. 'All our attacks were low-level ones, carried out at 200 feet, a method which gave us maximum flexibility; we picked a target, flew straight at it and over it low down, releasing bombs to arrive on the target more or less at the same time as we passed over it,' wrote Panton. He also described the scenes that he witnessed as he flew on his missions. 'We could see the lines of shipping crossing and re-crossing the Channel, bombs and shells exploding among the lines of soldiers on the beaches and around the shipping standing off them and air battles in the blue sky above us. It was gigantic awesome spectacle.' On his third sortie Panton experienced an astonishing incident.

Having lined up my target, I found I was following another Blenheim from an unknown squadron. Not knowing what delay had been set on his bombs, and not wanting to be blown up by them, I eased off on his port side. As I pressed my release button, the other Blenheim's bombs exploded, and as I passed over the German guns, a soldier appeared in the air beside the cockpit 200 feet up, still running, with a ludicrous look of outraged surprise on his face, which I could clearly see under his helmet.[21]

The magnificent evacuation saw more than 300,000 Allied troops lifted from the beaches by 4 June. But as Churchill told the Commons, 'wars are not won by evacuations'.[22] Dunkirk was soon followed by the fall of France, which meant that the entire northern coast of continental Europe, from the Spanish border to the tip of Norway, was in German hands. The strategic balance of the maritime war was transformed in the Reich's favour, with Coastal Command put even further on the defensive. In particular, the seizure of France gave an enormous advantage to the Kriegsmarine and the Luftwaffe. Not only were the Western Approaches and the English Channel turned into hostile waters for Britain, forcing the Atlantic convoys to adopt longer northerly routes, but even more importantly, Dönitz's U-boat force could now use the French ports in the Bay of Biscay, which were 450 miles closer to the Allied sea lanes than its bases in Germany. After a huge logistical operation that brought supplies and materials to western France, the first Atlantic U-boat port began operations on 6 July. A dark new chapter in the submarine war had opened, soon threatening the very existence of Coastal Command as part of the RAF.

But it was the survival of Britain, isolated and battered, that was at stake in the immediate aftermath of the Reich's triumph in the West. Thwarted in his hopes that the British government would sue for peace, Hitler ordered plans to be drawn up for a full-scale invasion, code-named Operation Sea Lion. An essential prerequisite of the proposed assault, which was due to take place in September, was the Luftwaffe gaining air supremacy over southern England in order to protect the landings. The pulverizing recent victories of the German war machine led Hermann Goering, the bombastic Luftwaffe chief, to think that the task could be accomplished in a matter of weeks, but he had badly underestimated the resilience and determination of the RAF once the Battle of Britain began.

For Coastal Command, reconnaissance was still the main role, but this was heavily supplemented by attacks on enemy shipping in Channel ports as well coastal land targets such as marshalling yards, supply depots, barracks and aerodromes, to undermine the preparations for the invasion. According to Bowhill, Coastal Command performed 15,243 hours of operational sorties in July, another 13,676 hours in August, and 13,787 hours in September.[23] His force flew on average forty visual reconnaissance missions a day, co-operated with Bomber Command on mine-laying, and dropped 231 tons of bombs during the battle. For these duties, several steps were taken to strengthen the force. Because German fighters now posed a far greater threat from their bases in northern France and the Low Countries, Avro Ansons were fitted with extra side guns and some also had a free-mounted 20-mm cannon installed in the floor of their cabin to ward off attacks by E-boats. Anti-shipping and reconnaissance operations in the north were boosted by the deployment of two squadrons from Bomber Command, numbers 21 and 57, to Lossiemouth in Scotland. In July the four Blenheim squadrons, which did heroic work patrolling the French coastline and escorting Sunderlands, were reinforced by two further Blenheim squadrons from Army Co-operation, specifically to concentrate on surveillance of the invasion ports where the Wehrmacht was gathering a vast armada of almost 2,000 barges for Operation Sea Lion. The barges were also a key target for the Beauforts, which finally went into action as torpedo bombers, the technical difficulties having at last been resolved. On 11 September five Beauforts of 22 Squadron, led by Flight Lieutenant Dick Beauman, set out on their first torpedo mission, aiming for an enemy convoy off Calais. Three of the torpedoes failed to release and one hit a sandbank, but Beauman's badly damaged a 6,000-ton freighter. Despite heavy flak, all the Beauforts returned safely. Almost a week later, on the night of 17 September, 22 Squadron launched another attack by Beauforts, this time led by Rex Mack. The target was Cherbourg, the most heavily defended of the

Channel ports, as Mack soon discovered. Having entered the harbour through its western entrance, 'I had hardly got in, flying at about 50 feet, when the Germans opened fire. I was so close that I could actually see them and I watched a German gunner, one of a crew of three manning a Bofors gun, trying to depress the barrel,' said Mack. But the gunner could not get it down sufficiently and the flak passed over the Beauforts to hit a fort at the other end of the breakwater. Then Mack saw the target, a large troopship.

I dropped the torpedo in perfect conditions, for I was flying at the right speed and the right height. Half a second after I had dropped it five searchlights opened up and caught me in their beams. I pulled back the stick and put on a lot of left rudder and cleared out. The trouble about a torpedo attack is that when you have released the torpedo, you have to fly on the same course for a short time to make quite sure that it has, in fact, left the aircraft. I remember counting one and two and three and forcing myself not to count too fast. Then we were away.[24]

Inevitably, given what was at stake, there were tensions during the summer of 1940 between the service chiefs, with Bowhill complaining that he was not treated with the same respect as Sir Hugh Dowding, head of Fighter Command, or Sir Charles Portal, head of Bomber Command. That resentment had been exemplified in June when the Air Ministry decided to base three fighter squadrons at Coastal Command's station at St Eval, Cornwall, a move that required Bowhill to move some of his operations elsewhere. 'Accommodation for these fighter squadrons is to take priority over all other commitments at St Eval,' ruled the ministry.[25] Bristling at this remark, Bowhill wrote to Sholto Douglas, the deputy chief of the Air Staff, 'I wonder if it is fully realized in certain branches of the Air Ministry the vital importance of defending our shipping from the menace of the submarine and the amount of flying we have to do to ensure that our shipping is comparatively safe.' Bowhill further expressed his annoyance at the lack of consultation. 'I should have been informed. I notice that Dowding is always asked about his aerodromes and also Portal. I am not obstructing in any way – far from it – but such snap decisions hamper my Command considerably.'[26] Douglas told him that, though he recognized the importance of Coastal Command's work in defence of shipping, 'we have got to reorientate our fighter defence to look south as well as east'. A fighter station was therefore necessary in Cornwall, and St Eval was the only possible location because 'aerodrome accommodation is strictly limited in the west of England'.[27]

The following month Douglas wrote to warn Bowhill against conducting his own independent bombing campaign against targets in occupied Europe without reference to the Air Ministry. Having reminded Bowhill that 'the primary role of your squadrons is reconnaissance', Douglas stated that the RAF's accepted policy was 'that subsidiary offensive operations undertaken by your Command should be directed primarily against ships at sea or concentrations of shipping in harbour'. It was vital that operations should be conducted 'in conformity' with the wider war strategy because 'however important these objectives may appear, unless they are relating to the general bombing policy, their attack may be an unjustified diversion of effort and result in the dispersion of the limited bomber force which we have available'.[28] In reply, Bowhill said he 'fully realized' that reconnaissance was his command's key duty, but added that recent subsidiary offensive operations have been directed 'primarily against concentrations of barges and small vessels in the inland waterways of Holland, Belgium and north east France'. He further explained that his crews were sometimes hindered by 'insufficient' information and short notice from the Air Ministry about the chosen targets. Precisely because bombing was a subsidiary role, his command needed 'a little more time' to organize raids than Bomber Command.[29]

At the end of the month Bowhill protested to Portal that official demands for Coastal Command's support in designated bomber missions could be unrealistic: 'You will appreciate that with the primary role of reconnaissance considerably increased as a result of the threat of invasion, the number of aircraft that can be made available at any time for bomber operations is comparatively small.'[30] Bowhill was also unhappy with the co-ordination of mine-laying operations on the enemy coast, whereby Bomber Command retained operational control of its Hampden squadrons responsible for this task while the details of targets were provided by Coastal Command acting on instructions for the Admiralty. Even though Coastal Command's Beauforts were now functional, the scope for inefficiency was worsened by hold-ups in the supply and distribution of mines. 'On many occasions, in both Commands, aircraft and crews were kept standing by on the promise of the delivery of the mines, when they could have been deployed on other vital operational tasks.' A change was duly made in mid-August whereby Coastal Command was put in authority of both the information on targets and the distribution of mines, and arrangements 'proceeded more smoothly for the next six months', he wrote.[31]

Through mine-laying, reconnaissance and its own bombing raids, Coastal Command helped degrade Germany's military capacity, provided vital intelligence, disrupted supply lines and strengthened Britain's resistance. Crucially, more than 10 per cent of the Reich's invasion fleet in the northern continental ports was destroyed. By mid-September the Germans recognized that air superiority could not be achieved, without which an assault on Britain was impossible.

On the 17th, two days after the Luftwaffe had sustained crippling losses at the hands of the Spitfires and Hurricanes, Hitler indefinitely postponed Operation Sea Lion. It was the Reich's first defeat of the war. Like the rest of the RAF, Coastal Command paid a heavy price for its defiance, losing 148 aircraft and 280 men in the battle, more than half the total of Fighter Command's casualties. Given the pivotal circumstances of the struggle, such attrition had been inevitable, but on 16 October the outgoing head of the RAF, Sir Cyril Newall, who was about to be replaced by Portal, told Bowhill that the time had come to preserve his resources for the fight that lay ahead, when other burdens would be placed on his command.

The loss of highly skilled reconnaissance crews should be avoided where possible, the more so in view of the expansion of your command during the coming year when such personnel will be worth their weight in gold. I realize that we have been passing through a critical phase when a measure of risk had to be taken in pressing home attacks against the invasion ports. But now that the immediate threat of invasion has somewhat receded and the weather is deteriorating, I think those risks are less justified.

Newall concluded with words of praise for 'the offensive spirit' and 'the high standard you have already set',[32] qualities that would now be needed in another great battle, that of the northern Atlantic.

3

Control

Although it was the height of summer, the rain was falling heavily when Flight Lieutenant Ernest Baker was brought with his crew from 210 Squadron by dinghy to their Sunderland at Pembroke Docks. The Battle of Britain was now raging in the skies over southern England but his mission would take him far from the scene of combat between Fighter Command and the Luftwaffe. On this bleak morning of 16 August, with the dark clouds hanging just 400 feet above the sea, Baker had been instructed to fly a patrol down to the Bay of Biscay, picking up a convoy and looking for U-boats. Having taken off at seven o'clock, the crew had glimpsed no sign of the enemy after six draining hours in dismal weather. Then suddenly the second pilot shouted that he had spotted a U-boat to port. 'I put my foot on everything,' recalled Baker. His account continued:

> The U-boat was on the surface when we sighted it and they must have sighted us at the same time, for they started to do a crash dive. By the time the submarine was down, I was diving low over the top to attack. The result was terrific. The whole of the surface of the sea seemed to shudder for yards around and then suddenly blew up. In the middle of the boiling sea, the submarine emerged with its decks awash and then sank rather like a brick. I did a steep turn and came over it again just as it was disappearing. The explosion actually blew the submarine right out of the water.

Baker dropped more bombs right over the frothing target.

> Large air bubbles came rushing up – one was over 30 feet across. Great gobs of oil began to spread over the surface until a wide area was

covered. I waited for about an hour until there was no more air or oil coming up and then I fetched a destroyer from the convoy and signalled what had happened.[1]

After carrying out an ASDIC sweep, the Royal Navy ship reported no contact.

It had been the first attack by Coastal Command on a U-boat using airborne depth charges. Yet the bubbling water and widening oil slick gave only the illusion of destruction. Remarkably, the German vessel U-51, skippered by Dietrich Knorr and on its fourth war cruise, was not sunk by Baker's Sunderland but escaped, only to be fatally hit four days later near Nantes. Tellingly, it was not another Coastal Command plane that was responsible for the kill but the torpedoes of a Royal Navy submarine. U-51's survival from the Sunderland's apparently devastating assault was a tribute to the toughness of the submarine's design, with its thick steel pressure hull. But it was also a reflection of the weakness of Coastal Command's anti-submarine armoury and tactics, which negated the courage of the crews. In mournful tones, Bowhill wrote in his monthly summary for July 1940:

> The results of actions against the U-boats continue to be unsatisfactory. It is an outstanding fact that 70 per cent of the U-boats attacked by my aircraft are getting away without material damage. I am more than ever convinced that the weapons in use to date have been inadequate for purpose.[2]

He was fully justified in his belief. Despite the growing awareness of the U-boat threat, the anti-submarine bombs were still almost impotent and ASV radar sets ineffective beyond a range of only 3.5 miles. At the same time, the 450-pound naval depth charge, modified for Coastal Command's use by the fitting of a streamlined nose cap and an air tail, was no panacea, as Baker's experience proved. Over 700 had been supplied to the maritime force, but its Amatol explosive charge lacked power, it was too heavy to be carried by any plane other than the Sunderland, and the entrenched theory that it should be dropped from 100 feet turned out to be disastrously mistaken, an illustration of the absence of proper operational research within the force.

The reality was that Coastal Command still had to live with the legacy of RAF policy in the pre-war years, with its focus on bombing strategy, its complacency towards enemy submarines and its low priority for maritime air power. Bowhill wrote:

> The situation regarding numbers and types of aircraft at my disposal caused me grave concern, not only because the strength was still below the minimum necessary to undertake the initial requirement of the co-operation with the Navy but because the war had revealed many new tasks that had not been envisaged.[3]

Sir John Slessor, one of Bowhill's successors, felt that it was 'nothing short of amazing the extent to which the U-boat menace was under-rated' at this time.[4] Only the Sunderlands were capable of operating beyond a 500-mile radius, but they were still in short supply; by July 1940 there were still just thirty-four of them in service. At a senior level the Command's sense of grievance shone through its discussions about the Air Ministry's failure to provide sufficient and effective long-range flying boats to combat the Reich's U-boat fleet. In a perceptive memorandum of 22 February 1940, Air Commodore Ivor Lloyd, the head of planning at Coastal Command, emphasized the need for greater endurance. 'Within the next year, the Germans will build submarines of sufficiently heavy tonnage to operate in the mid-Atlantic and prey on our convoys, and we shall have nothing with which to reach them.'[5]

This feeling of neglect was all the more dangerous because Dönitz had dramatically intensified his campaign since the fall of France, taking advantage of his ability to deploy his U-boats much closer to the Western Approaches and the Atlantic. There had been a brief lull in the submarine war during the conquest of Norway, when he was required to send much of his fleet to Scandinavian waters, but now he was ready for a deadly new phase, backed by a growing force and new tactics. Dönitz had forty-eight U-boats in June, to which another twenty-four were added by October. The geography of the war had shifted decisively in his favour. Within a week of the armistice in

France, his U-boats began to establish their bases in five Atlantic ports, namely Brest, Saint-Nazaire, Bordeaux, Lorient and La Rochelle, where he ordered the installation of anti-aircraft defences and the construction of vast concrete bunkers in each to act as submarine pens. These were built by the 15,000 engineers and forced labourers from the Todt organization that handled large infrastructure projects with an astonishing efficiency. In another step that exemplified his unrelenting focus on the Atlantic campaign, he set up his headquarters in the nineteenth-century Villa Kerillon, which was known locally as the Château des Sardines and occupied a position overlooking the harbour at Lorient.

The U-boats soon started to wreak even greater havoc on the Allied shipping as they cruised the ocean to the west, out of reach of the RAF. What made their attacks all the more lethal was Dönitz's adoption of the *Rudeltaktik* or wolf pack system. While many of his submarines still hunted as lone killers, others preyed in groups, known as wolf packs, gathered along patrol lines that spread across the expected path of the convoys and were co-ordinated by messages sent from Dönitz's control centre at Lorient using the supposedly unbreakable Enigma code. One prime feature of most U-boats was that they had to spend much of their time on the surface in order to recharge their batteries, to replace stale air and to use their radios, which were not operable underwater. While potentially increasing the vulnerability to being spotted, surfacing had two clear benefits in combat. First, the Royal Navy's ASDIC was nullified and, second, a surfaced U-boat had a much greater speed than a submerged one. In fact, a Type VII U-boat, which formed the basis of Dönitz's fleet, could only travel at a maximum of 7 knots underwater, slower even than a convoy, whereas on the surface it could reach more than 17 knots. Moreover, the theoretical risks of visibility were greatly reduced by Dönitz's instruction that U-boats should launch their strikes against convoys at night where possible, which had the advantage that enemy aircraft, lacking any method of illumination, had little chance of any sighting in the dark.

In terms of weapons, the U-boats were now packing a sharper punch compared to the start of the war. Type VIIs generally carried fourteen torpedoes, whose reliability had greatly improved by mid-1940 after their use in early campaigns had been plagued by technical faults, particularly failures to explode and premature detonations. Dönitz's Atlantic fleet was further boosted by support from the Focke-Wulf 200, known as the Condor, a large four-engined plane that had originally been built as a transatlantic airliner, but had been converted into a maritime patrol aircraft with the installation of machine guns, cannon and a central bomb bay. Despite its range of 2,200 miles, its slowness and weak structure should have made it an easy target, though Coastal Command's lack of aircraft meant that Condors, like U-boats, could roam with comparative and savage impunity. Operating from Bordeaux airport, they became a menace to unarmed merchant ships, sinking their first freighter off Ireland in late August, with more kills in the autumn. Coastal Command's burden was made all the greater because the German surface fleet was not only growing but could also use the Atlantic ports. It was in August 1940 that the *Bismarck*, then the largest battleship ever built in Europe, was commissioned. A more dubious addition to the Reich's maritime arsenal came on 10 June when Italy declared war on the Allies, bringing Mussolini's Regia Marina into the fray. By 18 October Italian submarines were operating out of the western French ports, but with nothing like the unforgiving efficiency of the U-boats.

That dominance reached an early zenith in the summer and autumn, a period Dönitz's crews dubbed the 'Happy Time' because of the toll they exacted. Between the beginning of June and the end of October 1940, 274 Allied ships were sunk in the Atlantic, a rate of almost two a day, totalling 1.4 million tons, for the loss of just six U-boats. In September 1940 the fast convoy HX72 came under attack and eleven of its forty-three ships were sunk. Even worse followed in October, when a seven-strong wolf pack attacked convoy SC7, sinking twenty of its thirty-five ships and damaging a further six. During that month 352,000 tons of shipping were sunk by the U-boats, up from 190,000 tons in June.

'The only thing that ever really frightened me during the war was the U-boat peril,' wrote Churchill in his memoirs.[6] His concerns were revealed at the time at a meeting of the Cabinet Defence Committee on 31 October, at which he emphasized that Britain's survival 'depended on the maintenance of life of this island' and keeping 'our sea communications open'. There had, he added, 'been a serious recrudescence of submarine warfare and recent losses had been heavy'.[7] The sense of crisis at Coastal Command was inescapable. 'My resources have been taxed to the utmost' by the submarines 'working further out into the Atlantic than hitherto', complained Bowhill in early October.[8] A fortnight later he warned Portal of the 'very grave U-boat menace which has developed lately against our trade'.[9] During the autumn he made repeated requests for support from Bomber Command to attack the German-occupied ports in the Biscay areas, without much success, as he later commented with acerbity. 'It was not found possible to direct other than a few light raids by Bomber Command on these concentrated wasps' nests.'[10] In the front line, the diary of Roger Morewood from 248 Squadron, flying Blenheim reconnaissance patrols from the Shetland Islands, captured a mood of frustration and impotence. 'Nothing of value,' he wrote after one mission on 11 September. 'In the grand scheme of things, what were we achieving?' he asked in another.[11]

Even so, the picture was not entirely bleak. The U-boats were not invincible. While Coastal Command attacks rarely resulted in a kill, the mere appearance of RAF planes over the sea could act as a deterrent, forcing U-boats to submerge and allowing convoys to proceed unhindered. And occasionally Bowhill's aircraft could be more punishing. On 1 July 1940 a Sunderland of 210 Squadron, captained by the Australian Bill 'Hoot' Gibson, claimed the force's second joint kill of a U-boat. Flying on patrol from their base at Mount Batten, Cornwall, Gibson's crew were ordered to a location south-west of Ireland, where a ship in a convoy had been torpedoed. Soon after the search began, the second pilot sighted a U-boat on the surface. Gibson roared down on the target and managed to drop four 250-pound anti-submarine bombs with cool precision. As they exploded, the Sunderland circled the scene. Another crew member, Bill Vout, recalled:

Suddenly the bow of the submarine broke surface at a very steep angle before levelling off. Hoot released a second salvo which fell about forty yards from the sub's midships. I saw the U-boat's crew pouring out of the conning tower and it looked as if each was placing his hand on the next's shoulder when suddenly they all jumped overboard and swam clear. The U-boat began to settle by the stern, slowly at first but then, gathering momentum, it tipped up the bows and slid under the sea at the same steep angle as it had risen.[12]

The ill-fated vessel, U-26, which had already sunk eleven Allied ships, had been unable to escape from Gibson's Sunderland because it had already been badly damaged by depth charges dropped by the Royal Navy corvette HMS *Gladiolus*. The German survivors were picked up by the Navy, which shared the kill with Coastal Command.

There were other signs of progress in developing the Cinderella Service. Much as Bowhill might complain, his command had grown from nineteen to twenty-six squadrons in the first year of the war, including the loan of four Blenheim squadrons from Fighter Command and one from Bomber Command. Another addition was the Armstrong Whitworth Whitley, a twin-engined bomber that had first gone into temporary service with the Command in 1939 when 58 Squadron was briefly transferred from Bomber Command to replace some of the ageing Avro Ansons. In the autumn of 1940 more Whitleys became available as new heavy bombers like the Stirling and the Halifax were produced, though its long, boxlike fuselage and thick wing meant it lacked agility. William Day, who flew with 58 Squadron, was not an enthusiast: 'As a combat aircraft it left a lot to be desired from the speed and bombload point of view. It was not built for comfort. On occasions the guns would ice up.'[13] Even so, the Whitley evolved into a useful maritime patrol and reconnaissance aircraft, the Mark VII version, with extra fuel tanks and advanced communications, eventually equipping four squadrons in Coastal Command.

The geographical scope of Bowhill's force had also been significantly widened. A presence was established in Gibraltar when 200 Group, previously under the control of the RAF's Mediterranean headquarters, was transferred to Bowhill, though at first the new Coastal Command base only accommodated Saunders-Roe London flying boats and Fairey Swordfish torpedo biplanes. Another new station was opened in Iceland, which Britain had invaded in May 1940, fearing that the Reich was about to take over the island. As in

Gibraltar, the initial Coastal Command force was limited, comprising just one squadron of single-engined Fairey Battle light bombers, but later in 1940 detachments of Sunderlands and Hudsons were deployed there as the island grew into a vital link in the Atlantic's aerial defences. Bowhill was also able to strengthen his protection of the North-Western Approaches by installing two Blenheim squadrons at Aldergrove in Northern Ireland and another in Cornwall.

More and better equipment was becoming available. All the Command's aircraft had by now been fitted with short-range R/T (radio/telephone) so they could be in direct contact with the Royal Navy's vessels without using Aldis lamps. Visual technology was advancing as much as audio communication. The Mark I ASV radar was in service with twenty-four Hudsons and twenty-five Sunderlands in late 1940, but a more reliable Mark II set had been developed, with a greater range of up to 35 miles due in part to the rearrangement of its aerials on the airframe so they looked sideways rather than forwards. The first longer-range Mark II was used on 502 Squadron's Whitleys, whose flat sides suited this new configuration, and proved such an effective tool that in October Bowhill made 'a most urgent and immediate request that a further Whitley squadron be added to the Command'.[14]

In the autumn of 1940, shaken by the U-boat losses and perturbed by the continuing weakness of Coastal Command, several chiefs of the Admiralty, led by the first Lord Albert Alexander, contemplated a more radical measure. What they sought was a takeover of Coastal Command, turning it from a branch of the RAF into a subsidiary of the Royal Navy, like the Fleet Air Arm. In their bold demand they were backed up by Lord Beaverbrook, the *Daily Express* proprietor and minister of aircraft production since May 1940. As with the circulation of his paper, the Canadian press baron had performed wonders with output from the fighter and bomber factories, but respect for his dynamism was undermined by dislike of his conspiratorial ambition mixed with his mercurial inconstancy. 'The only truly evil man I have ever met,' was the verdict of Clement Attlee, Churchill's deputy.[15]

The fraught saga of control of Coastal Command was a continuation of the long duel between the RAF and the Royal Navy that stretched back to the abolition of the independent naval air service in

1918. Determined to uphold the status quo was the new chief of the Air Staff Sir Charles Portal, a highly articulate, self-assured leader with a streak of icy aloofness and an unswerving belief in the Trenchard doctrine of the bombing offensive. After outstanding service in the Royal Flying Corps during the First World War, his natural authority, self-discipline and fierce work ethic saw him rise to the top of his service in October 1940, 'the accepted star of the Royal Air Force', in the words of Winston Churchill.[16] His opposite number as head of the Royal Navy was Sir Dudley Pound, who also served as the chairman of the Chiefs of Staff. A much less commanding figure than Portal, solid rather than brilliant, Pound had enjoyed an impressive naval career, including spells as flag captain of the Grand Fleet and head of planning at the Admiralty during the First World War, but was in poor health for much of his time in charge during the Second. Appointed First Sea Lord in June 1939, he was afflicted by osteoarthritis and fatigue, prompting senior strategist Alan Brooke to comment in his diary, 'Pound is quite the slowest and most useless chairman one can imagine'.[17] Even more damning was the judgement of Commander Robert Bower, who served in the Naval Liaison section at Coastal Command headquarters in 1940.

When I saw Pound just after the war started, he hobbled into the operations room at Coastal Command and I noticed with horror that he had become a worn-out old man. His hair was snow white and wispy, his face seamed and ashen and there was a noticeable distortion in one eye.[18]

Yet for all his infirmities, Pound's integrity and unruffled temperament won Churchill's trust, while his broad vision made him a strong advocate of maritime aviation.

Unlike his political master Alexander, Pound was lukewarm about the proposed takeover, fearing it would be a major distraction that would produce no more aircraft. In fact, Portal privately said at the height of the furore that the Admiralty was 'only playing second fiddle to Lord Beaverbrook'.[19] But during the last two months of 1940 the idea gathered momentum in Whitehall and soon attracted the interest of Churchill, who had concerns about the efficiency of

Coastal Command under RAF control. Against the backdrop of mounting losses to the U-boats, Alexander too was deeply worried about shortages of maritime aircraft. On 4 November he circulated a paper to the War Cabinet entitled 'Strengthening of Coastal Command', in which he observed that

> whilst the Coastal Command has given the Navy every possible assis-
> tance with the forces at their command, no means of meeting the
> Navy's urgent requirements can be within reach on the present Coastal
> Command's strength. That Command's strength has increased from
> 150 to 300 planes since September 1939. In my view the number
> should be brought much nearer to 1,000 planes in operation at the
> earliest possible moment.

In practice, he argued, 'this would mean that of the 100 new squad-rons to be put into service by June 1941, fifteen of them should go into the Coastal Command'.[20] The following day his paper was discussed at a meeting of the Defence Committee, with the prime minister in the chair. It was after reiterating his call for a substantial increase in aircraft that Alexander described Coastal Command as the Cinderella Service of the RAF: this was the first time the term had been used. In response, Sinclair not only denied the Cinderella accus-ation but also put forward the classic argument for the primacy of strategic bombing: 'Any undue expansion of the naval co-operation force would inevitably hamper the building up of Bomber Command's strength and would sacrifice the possibility of its being employed effectively on strategic operations.' Sinclair's stance provoked Beaverbrook to a dramatic intervention. Never an admirer of the Air Secretary, he urged the complete handover of Coastal Command to the Royal Navy.[21] Interestingly, Pound did not express his support for the plan and instead focused on the immediate need for more aircraft.[22] Churchill was in two minds: on one hand, he said, there would undoubtedly be 'advantages in having the whole of protection under one operational control. The Coastal Command had not received the scale of equipment that they should have.'[23] On the other hand, 'it would be a poor economy to duplicate training grounds or set up competition between the services in the market for aircraft'.[24] He concluded that a swift investigation by his office should be held into the proposal.

The political wheels were now in motion for a collision, with Beaverbrook at its centre. He followed up his appearance at the committee with an incendiary paper of his own, 'A Naval Air Force', where he stated: 'It is not a satisfactory answer to say that the RAF can fulfil the task of supplementing the surface craft of the fleet. It has failed to do so. The Coastal Command is quite inadequate'. It was a claim that was repeated in articles in the *London Evening Standard*, another of his papers.[25] Many involved with the RAF were furious at his conduct. Slessor, then director of plans, privately denounced what he called 'Beaverbrook baboonery' based on a 'totally irresponsible and irrelevant demand' borne of 'crass ignorance of air or sea warfare'. Regretting that the affair 'did not even serve to convince Winston what an ass Beaverbrook was', Slessor also called the prime ministerial investigation 'a mountain of nonsense' that 'rehashed all the old, stale, anti-air force arguments'.[26] Almost as scathing was the Coastal Command naval liaison officer, Captain Peyton-Ward, who said that Beaverbrook's paper lacked 'both restraint and sound argument'.[27] Lord Trenchard, the founding father of the RAF, was so appalled that he called on Sinclair, who relayed their conversation to Churchill. 'In his opinion, such dismemberment of the Royal Air Force would greatly impair it and would weaken the very instrument which offers the best hope of victory.' Trenchard therefore wanted 'an assurance that the government has no intention of severing Coastal Command from the RAF'.[28]

That is exactly what Portal also wanted. He had only been in post a few weeks, but had marshalled a powerful defence of the RAF at meetings and in writing. On 24 November he privately told Sinclair that 'nothing but great harm to the Royal Air Force and the country can result unless this matter is dropped completely and finally now'. If the government decided on a full inquiry to consider it, then he and his deputy Sir Wilfrid Freeman 'would feel bound to tender our resignations'.[29]

Another voice in the chorus of disapproval, inevitably, was that of Bowhill. In his own response of 19 November, he wrote that 'there would be no operational advantage in the suggestion' since the 'present system works well'. Increased costs and waste would be 'unavoidable', he wrote, before asking, 'surely wisdom demands that we should husband our resources – keep our air effort under one central organization and direction – so we can guard here, strike there?'[30] Yet there was a fundamental gap between the fine rhetoric of the RAF and the reality of Coastal Command's long neglect. For all the anger directed at him, Beaverbrook had both touched a nerve at the Air Staff and emboldened some at the Naval Staff. Writing to the War Cabinet on 20 November, Alexander stated 'we concur' with Beaverbrook's arguments, adding that 'the Admiralty have always been in favour of having full control, not only of Coastal Command, but of all aircraft whose normal function is to fly over the sea'.[31]

After a month of feverish documentary and verbal contention, the dispute came to a climax on 4 December 1940 at a crucial meeting of the Defence Committee, which Churchill again chaired. In his contribution, Sir Charles Portal ran through a series of problems with 'a complete transfer of the whole Command', such as the loss of flexibility, the 'disastrous blow' to the RAF's *esprit de corps*, and the psychological impact of transferring 28,000 men to another service. But he sensed the tide was turning and so made a significant concession in admitting that he was 'perfectly prepared to see the Royal Navy in operational control of Coastal Command'.

In those words lay the outline of the settlement that was to last the rest of the war. Churchill seized the moment at the meeting's conclusion:

> The Prime Minister said that it might have been desirable, if he had been starting afresh in peacetime, to make the great change proposed. It would be disastrous at the present moment to tear a large fragment from the Naval Air Force. This was not the time for interservice controversy.

But he agreed that 'complete operational control must be secured to the Admiralty', with any differences that arose to be settled by the Defence Committee.[32]

This outcome was an awkward but creative compromise, perhaps the only pragmatic solution that could have been reached in the pit of war. Afterwards Churchill told his foreign secretary Anthony Eden that 'it would never be possible to hand over Coastal Command to the Admiralty' because of the 'very grievous inter-service wrangle' it would have generated.[33] Both Beaverbrook and Alexander were unhappy and dissented from the decision. Slessor thought the whole affair was a farce that 'produced this ridiculous mouse in the shape of a really quite meaningless form of words'.[34] Others argued that the new arrangement made no difference since there was already good co-operation on the front line. Indeed, that point was emphasized in a joint note that Pound and Portal sent Churchill just after the meeting:

> We are agreed that under present conditions the existing system of operational control is the best that can be devised. Under this system the Admiralty issues directives from time to time, supplemented by urgent instructions to meet particular situations. The Air Officer Commanding-in-Chief, Coastal Command, is responsible for translating Admiralty requirements into orders for air operations.[35]

Although the question was settled at a service level, within the political arena the dispute rumbled on for the next two years, mainly in the form of interventions in Parliament from advocates of Admiralty control. The row over operational control had given a shock to the RAF, which had only narrowly avoided paying a heavy price for its parsimony towards its maritime wing. But the struggles for Coastal Command would continue.

4

Research

S OON AFTER THE climactic Defence Committee meeting, Portal wrote to Bowhill,

> We have had an unpleasant fortnight over the ownership of Coastal Command, as well you know and, having survived the broadsides, we must, I feel, avoid compromising our position. We are being pressed to help the Navy against the submarine and Focke-Wulf menaces. I am in full agreement that this is as important and pressing a requirement as any with which we are now confronted. To that end, therefore, we have been forced to divert, much against our will where the air war is concerned, a ponderable proportion of the very limited bomber effort at our disposal.[1]

Apart from the transfer of operational control and the RAF's reluctant diversion from attacking Germany, there were other indicators of the greater priority for the maritime war. One was the move of Coastal Command's No. 15 Group from Plymouth to Liverpool as part of the creation of a new combined headquarters for the Western Approaches, covering the vital supply lines in the Atlantic. Jointly led by the affable, innovative Admiral Sir Percy Noble and Air Vice-Marshal James Robb, a highly experienced, sometimes outspoken, officer, the headquarters was accommodated in a vast bunker beneath Derby House in the centre of Liverpool, with almost a hundred rooms and a central hub whose reinforced concrete roof was over 7 feet thick, hence its nicknames, the Fortress or the Citadel. Like Coastal Command's headquarters at Northwood, the Derby House situation room contained a huge wall chart that showed the movements of Allied and enemy vessels and was constantly updated by a team of Wrens using wooden markers and working on wheeled ladders, which were so high that in 1943 one of them, Patricia Lane, fell to her death when she lost her footing. Gathered from a range of sources, including RAF photo reconnaissance reports, the information was fed to Derby House through a secure network of teleprinters and telephones from Coastal Command's headquarters at Northwood and the Admiralty's Operational Intelligence Centre in Whitehall, whose Submarine Tracking Room was headed by Commander Roger Winn. A brilliant lawyer before the war, Winn had suffered polio as a child, leaving him a legacy of crippled legs and a heavily stooped posture, but this did not prevent him carrying out his duties with remarkable diligence and an uncanny grasp of German intentions. A similar process for disseminating intelligence was instituted at the Coastal Command's other combined naval group headquarters, of which there were now four. In addition to No. 15 based in Liverpool, No. 16 at Chatham and No. 18 at Rosyth, a new No. 19 Group was set up at Plymouth, covering the vital theatre of the Bay of Biscay.

To maintain the supply of personnel for its extensive operations and instruct crews in the use of ever more complex equipment, Coastal Command built up a large training organization, overseen by No. 17 Group headquarters in Gosport and featuring specialized bodies such as the School of General Reconnaissance, the Torpedo Training Unit, the Combined Anti-Submarine Training Centre and the Flying Boat Training Squadron. In the early years of the war, like in the rest of Coastal Command, training was restricted by the lack of aircraft, facilities and crews, which meant that squadrons were badly under strength. As the conflict intensified, however, increasing importance was attached to two key elements of the programme. The first was the massive Empire Training Scheme, which began in December 1939 and took raw RAF recruits and gave them extensive flying instruction in the Dominions free from the risk of enemy attack. In Canada alone, the principal centre for the scheme, over 131,000 Allied personnel received training. The second were the Operational Training Units (OTUs), which grew from a single, overstretched outfit in 1939, turning out just one new crew a month, to a network of six by the summer of 1941. In addition, greater capacity meant that the length of OTU courses could be doubled from four to eight weeks, though many of the training aircraft were obsolete Stranraers and Lerwicks.

In defence of supply lines, Coastal Command was also extending its reach overseas. Obsolete Fairey Battles began to be replaced in Iceland by Hudsons in early 1941, helping to shrink the 'Atlantic Gap' where U-boats were out of the range of the RAF. One of those who flew Hudsons from the Coastal Command base at Kaldadarnes was Hugh Eccles, who recalled that

> the airfield consisted of one main runway made of crushed lava dust, surrounded by peat bog, and at the perimeter was a fast-flowing river. The facilities were very primitive. An old farmhouse had been taken over as an officer's mess, with several Nissen huts erected around it.

Of his duties in 269 Squadron he said,

> Ninety per cent of our work was convoy escorts, as all North Atlantic convoys were passing through our area. At times I was escorting convoys of 100 ships. It was a very hard-pressed time. I was normally doing 15 flights a month while I was in Iceland. A typical trip would be to take off from Kaldadarnes, go up to 1,000 feet, then get to the position where the convoy would be. The important thing was to meet the convoy and I would say we did it seven out of 10 times. Having arrived at the convoy, we would do a search formally, which involved flying 20 miles ahead of the convoy and them coming back again, making a kind of square pattern. Then we would fly round the tail of the convoy, to see if there were any U-boats on the surface, before we went round the circuit again. Most of the escort duties were pretty routine.[2]

Joe Collins of 59 Squadron was based at Camp Geck near Reykjavik from 1943, as the Atlantic campaign reached its climax. 'We suffered many hardships: no lighting, no water, no sanitation.'[3] Edward Nichols, who served as a Whitley rear gunner with 612 Squadron, was shocked on his arrival in Iceland in December 1941 by the cold on the island. 'I woke up after my first night to six feet deep snow outside the hut.' His living quarters were a prefabricated Nissen hut with a Queenie cast-iron, coke-filled stove for heating. 'We provided more heat between us than that ruddy stove; we could never keep it going at night.' To avoid the damp, the beds were propped up on empty two-gallon petrol cans, and even the chairs were made of wooden crates. The space between the huts was lumpy, hard frozen earth, topped with a layer of snow. Icicles hung everywhere from windows and roofs. 'It was bleak,' wrote Nichols.

> Ablutions? We could be excused not washing or shaving. They were primitive to say the least. Supposed to be showers, they exuded a brown-tinted pathetic little stream of either freezing – which it mainly was – or boiling water. The toilet, bogs are a fair description, consisted of a standard Nissen hut, RAF issue, airman for the use off. Down each side, six cubicles at the front, each cubicle with a wooden seat, wall to wall with the usual shaped hole in it, bucket underneath.

Nichols also recalled a ferocious storm that swept across his base one night in January 1942.

> The whole of our area was smothered in sleet and snow with winds reaching speeds of 135 mph or more in terrifying gusts. Amid tremendous noise, the planes had to be held down by cement blocks supplemented by heavy vehicles and teams of forty men each to hold them down.[4]

Much further south, in January 1941 three Sunderlands of 95 Squadron were sent out via Gibraltar to Freetown in West Africa to strengthen the protection of the supply lines there. This was a very different assignment from the freezing one in Iceland, as recounted by wireless operator Geoff Walker.

> It was a tropical paradise of white surf, golden sands, waving palm trees and a warm ocean. The daily routine of springing lightly from under the 'mozzy' nets, having checked first for snakes by leaning over one side of the bed and bashing a shoe on the floor, before dashing to the showers and then a glass of water with a dash of Dettol in it, drunk to wash down the issue yellow Mepacrine tablets, kept most of us free

from the dread 'lurgi'. Of course the most potent remedy was the weekly bottle of Johnnie Walker or Bourbon – no germ could survive in those concoctions.[5]

James Kernahan of 228 Squadron enjoyed the rations but not the tedium of his patrols. 'In West Africa you had oranges, bananas and sweets, all things you never saw in England. The worst thing was the boredom, continually searching the ocean with your eyes until you'd lose the horizon.'[6]

Gibraltar itself, with its strategic position at the gateway to both the Atlantic and the Mediterranean, was becoming increasingly important to Coastal Command, so much so that Bowhill, in a reversal of the great political battle of the previous winter, even wrote to the Admiralty urging that he be given operational control of the base in order to ensure that 'the men on the spot' conform 'to the accepted principles which have proved successful over here as regards the protection of shipping'.[7] Predictably, the government rejected the idea, but Coastal Command's workload in the Mediterranean was expanded, as some of the Sunderlands of 228 Squadron were sent to an advanced base in Malta, mainly to keep a watch on the Italian fleet and harass the Axis supplies for the increasingly intense North African campaign. When the Allies had to quit Greece in April 1941 after another military defeat, it was the Sunderlands of 228 Squadron that were at the forefront of the evacuation.

The creation of new bases was accompanied by the promise of more aircraft. One clear result of the furore over operational control was that the Air Ministry had to increase Coastal Command's share of the planes coming off British production lines and from the USA's swelling provision of reinforcements under the Lend-Lease programme negotiated by Churchill and President Roosevelt. Of the additional 100 squadrons due to reach the RAF by June 1941, Coastal Command was promised fifteen. In the immediate term, new units of Whitleys, Beauforts and Blenheim Mark IVs, then being phased out by Bomber Command, were handed to Bowhill. More importantly, three far more successful planes – the Wellington, the Beaufighter and the Catalina – entered Coastal Command's service in early 1941, becoming synonymous with the force's burgeoning power. The versatile

Vickers Wellington, which had already performed duty as an unorthodox aerial minesweeper, now started duty as a maritime workhorse, equipped with ASV radar. The first Coastal Command squadron to use the Wellington was 221 Squadron, based at Bircham Newton. From 23 February, No. 221 flew convoy escort patrols before adding shipping reconnaissance along the Dutch coast in March and then moving to Northern Ireland in May, from where it undertook anti-submarine work. Partly designed by Barnes Wallis, later the mastermind of the Dambusters' bouncing bomb, the twin-engined Wellington was so useful because its geodetic airframe, a lattice steel structure covered in doped fabric, could absorb large amounts of punishment. 'I thought it was a great aircraft, very reliable and tough. We once came back on one engine, flying at about 1,000 feet. I would have been happy to fly anywhere in a Wellington,' recalled navigator Peter Beswick.[8]

Equally rugged was the Beaufighter. Developed by Bristol's design team, headed by Leslie Frise, from the unsatisfactory Beaufort by the installation of a shorter nose to move back the centre of gravity, it had a pair of more powerful Hercules engines and stronger armament, including four 20-mm cannon and six 7.7-mm machine guns mounted in its wings. The relative quietness of its radial engines, combined with its heavy armament, brought it the nickname Whispering Death among some of the enemy that encountered it in action. Despite its size and firepower, it was manoeuvrable, fast (it was capable of 350 mph) and effective in a variety of roles, from long-range fighter escort to torpedo bomber, though it was as an anti-shipping strike aircraft, complete with rocket projectiles, that it proved most deadly over water. After some teething problems, Mark I Beaufighters began to enter Coastal Command's service from December 1940, with 252 Squadron, based at RAF Chivenor in Devon, one of the first recipients. 'It was a bulldog of a warplane, immensely tough and able to withstand any amount of damage,' recalled Jim Blake of the squadron, which soon moved to Malta to join the fight against the Axis in the Mediterranean.[9] Of his initial flight in a Beaufighter, Norman Carr of 143 Squadron said that 'the power seemed unbelievable on first take-off'. He went on to describe the plane as 'immensely strong and powerful' as well as 'reliable and able to take an awful beating and still get you home in one piece'.[10] But Portal warned that the Beaufighter, for all its qualities, was no panacea. 'On no account should it be supposed that the use of the Beaufighter will enable us to defeat the German attacks on our shipping. In my opinion the use of shore-based fighters will never offer adequate protection against the kind of attacks we must now expect,' he told the Chiefs of Staff Committee pessimistically in March 1941.[11]

Against the backdrop of limited Sunderland production because of the pressure on Shorts to build bombers, Coastal Command was also crying out for another modern flying boat for reconnaissance and patrol duties. The answer was the introduction of the Consolidated PBY4 seaplane, powered by two Pratt & Whitney Wasp engines, which had been in service with the US Navy since 1936. Like the Wellington and the Beaufighter, it was tough and versatile but was also distinguished by its long range of over 2,500 miles and the excellent visibility provided by its high, parasol wing and large blisters on either side of its fuselage. The aircraft had first been purchased by the Air Ministry in 1939, and within the RAF quickly became known as the Catalina after an island off the Californian coast close to Consolidated's base in San Diego. Bowhill had mixed feelings about the import, telling Sir Wilfrid Freeman in February 1940,

> My objection to the PBY4 is that at the best this aircraft – which has already seen five years service in the American Navy – does not compare as a military proposition with the Sunderland or the Lerwick in armament or navigational facilities, but where the Americans do definitely have the advantage over us is in their engine design, which makes for greater economy in fuel consumption and maintenance.[12]

Despite Bowhill's reservations, the Catalina went on to perform impressively for Coastal Command and was especially valued for its ability to operate from almost any stretch of water. Having entered service in April 1941, over 700 of the type saw action in the RAF.

One intriguing but abortive proposal to bolster Coastal Command in its fight against the intimidating Focke-Wulf Condor was put forward by Robert Mayo, the technical adviser to Imperial Airways, who before the war had successfully conducted experiments with a seaplane carried for part of its journey on the back of a Short Empire flying boat before the two aircraft separated. Known as the Short–Mayo composite, this innovation enabled the airline to carry mail long distances without the need for refuelling, though the outbreak of hostilities prevented it being put to practical civilian use. Mayo felt, however, that the composite had military potential, and suggested that, to give long-range fighter cover, a Spitfire–Whitley bomber composite be developed. Bowhill, anxious about the damage caused by the Focke-Wulf, was an enthusiast, telling Freeman that 'any idea which may be possible should be tried out – as you will be fully aware we must do everything to overcome this menace to our shipping'.[13] But Freeman, while assuring Bowhill that the government treated the idea of the Spitfire–Whitley composite 'very seriously', believed it would take too long, probably more than six months, to come to fruition because both the undercarriage and the fuselage of the Whitley would have to be 'greatly strengthened'. Nor did Freeman have much faith in Mayo. 'I found him to be such an over-optimist as to almost earn the name "liar".'[14] The final death knell was sounded when Churchill himself imposed a veto on any further work on the project in April 1941.

The aerial campaign by the Condor, which not only attacked shipping but provided vital reconnaissance, was part of the Reich's increasingly successful maritime war, led by Dönitz and his deadly U-boat wolf packs. In January 1941 the Germans sunk fifty-nine Allied and neutral ships in the Atlantic with a tonnage of 273,000. The following two months saw 132 ships lost on the Atlantic routes, totalling 682,000 tons, though five U-boats were also destroyed. There was no let-up in the carnage during April, May and June, as the Germans accounted for 184 vessels in the Atlantic, with a combined weight of 947,000 tons. The U-boats may have been the most dreaded element of the enemy's forces, but Axis aircraft were also exacting a savage toll. During the first six months of 1941 air attacks were responsible for the sinking of no fewer than 294 Allied ships in all theatres, including northern Europe and the Mediterranean. Operating together, the submarines, planes and surface raiders could be a devastating combination, as shown by the experience of convoy HG53 that left Gibraltar on 6 February 1941 bound for Liverpool. It was soon sighted by

U-37, which not only began to shadow the procession of twenty-one ships but also provided homing beacon signals for a formation of five Condors from the nearby German air base at Bordeaux. Having found the convoy, the Focke-Wulfs bombed it from 150 feet, a ferocious assault that was joined by the Kriegsmarine's heavy cruiser the *Admiral Hipper*, which was guided on to the target by U-37's beacon signals. Nine British ships, almost half the convoy, were lost.

Coastal Command knew that it was up against a formidable foe. In parts of the service confidence started to wane, a trend worsened by the perception of the low priority given to the Command and the futility of some of its missions. In a letter of 25 February 1941 to Freeman, Bowhill wrote, 'We are asking a tremendous lot of pilots to fly continually long distances over the sea, hour after hour, in aircraft which they know will not fly on one engine. This does and must produce nervous strain.' Bowhill further grumbled about shortages of Sunderlands, the slowness of Whitley and Wellington deliveries and the unreliability of his Beauforts.[15] His frustrations were mirrored in his squadrons. 'We were only too painfully aware of the successes of the U-boats, which were now hunting in their feared wolf packs,' wrote Ted Cowling, a Sunderland pilot in 210 Squadron about early 1941.[16] For William Middlemiss with 233 Squadron based in Northern Ireland, the chief memories were of cold and tedium. 'We did long, dreary trips over the Atlantic, watching the sea. We sighted a Condor once but could not get near it. And when we first arrived, we were stuck in Nissen huts without any heating. We were frozen.'[17]

The New Zealander Mike Ensor, who became one of the Command's most renowned pilots, was shaken by the lack of morale and purpose when he joined his first operational unit, 500 Squadron, based at Bircham Newton and flying Blenheims. 'Days drifted by without us being told what we were supposed to do or how to do it. Grumbling began, none too quietly either, and the atmosphere became poor.' According to Ensor, there was a readiness of crews to avoid hazardous trips, while senior officers 'looked and sounded miserable' at briefings and were 'conspicuously absent when danger beckoned'. But the worst problem was the obsolete Blenheim. 'Let's face it. The Blenheim was not a machine to go to war in, not in winter, not across water and not least of all against the Germans.'[18]

Another famous Command pilot, Patrick Gibbs, who flew Beauforts in 22 Squadron in 1941, was equally disillusioned with the cost of sorties against enemy shipping, protected by heavy flak and fighters. 'With monotonous regularity we kept losing crews and aircraft without sinking any worthwhile targets.'[19] Indeed, anti-shipping operations in the first half of that year were ineffectual, with just five enemy vessels sunk and four damaged.

The pressure to take the offensive against the U-boats and German navy by targeting the French coast heightened the strain on Coastal Command. By mid-1941 Dönitz had ensured that the Biscay ports were heavily defended, which meant that raids could be hazardous. Alan Wilson, who flew Beauforts with 217 Squadron, based at St Eval in Cornwall in 1941, remembered how useless the 250-pound bomb was in action against the Kriegsmarine's *Scharnhorst* and *Gneisenau*, when the two huge battleships were anchored at Brest: 'The bombs just bounced off the decks of those ships. It was quite dangerous over Brest. There was a lot of flak. I don't think we had much success.'[20] In fact, so dangerous were these missions that 217's commander, Guy Bolland, refused to obey an order in March 1941 to attack the *Admiral Hipper* at the port by daylight with all available aircraft.

I was only too aware of how well that was defended by guns and fight-ers. There was no possible chance of any of my machines getting anywhere near Brest, and if they did and were lucky enough to hit the ships, the damage they inflicted on the enemy would be negligible. I decided to declare all my aircraft unserviceable.

His action was questioned by 19 Group at Plymouth, and Bowhill telephoned St Eval to protest. But Bolland stood his ground, and travelled to Plymouth to explicitly state his case. 'I told the Air Officer Commanding [Air Commodore George Boyce] that this was a suicide order and I was dead against it, as it would serve no useful purpose except to pander to the Navy's demand for action.' As Bolland admit-ted, 'it was a useless visit and one which cost my command'.[21] The mission went ahead and all three Beauforts were lost, though daylight raids were drastically reduced after that. In fact, Coastal Command's poor record in this theatre led to a change of air policy, as Freeman told Bowhill in April:

> It is the intention that Bomber Command will take over the bombing attacks on enemy harbours and that your striking force should only be employed in the torpedo and bomber role against ships at sea, with the exception that should the opportunity ever occur, a torpedo attack on enemy shipping in harbour may be attempted.[22]

In the face of such apparent helplessness, there were episodes of extraordinary valour, even while Bolland's forebodings were proved right. On 6 April 1941 Kenneth Campbell of 22 Squadron took part with a formation of Beauforts in an attack on the *Gneisenau*, which was anchored on the north shore of Brest harbour and protected not only by its own guns but also by an array of batteries and three anti-aircraft ships. The Admiralty feared that the battlecruiser was about to break out and sail westwards across the Atlantic to devastate Allied shipping. Only two of the planes reached the port at first light, and managed to fly through the initial rounds of flak from the outer shore batteries. But then the pilot of one of the Beauforts turned back, deterred by both the growing intensity of the continuous barrage and his inability to see the *Gneisenau* because of a low mist that hung over the water. Campbell's crew were now on their own. Undaunted, they dived down to almost sea level, sighted the vast grey vessel and sped towards their target in the face of a stream of heavy and light shells as well as tracer machine-gun fire. When they were less than 500 yards from the ship, Campbell released the Beaufort's torpedo, then banked steeply to avoid the hills that lay immediately behind the shoreline. His manoeuvre was to no avail. His plane was shot down and, according to one eyewitness, crashed on the deck of the *Gneisenau*, but not before its torpedo had caused severe damage below the waterline, requiring the cruiser to be brought back to dry dock for major repairs. The entire RAF crew died in action, but their bravery may have saved thousands of lives by keeping the *Gneisenau* out of the Atlantic for months. Campbell himself was posthumously awarded the VC, Coastal Command's first of the war. 'By pressing home his attack at close quarters in the face of a withering fire on a course fraught with extreme peril, Flying Officer Campbell displayed valour of the highest order,' read his citation.[23]

Despite individual acts of courage like Campbell's and the expansion of Coastal Command's fleet, the results of operations still disappointed. There was a growing sense in the Air Staff and government that Bowhill's force was neither maximizing the use of its resources, whether through serial inefficiencies or misguided tactics, nor coping well with its expanded responsibilities. What was needed was a more scientific approach, one that used hard data and scientific evidence to guide the Command's decision-making.

The first move in this direction had come in December 1940 when the Command set up a development unit, based at Carew Cheriton in Pembrokeshire, to undertake service trials of radar equipment and advise on how this technology could best be used. Quickly winning the respect of commanders, the unit saw its role expanded to provide trials for all the Command's new equipment and aircraft. This success soon led to the decision in early 1941 to recruit a scientific adviser, with a remit to focus on the war against the U-boats. The expert chosen can be regarded as one of the great unsung heroes of the Command's story because of his beneficial influence on operational practices and strategy. He was Patrick Blackett, a brilliant physicist who hailed from a middle-class stock-broking family. After outstanding service as a sailor in the First World War, during which time he became fascinated with the problems of technological warfare, he joined the world-renowned Cavendish laboratory at Cambridge University, beginning the work on cosmic rays and anti-matter that would eventually win him the Nobel Prize. From his earliest days at Cambridge, he placed great emphasis on the importance of statistics. 'You should treat your research like a military campaign. Make sure you have plenty of data,' he told his students.[24] But Blackett was no monomaniac. On the contrary, his interests in the arts and left-wing politics led him to mix in Bohemian circles in the 1930s, including the Bloomsbury Group, where his intense good looks were admired. 'He was tall and strikingly handsome in the film star mould,' recalled fellow scientist Solly Zuckerman, who worked on a range of vital research projects during the war, including the design of the civilian defence helmet and the destruction of the German transport network in occupied France during the build-up to D-Day.[25]

A socialist but never a pacifist, Blackett was recruited at the outbreak of war by the Royal Aeronautical Establishment at Farnborough, where he worked on the creation of a new bombsight. His growing renown saw him appointed in August 1940 as scientific adviser to Anti-Aircraft Command under Sir Frederick Pile, who was immediately impressed by Blackett's skill in developing gun-laying radar for the defence batteries. Another figure impressed by Blackett was Lord Hankey, the former Cabinet secretary who had built a formidable reputation for administrative efficiency before switching to politics and becoming Chancellor of the Duchy of Lancaster in Churchill's wartime government. In January 1941 Hankey wrote to the Air Secretary Sir Archibald Sinclair to suggest that Coastal Command should have its own scientific adviser, given how 'very useful' Blackett had been to Pile. Explaining that he knew Bowhill 'very well', Hankey wrote that 'he tells me he would like nothing better than to have the services of a first-class scientist on his staff'.[26]

Sinclair was immediately taken with the idea. After the consideration of some other names, his ministry suggested that Blackett could be loaned by Pile to Coastal Command for three months in the Western Approaches headquarters in Liverpool, a sufficiently long period 'to hasten the development of anti-submarine work'.[27] The task of informing Pile about this plan fell to Joubert, the assistant chief of the Air Staff. In a letter of 12 February 1941 Joubert told Pile that though 'a combined drive' by the Royal Navy and Coastal Command was under way 'to stop the rot' in the Atlantic, there 'has been a lack of scientific direction'. But the campaign, he argued, would be enhanced by the temporary appointment of Blackett, 'the best man for the job' both because of his naval and scientific record, and his strength of character. 'This, of course, will leave you without your magician – a situation which will be very upsetting to you,' Joubert wrote sympathetically, but he expressed the hope that Pile would concur because 'we are getting into a really desperate situation as regards shipping at the moment'.[28] Pile reluctantly agreed. However, there was a more difficult hurdle to overcome since Professor Blackett was nominally still employed by Lord Beaverbrook's Ministry of

Aircraft Production. The mercurial press baron was not happy about the request, as he told Sinclair. 'There is a very heavy demand going on from the Air Ministry for personnel from this Ministry. There is no return flow. The answer on this side is always "yes". The answer on that side is always "no".' But Beaverbrook gave way. 'You may have Professor Blackett for six weeks.'[29]

Blackett stayed at Coastal Command much longer, widening his role from lone adviser to head of an influential Operational Research Section, which was formally established in June 1941. For this new body, he hired an eclectic bunch of scientists and mathematicians, including Dr Cecil Gordon, a geneticist who specialized in fruit flies. His most important recruit was a stocky Welshman called E. J. Williams, who managed at the same time to be shy, inhibited, argumentative and impetuous. 'There was a wildness and unexpectedness about his behaviour,' wrote Blackett, reflected in the way Williams 'drove a car with complete disregard for the laws of dynamics'.[30] But Williams's restless, enquiring spirit was to be crucial to the Operational Research Section's work, particularly on maintenance schedules and the optimum height at which depth charges should be set to detonate.

An intellectual genius, Blackett was also a highly practical man. For him, solid improvements were more important that shiny inventions. 'Too much scientific effort has been expended hitherto on the production of new devices and too little in the proper use of what we have got,' he once said.[31] One of his first insights arose after he had studied the vast wall chart at Derby House, showing the known movements of all ships and submarines over the Atlantic. With his analytical mind, he calculated that the number of U-boat sightings by Coastal Command planes should be four times higher than their current level. The reason for this gap, he concluded, was that in three out of four cases the U-boat spotted an RAF plane early and was therefore able to dive before any radar contact was made. Blackett then asked what colour Coastal Command's aircraft were painted, and was told that, as in Bomber Command, they were black to reflect as little light as possible from any searchlights. But unlike the Bomber's nocturnal missions, Coastal Command's patrols were also conducted during the day. Blackett therefore urged that the Command's planes engaged in anti-submarine warfare should be painted white. Subsequent trials showed that the white camouflaged aircraft would be likely to catch submarines on the surface on 30 per cent more occasions than black ones. The visual change was implemented.

More importantly, the Operational Research Section conducted a comprehensive analysis of how depth charges were deployed with the aim of raising the dismal kill rate. Until now, Coastal Command's advice was that they should be set to explode at between 100 and 150 feet, based on the calculation that this was a depth that an average submarine would reach in a dive lasting two minutes, having been sighted by an attacking aircraft. Yet, as Blackett's fellow physicist Bernard Lovell pointed out, 'the fallacy was that in these cases, after two minutes had elapsed, the aircraft had poor information on where to drop the charge so the effective accuracy was very low'.[32] Blackett's team further showed that in 40 per cent of cases, the U-boat either stayed on the surface or had been out of sight for less than fifteen seconds, so the setting was far too deep. In fact the 100–150-feet setting represented the worst of all worlds: targets in the right place were at the wrong depth while targets at the right depth were in the wrong place. In a groundbreaking paper, Williams demonstrated that if the charge was dropped from low level and the setting fixed at 25 feet, the lethality of attacks on submarines would increase by two and a half times. Again, this proved Blackett's theory that significant operational gains could be achieved by simple tactical changes, though it was not until September 1941, after a series of trials, that a charge with a much shallower setting was adopted across Coastal Command. Edward Shackleton, who served as an intelligence officer at St Eval and later became a Labour government minister, said of Blackett's impact: 'in the first two years of the war, the RAF hardly sank a submarine. It was only when the operational research people got busy that we changed our tactics.'[33]

The arrival of Blackett coincided with a greater sense of urgency towards the submarine war, as the damage to the merchant fleet appeared to threaten the nation's survival. The historian Andrew Roberts has pointed out that the United Kingdom had 'to import two-thirds of all her food, 30 per cent of her iron ore, 80 per cent of her soft timber, 95 per cent of her petroleum products and 100 per cent of her rubber'.[34] By March 1941 Britain had lost 3.2 million gross tons of shipping since the start of hostilities but only thirty-six U-boats had been sunk, less than two a month, while the Focke-Wulf Condor continued to roam the skies. The Germans were also ahead of the Allies in naval intelligence, their B-Dienst cryptanalysis service having penetrated the British naval codes since the start of the war, whereas the Kriegsmarine's Enigma code remained uncracked in the first two months of 1941. During a visit to Chequers at the beginning of March, the Australian prime minister Sir Robert Menzies witnessed Churchill's anxiety about the Atlantic, as he recorded in his diary: 'The PM in conversation will steep himself (and you) in gloom on some grim aspect of the war, tonight shipping losses to Focke-Wulf planes and U-boats – the supreme menace of the war.'[35] In his own war memoirs, Churchill wrote that he would have 'exchanged a full-scale invasion for this shapeless, measureless peril, expressed in charts, curves and statistics'.[36] Determined to galvanize the fight to protect Britain's lifelines, Churchill issued a memorandum on 6 March that became known as the Battle of the Atlantic Directive. It declared:

> We must take the offensive against the U-boat and the Focke-Wulf wherever we can and whenever we can. The U-boat at sea must be hunted, the U-boat in the building yard and the dock must be bombed. The Focke-Wulf and other bombers employed against our shipping must be attacked in the air and in their nests.

To that end,

> all measures approved and now in train for the concentration of the main strength of the Coastal Command upon the North-Western Approaches and their assistance on the east coast by Fighter and Bomber Commands will be pressed forward. It may be hoped that with growing daylight and the new routes to be followed, the U-boat menace will be reduced.[37]

Churchill's clarion call was reinforced by the creation of a Battle of the Atlantic Committee, chaired by the prime minister and made up of the service ministers as well as naval and RAF chiefs. This body, which held its first meeting on 19 March, dealt largely with operational issues and put further impetus behind the growth of Coastal Command. Over the next six months the force would grow from thirty-one squadrons to forty-six. To strengthen the North-Western Approaches, Bowhill won approval to shift eight of his squadrons from southern England to Northern Ireland and Scotland. These reinforcements also enabled him, in fulfilment of the spirit of Churchill's Atlantic Directive, to go on the attack against the Focke-Wulf Condors and the U-boats, as he recorded in his despatch:

Offensive sweeps were carried out into the Atlantic to a depth of 400 miles. Individual escort was provided for convoys out to 300 miles but such escort was at a distance of 15 to 30 miles from the convoy and was made a priority in the later afternoon up to sunset.[38]

More squadrons were equipped with ASV Mark II. From May 1941, just as the Operational Research Section was devising new tactics, the supply of 250-pound depth charges began to reach Coastal Command in large numbers. The Command's presence in Iceland was expanding rapidly, with both an airfield and a seaplane base opened at Reykjavik in addition to the facility at Kaldadarnes, further stretching the radius of Sunderland operations and forcing the U-boats to move further west and south. In fact, Bowhill could boast that, thanks to greater air cover, he had by the spring of 1941 'established fair immunity from attack by U-boats for our shipping out to 250 miles from our coast'.[39]

Other developments were in the pipeline which would dramatically boost Coastal Command's fighting capacity. One was the invention of a powerful airborne searchlight by Humphrey de Verd Leigh, a personnel officer at the Command's headquarters. On his own initiative he had begun experiments with this method of illumination, which would come to fruition in 1942, transforming the fight against the U-boats at night in the Bay of Biscay. Another was the progress by Bletchley Park in deciphering the Enigma code from March 1941 on, after a raid by the Royal Navy and two Commando units on the German-occupied Lofoten Islands off the Norwegian coast, with the aim of destroying enemy shipping and the production of fish oil, vital for high explosives. During this daring combined operation, code-books and a set of Enigma rotor wheels were captured from a German armed trawler before it sank, providing the Allies with their first real insight into the enemy's naval communications. 'It seems that the British are getting around the locations picked out for attacks. This leads one to suspect that our ambush points are known to the enemy,' wrote Dönitz in his diary in April 1941, though his suspicion fell on a potential traitor or spy within his fleet rather than on Britain's cryptologists.[40]

Just as important was the promised advent of the American long-range bomber, the Consolidated B-24, known to the RAF as the Liberator, which had first flown in December 1939. The plane featured a spacious, slab-sided fuselage for the crew of ten, heavy armament, four Pratt & Whitney Wasp engines, twin oval fins on its tailplane, a tricycle undercarriage and a revolutionary high shoulder wing, designed by David Davis, a freelance aeronautical engineer. Its unrivalled performance was recalled by Squadron Leader Tony Spooner in a post-war interview.

We had a war-winning aircraft in the Liberator. It was magnificent with an enormous range and four very reliable Pratt and Whitney radial engines which almost never failed. Its superb radar could show U-boats in the Atlantic relative to the aircraft's position. We had far better depth charges, a low-level bombsight and we were armed to the teeth.[41]

But it was not an easy plane to fly, and was nicknamed the Flying Coffin by some American crews because of its vulnerability to enemy fire and its single exit at the rear. The French government had been sufficiently impressed by the early design to place an order for 120 of them. Before any could be delivered France had fallen to the Reich, however, and this meant that the contract was taken over by Britain. Inevitably, as the first B-24s had become available in early 1941, Bomber Command had prior claim on them, but they deemed the aircraft unsuitable for night bombing missions, partly because of its susceptibility to flak and partly because of the long, bright flames from its exhausts. When an initial batch of Liberators was offered to

Coastal Command, Bowhill too expressed his doubts. An item in the minutes of Churchill's Battle of the Atlantic Committee in early April read, 'He [Bowhill] was not very satisfied with what he had heard of the Liberator, but he did not know enough of its capabilities yet. It might do.'[42] The Liberator could not immediately enter service, for the plane had to be modified for anti-submarine use, a requirement that involved the installation of ASV radar, four 20-mm fixed cannons and equipment to carry depth charges in the bomb bay. By August the first Liberators were ready for deployment, and were sent to RAF Nutts Corner in Northern Ireland, where 120 Squadron had reformed.

By then the Catalina, Consolidated's other plane in Coastal Command, had been in action for several months and had played a central role in one of the most significant maritime exploits of the early war. On 20 May 1941 the Admiralty received a report from the naval attaché in Stockholm that the German battleships *Bismarck* and the *Prinz Eugen*, two of the largest vessels ever constructed by a European power, were moored at Bergen on the Norwegian coast, a finding confirmed both by a photo reconnaissance Spitfire and by decrypts from Bletchley Park. As the Admiralty recognized, the two ships, escorted by a flotilla of destroyers, were making preparations to raid the Allied shipping lanes in the Atlantic. Given the havoc these ships could cause, a concerted effort had to be made to stop them. Coastal Command therefore ordered Whitleys and Hudsons based at Wick, Scotland, to carry out an attack on the night of 21/22 May, using 250-pound semi-armour-piercing bombs. But in poor weather the mission proved abortive and the German force was able to reach the Atlantic, having evaded further patrols carried out by Coastal Command between the Shetland Islands and Iceland. The Admiralty's worst fears were now realized, as the Royal Navy made contact with the enemy. In a ferocious encounter in the Denmark Straits early on 24 May, HMS *Hood*, the pride of the fleet, was struck in her aft ammunition magazines by a shell from the *Bismarck*. She exploded and sank within three minutes with the loss of more than 1,400 lives. The *Prince of Wales* was also badly hit, though she stayed afloat and was able to return fire on the *Bismarck*, causing serious damage to her fuel tanks, hull and turbo generator gear.

The action was witnessed by Flight Lieutenant R. J. Vaughan of 201 Squadron, based in Iceland, flying overhead in his Sunderland. Having watched the huge explosion on the burning *Hood*, Vaughan was forced to find cloud cover at 2,500 feet from enemy anti-aircraft fire. 'On emerging from the cloud five minutes later, the *Hood* had almost completely disappeared and only part of the bow was showing,' he wrote, before expressing his admiration for the *Prince of Wales*'s gunners in firing back at the *Bismarck*. A hit in the stern, he said, 'was the most accurate salvo I had observed in the action'. Even so, the scene was a harrowing one. 'We flew over the wreckage of the sunken ship, observing one large red raft and a considerable amount of wreckage amidst a huge patch of oil. From the height we were flying no survivors could actually be seen.'[43]

Triumphant but battered, the *Bismarck*'s captain Admiral Günther Lütjens decided to head for France, where his ship would have to undergo major repairs. But the Royal Navy and Coastal Command were in pursuit, bent on vengeance for the loss of the *Hood* and helped by the seeping oil, which enabled another patrolling Sunderland to identify the *Bismarck*'s path. At midnight on 24/25 May, eight Fairey Swordfish from the carrier HMS *Victorious* launched a torpedo attack that succeeded in inflicting further damage on the *Bismarck*, causing more flooding and a loss of speed. The wounded German battleship then had a stroke of luck, as bad weather intervened and the Allied chasers lost contact. It was at this moment that Bowhill, a former sailor himself, played a master stroke, as he recalled after the war:

> After careful analysis of the position and the probabilities of what the *Bismarck* would do after contact was last made at 0306 hours on 25 May, I decided that in my opinion her most probable course would be to make for the Bay of Biscay ports. I therefore ordered two crossover patrols to cover the area.[44]

This was further south than that estimated by the Admiralty, who, due to a misinterpretation of encoded signals from the *Bismarck*, thought the ship was sailing for Germany via the Iceland–Faroes gap. Bowhill's instinct proved correct. Against a backdrop of mounting urgency to find the *Bismarck* before she reached port, the patrols were carried out by Catalinas from 209 Squadron, then based on Lough Erne in Northern Ireland before its move to Iceland in August, and 240 Squadron from Oban. It was one of 209's planes, captained by Pilot Officer Dennis Briggs, that sighted the enemy battleship. After taking off at 3.25 on the morning of 26 May, his crew had engaged in a long, difficult search for hours through heavy cloud cover. But approximately 790 miles west of Brest the clouds parted and Briggs, flying at 1,500 feet, saw the *Bismarck* directly below. Immediately the ship's anti-aircraft guns opened up, forcing the Catalina into evasive action. Briggs later gave this account of the incident:

> The first we knew of it was a couple of puffs of smoke just outside the cockpit window and a devil of a lot of noise. And then we were surrounded by dark, brownish-black smoke as she popped off at us with everything she'd got. The explosions threw the flying boat about, and we could hear bits of shrapnel hit the tail. Luckily only a few penetrated. My first thought was that they were going to get us before we'd sent the signal off, so I grabbed a bit of paper, wrote out the message and gave it to the wireless operator.[45]

The signal was sent to the Navy, whose ships now raced to the location. As another Catalina continued to shadow the *Bismarck*, the aircraft carrier HMS *Ark Royal* steamed towards the target before despatching three units of Swordfish torpedo bombers that evening. This time the damage was terminal. One torpedo demolished the *Bismarck*'s rudder, with the result that the ship could not be manoeuvred and kept going round in circles. In this stricken state, she was easy prey for the advancing Royal Navy destroyers, which finished her off on 27 May. The *Prinz Eugen* was more fortunate. Despite one possible sighting by a Catalina of 210 Squadron, she managed to reach Brest.

Nevertheless, at a low point in the war, the sinking of the *Bismarck* was a major boost for the Allies. In the House of Commons, Churchill praised the co-operation between the Navy and the Air Force: 'From the moment the *Bismarck* was known to be at sea, the whole apparatus of ocean control came into play' and 'very far-reaching combinations began to work'.[46] Yet, after this triumph, Bowhill did not remain much longer at Coastal Command. In June, to his regret, the government decided to transfer him to Ferry Command, a vital post but one that was out of the front line. On 12 June, just two days before he left, he put in writing his complaint about the treatment of Coastal Command, which in his view had been 'saddled with any cast-off aircraft that the Air Ministry do not know what to do with'.[47] He was being too negative. Despite some doubts about his organizational abilities, he had presided over a transformation of his force during almost four years in charge. Coastal Command was ready for a new phase – and a new commander.

5

Atlantic

IN THEORY, THE man chosen to succeed Bowhill could not have been more suited to the role. Sir Philip Joubert de la Ferté had not only been the first chief of Coastal Command when it was established in 1936 but he was also a highly experienced, courageous officer who had fulfilled an impressive range of responsibilities since joining the Royal Flying Corps in 1913. During the First World War he was mentioned in despatches no fewer than seven times; the first such citation occurred within a week of the outbreak of hostilities when he had made aviation history by undertaking the first ever reconnaissance flight behind enemy lines. After service in France, he was transferred in 1916 to Egypt, where he showed a flair for improvisation and shrewd husbandry of limited resources, qualities that he further displayed as a commander in Italy. During the interwar years his gift of leadership and creative mind propelled him rapidly up the Air Force's hierarchy, with successful spells as commandant of the RAF staff college at Andover and commander of the RAF in India. Soon after the start of the Second World War he was made assistant chief of the Air Staff (ACAS) with oversight of naval liaison and the practical application of radar, particularly for night fighters, a task which again utilized his interest in technology.

It was as the ACAS that he became a household name in Britain because another of his duties was to give regular BBC radio broadcasts and write national newspaper articles about air affairs. His eloquent originality as a communicator was helped by his imaginativeness and unconventional background. Born in Darjeeling, the son of an Indian civil servant whose father was French, Joubert himself was a fluent French speaker, a key asset on the western front during the First World War. Some of his radio talks could be controversial, however, as in October 1940 when he predicted increasing success by the RAF against the Luftwaffe's night bombers. As the Blitz intensified that winter and the death toll mounted, his forecast looked badly mistaken. Indeed, Churchill was moved in early December to complain to Air Secretary Sir Archibald Sinclair that Joubert should concentrate on his main job of improving Britain's air defences.

> Sir Philip Joubert de la Ferté's broadcasts no doubt give a great deal of pleasure to his audiences but when I see how completely he has failed to produce any results in the night-fighting against bomber attacks and how unsatisfactory is the air action on the North-Western Approaches in respect of which he has important liaison duties, I wonder if it would not be better if he confined himself more precisely to those professional duties upon which our safety largely depends.[1]

A few days later Joubert provoked even greater prime ministerial ire with an article in the *Sunday Express*. 'Disciplinary action in regard to this officer is overdue. The very important, nay vital work with which he is charged is not prospering and he has no business to neglect it for the sake of advertisement and publicity.'[2] But Churchill's annoyance did not prevent Joubert being appointed the head of Coastal Command on 14 June 1941, and given the rank of air vice-marshal.

Joubert was a figure of considerable suavity: 'a real old world gent,' in the words of the Coastal Command pilot Mike Ensor.[3] His friend and RAF colleague Sir Arthur Longmore, for a time the commander of the RAF in the Middle East, described him as 'charming, talented and entertaining'.[4] Yet for all his elegant sophistication, he also had a steeliness to his character which brought him into conflict with other senior officers and politicians. At the heart of this discord was the perennial struggle between the primacy of the bomber campaign and the needs of the maritime war. Throughout his time at the head of Coastal Command, he was engaged in a constant, draining fight for more aircraft and better equipment in the face of hostility from the Air Staff and most of the Cabinet, who clung to the belief that the destruction of the Reich's cities and industrial capacity was the way to win the war. 'For Churchill, Bomber Command was the favourite child,' wrote Joubert later.[5]

In fact, from the moment of his appointment, much of the Air Staff regarded Joubert with suspicion, fearing his ambition, independence and reluctance to subscribe to the official orthodoxy. Just before Joubert took up his post, Freeman urged Portal to interview him to ensure that he understood the government's priorities, writing: 'Joubert must while commanding Coastal Command adhere to the doctrines of the Air Staff. Bowhill was good in this regard and seldom went adrift and only did so in ignorance.'[6]

Against this background Joubert's belief that Bomber Command should support his force in the maritime war was coolly received. On his first day at Northwood, the headquarters of his command, he told Portal that Coastal Command should be able 'to call on Bomber Command' for attacks on submarine bases at the Biscay ports and this co-operation should be, within reason, given unquestioningly.[7] Portal replied that Joubert should consult Bomber Command as well as his group commanders before pushing for major policy decisions. Within less than a week Joubert set out his case in more detail to Richard Peirse, the head of Bomber Command: 'The ports are well within reach of our heavy bombers and I suggest that in the next moonlight period a reasonable part of Bomber Command's striking force should be devoted to this form of attack.' Joubert concluded, 'We are fighting for our bare existence . . . I feel we shall not get the better of the submarine menace unless we take all the measures I suggest with the utmost vigour.'[8] Peirse wrote back, telling Joubert that it was a question of priorities:

> I am firmly convinced myself that the better use for the limited available bomber force today and in the near future is to attack objectives in Germany. It is up to the Navy to protect seaborne trade and though I realize that my bombers must be deflected from their primary role against major menaces such as the *Scharnhorst* and the *Gneisenau* (which apparently cannot be dealt with by the Navy) the same cannot be said of the Biscayan ports.[9]

The Air Ministry was just as dismissive, maintaining that attacks on the Bay of Biscay ports would 'constitute a very considerable and unwarranted diversion from present planned operations'.[10]

Reluctance from Bomber Command to co-operate over the French ports was just one of an imposing range of problems that immediately faced Joubert as he tried to galvanize the campaign in the Atlantic where Britain, in his view, was 'still fighting a defensive – and consequently ineffective – war against the U-boats'.[11] Admittedly, Coastal Command's anti-submarine component had expanded substantially in recent months; by the time he took over there were 269 aircraft in the Northern Approaches and more than half of Coastal Command's fleet had been fitted with ASV radar. Moreover, the cracking of the Enigma naval code, reinforced by the Royal Navy's capture of U-110 in May, enabled the Admiralty to predict the Kriegsmarine's movements. Yet, given this increase in resources and the improvements in intelligence, the number of successful attacks on German submarines remained negligible, as was reported at a meeting of the Battle of the Atlantic Committee on 9 July. 'Tracking room evidence had shown an unusually large number of U-boats making for the French Biscayan ports, and by keeping a good search going, Coastal Command had achieved a good number of sightings. Unfortunately no sinkings appear to have resulted.'[12]

Some of this failure was down to technical deficiencies. Even long-range ASV was not proving as successful as originally hoped, only locating U-boats before visual contact was made in 20 to 25 per cent of cases. ASV was difficult to maintain, not trusted by crews who preferred to rely on their own eyes, and, crucially, did not work in the final 1,000 yards in the run up to the target, so it was little use at night when U-boats usually surfaced to recharge their batteries. The searchlight pioneered by de Verd Leigh was still far from the prototype stage, its development hampered by official interest in other types of airborne illumination. Nor had the suggestion of Professor Blackett's team for a shallow depth charge setting at 25 feet been widely implemented, partly because the standard naval fuse had a minimum setting of 50 feet. It was not until November 1941 that a 25-feet pistol was widely distributed, but even then there were teething troubles with premature detonations. In addition, Coastal Command crews had not yet found the ideal technique in terms of spacing and angle of approach for dropping a stick of charges on the target. At the meeting of the Battle

of the Atlantic Committee on 9 July, Joubert noted two other difficulties with the depth charges:

> The plane had to proceed at a slow speed to drop them. This meant
> that as you approached the submarine you were trying to ease down,
> while it was endeavouring to make a getaway. Furthermore, the opti-
> mum height for ASV was 1,500 feet but that was too high for depth
> charge attacks.[13]

As Bowhill had been, so Joubert was immediately confronted
by grumbles about mismanagement in Coastal Command, which
was undermining the benefits of expansion. Anxieties about the
Command's efficiency lingered, even reaching the heart of Downing
Street. On 21 July Churchill asked Portal about the impression of
Liberators 'lying idle because we had no crews to man them',[14] to
which Portal, echoing Joubert, explained that work had been needed
to convert 'these aircraft for the Coastal Command role which was
originally allocated to them', including the installation of 'elaborate
ASV, fixed cannon guns, depth charge dropping apparatus etc.'[15]

Part of Churchill's frustration with Coastal Command at this time
stemmed from his belief that Britain was now winning the Battle of
the Atlantic, and so more air resources should be devoted to the
bombing campaign. The prime minister's confidence, so early in the
war, was based on a number of factors, such as the strengthening of
the North-Western Approaches, which had pushed the U-boats
further into the middle of the Atlantic, as well as Roosevelt's willingness to dilute US neutrality in support of Britain. In July the president
announced that America would not only attack Axis U-boats and
raiders but would also occupy Iceland, thereby closing the 'gap'
further and freeing up British forces for deployment elsewhere. There
was also the impact of Hitler's dramatic invasion of the Soviet Union
in June 1941. This had not only shifted the focus of Germany's war
machine eastwards but had also heightened pressure on Britain to
lend its new ally support by attacking the Reich's homeland from the
air. Churchill's stance appeared to be backed up by statistics. In June
1941 Dönitz's force sank sixty-one ships in the Atlantic totalling
310,000 tons, but in July those figures had plunged to just twenty-two

ships and 94,200 tons. The toll in August was much the same: twenty-three ships totalling 80,300 tons. Late that month, Churchill's military aide Sir Hastings 'Pug' Ismay wrote to Sir Wilfrid Freeman to explain that the prime minister

> was inclined to think that the corner has been turned in the Battle of the Atlantic and that the drop in the rate of sinkings might be maintained. Meanwhile he is very concerned at the failure in production of bombers and the consequent steady decrease in the strength of Bomber Command. Taking these two considerations into account, he thought there might be a case for diverting to Bomber Command some of the effort at present going into Coastal Command.

What Churchill had in mind, wrote Ismay, was 'not just the diversion of any complete squadrons whose aircraft would be suitable for use in Bomber Command, but also a reduction in the number of new aircraft of suitable types now being specially equipped and supplied to Coastal Command'.[16]

Even the Air Staff, so keen on the bombing campaign, were doubtful about this. Freeman told Ismay that such a move would be counterproductive since the Wellingtons and Whitleys deployed to Coastal Command had undergone special modifications for maritime warfare. According to the Ministry of Aircraft Production, continued Freeman, 'it would take at least two months' to revert the fittings for Bomber Command use; nor were the Liberators equipped for Bomber Command work. If these three types were withdrawn from patrols on the North-Western Approaches, 'this area would have to be covered by long-range flying boats. This could not be done by the numbers we have.'[17] In frustration at the pressures on his force, Joubert described the government's position on the supply of Liberators as 'absurd. Out of 20 originally allocated we are to get 13 aircraft. These are still not forthcoming and with no possibility of replacement it is out of the question to form a squadron.'[18]

Churchill did not give up. In October 1941 he told the Admiralty that he was 'most anxious to increase' Bomber Command's strength. He suggested that it could be done through the 'transfer of 60 Whitleys and Wellingtons by a slow and gradual process back to

Bomber Command', now that new Catalinas, Sunderlands and Liberators were reaching Coastal Command.[19] This idea was force-fully rejected by A. V. Alexander, the First Lord of the Admiralty, who told Churchill directly that the suggested transfer of Whitleys and Wellingtons to Bomber Command would have 'a serious effect on the Battle of the Atlantic and I am therefore opposed to it'. The experience of recent months had shown that 'the close approaches to the United Kingdom have been made perilous to the enemy submarines, as in these waters our short-range aircraft are able to exercise adequate supervision', forcing the Germans 'further afield'. This meant it was even more necessary to have long-range aircraft. Yet the numbers were still too low, said Alexander, with 'just 27 Whitleys, 22 Wellingtons and 7 Liberators in Coastal Command's established strength at present'.[20] After meetings of the War Cabinet and the Battle of the Atlantic Committee, Alexander's view prevailed. 'It was essential that we retain these 60 bombers, especially for operations in northern waters,' he said on 28 October.[21]

What Joubert especially regretted about this pressure to shift resources to Bomber Command was the complacency that lay behind it. He believed that the lull in the U-boat war was only temporary and that Dönitz would soon renew his campaign with even greater vigour. Such concerns were shared by the Board of the Admiralty, which declared, 'We require every surface ship and every long-range aircraft we can possibly muster. Any suggestion that the corner has been turned is not supported by the facts.'[22] As early as the beginning of August, Joubert wrote to Portal, 'I have noticed with very great alarm a number of newspaper articles and paragraphs, some emanating from very high quarters, which appear to indicate a perfectly unjustifiable optimism in regard to the Battle of the Atlantic.' This view was badly misplaced, he said, because the Reich's 'enormous submarine-building programme is such that the enemy can flood the Atlantic with U-boats', which meant 'we cannot let up for a moment in this struggle. Coastal Command must retain, and indeed, increase the numbers of aircraft if it is to help the Navy keep this lifeline going.' Complaining about the drain of RAF resources to the Mediterranean theatre and North Africa, he wrote pithily: 'We could lose Egypt and not lose the war, but if we lose the Battle of the

Atlantic we are done.' His letter concluded, 'We are likely to suffer many losses yet and Coastal Command should be built up rather than reduced.'[23] In reply, Portal told him that he 'entirely agreed that no one should be too optimistic about the future of the Battle of the Atlantic. Far less should we think that it is already on the way to being won. We shall certainly do our best to build up the Coastal Command.' But he expressed the hope that the Americans' presence in Iceland, along with their growing protection of the convoys and their supply of new aircraft, would 'do much to relieve the strain on your resources'.[24]

Joubert's forebodings were correct. As he had warned, U-boat production was accelerating, so that in August Dönitz was able to put a daily average of forty-one submarines in the waters of the North Atlantic, compared to twenty-four in May. The result was that, after the brief summer decline, Allied losses began to mount dramatically again. In September sixty ships were hit by the U-boats, almost double the number in August, with a gross tonnage of 202,820 sunk. In October the U-boats accounted for fifty-one ships, totalling 156,554 tons. In hunting their prey, Dönitz's wolf packs continued to have invaluable assistance from the Focke-Wulf Condors, whose sorties could both provide reconnaissance on the location of convoys and inflict heavy damage themselves; indeed, over 40,000 tons of Allied shipping was sunk by Axis aircraft alone during September.

Yet the Condor was far from invincible even for less advanced aircraft, as was highlighted by the experience of Pilot Officer Ronald Down in the summer of 1941. Flying his Lockheed Hudson on escort duty for a convoy of twenty-seven ships, he sighted 'a large aircraft, about 4 miles away and very low in the water', which his navigator soon recognized as a Condor. Down increased his speed while the gunner readied himself behind the two .303 Brownings in the nose, and the navigator and wireless operator ran for the side guns. In Down's account, the RAF crew were 'overhauling the German fast, and at 400 yards they opened up with five short bursts from their front guns. The Condor replied, his tracer whipping past the nose of the Hudson in little streaks of light.' Down's plane drew even closer, continuing to fire.

When the two aircraft were separated by only about 40 feet, the Condor engines started to glow. For one moment they saw a white face appear at one of its windows. Then the big bomber turned away, into which the Hudson side-gunner opened fire. There was a wisp of smoke, a sudden belching of smoke and then flames from beneath the German's two port engines.

Down had to throttle back to avoid a collision; then, as he came out of a tight turn, he watched the Condor crash into the sea, four of its crew managing to reach its dinghy before they were picked up by the Royal Navy.[25]

Another aerial encounter with the Luftwaffe in 1941 was experienced by probably Coastal Command's most celebrated recruit, the globally renowned playwright Terence Rattigan, who served as a Sunderland air gunner and wireless operator in 95 Squadron based in Freetown, flying long patrols over the Atlantic. On one such sortie, Rattigan's Sunderland came under fire from a Heinkel He III bomber, firing from dead astern with its cannon and machine guns. 'We were an absolute sitter, but he missed us,' recalled Rattigan. The Sunderland pilot tried to take evasive action, but could not prevent the Heinkel making four further attacks. The tailplane was damaged, the intercom wrecked, and one engine failed. As the plane began to lose height, the pilot ordered the crew to jettison everything they could find. Rattigan immediately dived into his case and retrieved a set of papers before joining in the emergency removal of equipment, baggage and even the toilet seat. The exercise worked. Now sufficiently light, the Sunderland reached port 'with a few minutes of petrol to spare'.[26] The document that Rattigan saved, now decorated with a hole made by a bullet from one of the Heinkel's guns, was the partially completed manuscript for his play *Flare Path*, which became a huge hit when it was performed in the West End a year later. In a tribute to Rattigan's service, the author Robert Gore-Langton wrote, 'The chaps loved tail-end Terry for his kindness, his irreproachable manners and his professionalism. He appeared to have engine coolant in his veins, but later wrote of his hairier moments over the briny, "I was shitting myself along with everyone else."'[27]

Even more striking than the dogfights were Coastal Command's increasingly successful attacks on U-boats, as experience deepened and tactics began to improve under the influence of Blackett's Operational Research Section. During a patrol on 25 August a Catalina from 209 Squadron, now based in Iceland, sighted U-452 on the surface and roared over the submarine as it started to dive, dropping four 450-pound depth charges with the new recommended detonation setting of 25 feet. Rocked by the explosions, the U-boat was then strafed by the Catalina before a nearby armed trawler, HMS *Vascama*, rushed to the scene to finish her off with more depth charges. Though officially shared with the Navy, this was Coastal Command's first clear destruction of a U-boat.

The kill was followed two days later by one of the most astonishing episodes of the Command's war. That week, U-570 had sailed from Trondheim into the Atlantic on its maiden patrol, captained by Hans-Joachim Rahmlow. It was his first time in charge of a submarine, and the rest of his senior officers were equally untested. Compounding their inexperience were a host of technical problems that emerged as U-570 was ordered to intercept a large group of Allied merchant ships off Iceland. Aboard the U-boat, the air compressor had malfunctioned, the diesels were not tuned and the underwater listening devices had been knocked out. In addition, many of the crew were seasick and some were bedridden. In this debilitated state after several rough days at sea, on the morning of 27 August Rahmlow ordered his submarine to move close to the surface. Clearly visible from the air, the vessel was spotted by a Hudson of 269 Squadron, piloted by Sergeant Leslie Mitchell, who dived towards the target. To his anger, as he swept over U-570, his depth charges jammed in their bombing rack, but he was able to call out the location of the submarine to the rest of his squadron while he remained in the vicinity. Unaware of what had happened in the sky above, Rahmlow, still desperate for air or a respite, breached the surface at 10.50 a.m. without checking his periscope. Waiting for him was Squadron Leader James Thompson, skipper of another 269 Hudson, whose plane had picked up the U-boat on its ASV radar and now moved in for the attack. There was no jam this time; nor was there a direct hit as the four 250-pound depth charges exploded around the submarine. But that was enough to panic Rahmlow, who had ordered a dive as soon as he opened the bridge's hatch and heard the sound of the Hudson's engines. The shock of the detonations had not only knocked out U-570's electric motors and lighting but had also meant that seawater was leaking into the engine room and mixing with acid from the batteries to form a gas, which the crew mistakenly believed was deadly chlorine. Sick and shaken, Rahmlow gave orders to abandon ship and sent out an unencrypted message for help, though he also instructed that the boat's Enigma machine and its code books be thrown overboard. As the first of his men reached the conning tower, Thompson, still over-head in his Hudson, opened fire on them, thinking they were about to man the submarine's deck guns. 'I have lived all my life to see those bastards scrambling out of a conning tower,' said second pilot Jack Coleman, as the tracer hit the submarine and kicked up the water around it.[28] In desperation, the Germans waved an improvised white flag and put up their arms.

The scene was now an extraordinary one. As the RAF circled above, submariners clambered into liferafts or dumped equipment in the sea to lighten the U-boat and prevent it from sinking. More planes soon arrived, including a Catalina of 209 Squadron, to deter any attempt by the Kriegsmarine's surface ships or U-boats to mount a rescue in response to Rahmlow's uncoded message. With huge waves crashing against the paralysed submarine, the standstill continued for another eight hours until the Royal Navy turned up, first with an armed trawler, then with more ships. The German crew was taken aboard as prisoners, while the captured U-570 was towed to Reykjavik, where it underwent temporary repairs before sailing to England. Despite the loss of its Enigma machine, it provided a wealth of infor-mation to the British about U-boat technology. More incongruously, after stringent tests, it entered naval service as HMS *Graph*, the only submarine to fight on both sides during the war, another distinction to add to its record as the only U-boat to surrender to an aircraft.

The capture of U-570 was a shining, unique moment for Coastal Command. Apart from the boost to morale, the episode proved that the focus on shallow-set depth charges had been correct, as the Battle of the Atlantic Committee noted: 'These had produced a very satis-factory hammer effect', while anti-submarine bombs were 'useless'.[29]

Otherwise, the picture in the U-boat war began to look more positive during the remainder of 1941. Although submarine kills were still rare, Coastal Command's aircraft were undoubtedly a major deterrent, as revealed by the statistic that among the heavy shipping losses in September, just three of the fifty-one Allied vessels sunk that month were torpedoed within 350 miles of maritime air bases. The value of aircraft in convoy defence was further illustrated by the Royal Navy's use of the catapult-armed merchant (CAM) ship, equipped with launching gear but no landing deck. Dependent on exceptional courage, the makeshift CAM required a fighter pilot to set off and fly in search of the enemy until he ran out of fuel or reached the shore. Altogether, thirty-five of these ships saw action during the war. Equally innovative but more effective were the escort carriers, the first of which, the HMS *Audacity*, went on convoy duty in September 1941 with seaplanes flown by the Fleet Air Arm. Designed to meet the Navy's dire shortage of regular carriers, these auxiliary types were converted from fast liners by the installation of flight decks.

The protection of convoys on more southern routes was further enhanced by the expansion of Coastal Command's forces in West Africa through detachments from 96, 200 and 228 squadrons. Similarly, No. 19 Group's operations over the Bay of Biscay were reinforced in October by the transfer of the Catalinas of 209 Squadron to Pembroke Dock and the switch of the Hudsons of 33 Squadron, previously used for anti-shipping work, to St Eval in Cornwall to carry out anti-submarine duties. The rise in confidence was recognized by the Battle of the Atlantic Committee at the end of the month:

> Air attacks on U-boats continue to be carried out with increasing skill by aircraft based in the United Kingdom. The weapon situation is not yet satisfactory as we are having difficulty in getting both depth charges and bombs to explode shallow enough. These difficulties should shortly be overcome.[30]

Even the Liberator position began to improve in late September, when 120 Squadron based at Nutts Corner became fully operational, while the number of Sunderlands in Coastal Command had gone up to sixty-seven.

After a big increase in losses to the U-boats in the early autumn, the trend was dramatically reversed in November. Only thirteen ships totalling 62,200 tons were sunk in the Atlantic by the wolf packs that month. This decline was partly due to the Allies' countermeasures and partly to bad weather, but another crucial factor was the diversion of a large part of Dönitz's fleet to the Mediterranean to bolster the Axis campaigns in the Balkans and North Africa. Although Allied losses to U-boats doubled in December to 124,000 tons, the co-ordinated defence of the convoys was becoming increasingly adept, as illustrated by the case of HG76, comprising thirty-two ships, which left Gibraltar bound for Britain on 14 December, escorted by RAF Swordfish, seventeen destroyers, sloops and corvettes captained by the renowned Royal Navy U-boat hunter Frederic 'Johnnie' Walker, and the auxiliary carrier *Audacity*, which had American Grumman Martlet fighters on board. The progress of HG76 through the Straits was reported by German agents in Spain to German naval intelligence, prompting Dönitz to form a wolf pack, backed up by Condors, to intercept it.

But it was the Allies who made the initial deadly strike. As the distance from Gibraltar increased, Catalinas and Hudsons of Coastal Command, along with the Martlets, took over protection duties from the Swordfish, which had successfully beaten off three attempted attacks by the U-boats during the first night of the embattled voyage. Then on the following morning, a Sunderland on routine patrol spotted U-127 advancing to take up its position in the wolf pack's search line. The crew of the Sunderland alerted a nearby destroyer, which quickly found U-127 with ASDIC and sank it with depth charges. For a time after this the U-boats, harried by Coastal Command's planes, lost contact with HG76, but at noon on 16 December the convoy was sighted by a Condor. The wolf pack now moved in, ready to draw blood. There followed four days of continuous action, during which the RAF, the Fleet Air Arm and the Navy mounted a ferocious defence of HG76, enabling the convoy on the morning of the 22nd to come within range of a 120 Squadron's Liberator from Nutts Corner. The plane had an immediate impact as it chased off a Condor and attacked a U-boat. A second Liberator soon arrived to attack three more U-boats. Although it did not sink any of them, its aggression forced the submarines to dive and lose contact with the convoy. The following morning, 23 December, Dönitz called off his wolf pack and HG76 sailed unmolested to the Clyde.

Three ships and *Audacity* had been lost, but, with five U-boats sunk, the outcome was a decisive victory for the Allies – one that again illustrated the value of co-ordinated escorts and long-range aircraft. Indeed, the maritime war was exacting a heavy toll on Dönitz's forces. Five U-boats were sunk in November and ten in December, a reflection of the Allies' greater experience and grasp of technology. In one telling incident near the end of the year, U-451 was sunk off the North African coast with depth charges dropped by a Fleet Air Arm Swordfish. It was the first time that a German submarine had been destroyed by radar guidance at night. Events like that vindicated the opinion of Johnnie Walker, the hero of HG76, that 'aircraft are absolutely invaluable for anti-submarine warfare'.[31]

Far less progress was made in anti-shipping operations during Joubert's first six months in command. Indeed, since the start of the war there had been only a limited attempt to degrade enemy convoys, even though they were a vital part of the Reich's war effort, especially the import of iron ore from Spain and Sweden, as well as the maintenance of trade routes from the Far East. Coastal Command had lacked the planes, firepower and organization to cause serious disruption to this traffic, partly because the war against the U-boats was a higher priority and partly because of the drain of squadrons to other theatres. In addition, the German defences on the northern European coasts were formidable, embracing flak ships, anti-aircraft artillery, flying balloons and Luftwaffe fighters. Despite its importance, this offensive was a secondary consideration for Joubert compared to the Battle of the Atlantic. Nor was he alone in playing down the anti-shipping role. The government's own most recent directive for Coastal Command, issued on 2 September 1941, stressed that offensive operations were 'still subsidiary' to the primary role of reconnaissance.[32] According to Chris Ashworth, 'these months were a traumatic time for the anti-shipping forces of Bomber, Fight and Coastal Commands', with a total of 698 merchant ships attacked and 59 sunk for the loss of 123 aircraft and their crews.[33]

There were thirteen squadrons in Coastal Command responsible for anti-shipping work, two-thirds of them based in No. 18 Group in Scotland, but, much to Joubert's indignation, their strength was continually undermined by the demands from other theatres, especially the Middle East. In July he had complained about 'this constant drain on home squadrons', citing the recent transfer of trained Beaufighter crews to the Mediterranean,[34] while he later told Sinclair that the 'Beaufort situation is tragic, not only as regards shortage of aircraft but arising from unserviceability due to bad design'.[35] When, to make up for the absence of Beaufighters, Joubert made a request to the Air Ministry for some De Havilland Mosquitoes – the fast, versatile fighter-bomber that had recently gone into service – he was told it was 'out of the question'.[36] He was also plagued by shortages of torpedoes and the 'inadequate backing of torpedo trained crews';[37] and this meant that, from October 1941, torpedo operations had largely to be confined to the Norwegian coast. Nor had an experiment in an elite Coastal Command offensive unit, set up by the Air Ministry in early 1941, proved a success. Ideally, this unit was meant to comprise four long-range fighter squadrons, four bomber and four torpedo bomber squadrons, but again the removal of trained crews, shortfalls in Beaufighters and problems with the Beaufort hindered its effectiveness.

In his frustration, Joubert suggested that the force's Beauforts be replaced by more reliable Hampden bombers, which he believed were 'becoming obsolescent from Bomber Command's point of view' but in Coastal Command's hands would 'be excellent for torpedo work and mining in the Bay of Biscay and on the Norwegian coast'.[38] Freeman was having none of it. 'So far from being obsolescent the Hampden with its flexibility between bombing by day or night and sea mining, is extremely useful to Bomber Command. I am afraid that I cannot agree to your proposal that the Hampden should be handed to Coastal Command.'[39]

Just as fruitless was the creation of a Shipping Interception Unit in September 1941, with the aim of hitting enemy shipping in the Straits of Dover during periods of darkness or poor weather. The plan was that Beauforts, escorted by Hawker Hurricane fighters and equipped with ASV, would find the enemy, illuminate the target, then attack with torpedoes or bombs. After two missions with 'unobserved results', the trial was abandoned in December 1941 because the planes were needed elsewhere.[40] A month earlier, there had been more exasperation for Joubert when Coastal Command's anti-shipping work had been interrupted by the Admiralty's demand for intensified reconnaissance to keep watch on the German capital ships based in Trondheim and Brest, after intelligence reports that they could soon be on the move. In a hiatus that lasted ten days, 'all the long-range aircraft were collected from nine of the eleven operational Hudson squadrons, formed into a special flight and attached to No. 220 Squadron at Wick in order to assist the breakout patrols,' recorded Joubert.[41] But the breakout was not to occur for three more months – and when it did, Coastal Command would experience one of its darkest passages of the war.

Another early source of discord with Bomber Command was the lack of liaison from Richard Peirse's force over attacks on enemy surface vessels in European waters. In a clear statement of his belief in his command's absolute autonomy, Peirse had told Joubert in June that 'bombing is the bomber's role whether it is against shipping, industrial targets or in support of the army', adding that 'in principle and practice, the case for Bomber Command to specialize in bombing seems conclusive, just as conclusive is the case for reconnaissance to be the exclusive prerogative of Coastal Command'.[42] This rigid theoretical demarcation was bound to lead to conflict. As Joubert noted at one of his daily conferences with his senior officers, Coastal Command had 'constantly insisted' on the exchange of such information so that there was no 'overlap' in action, but 'Bomber Command did not play'; it was an attitude highlighted by the case of a Rotterdam convoy that was targeted by Bomber Command without telling Coastal Command. 'This divided control and usurping by Bomber Command of all right to any attacks on shipping is very detrimental to action against the enemy,' complained Jourbert.[43] As a result of his pressure, the Air Staff implemented a system whereby Bomber Command had the responsibility for attacks on shipping between Cherbourg and the island of Terschelling off the Dutch coast, while Coastal Command took charge of operations over the other waters around the British Isles.

The dangers of anti-shipping missions were graphically experienced by Alan Wilson of 217 Squadron, who was sent on patrol in his Beaufort near the French port of Lorient on 11 August 1941.

We found this tanker and went round once, dropped a bomb on it and then its flak caught us in the starboard engine which packed in completely. We turned around and decided to head for home. After we had gone five minutes, the other engine packed in. In fact, the Beaufort could barely keep up on one engine, and we were losing height.[44]

The plane had to ditch in the sea, but it stayed afloat long enough for Wilson and the two other crew members to escape through the hatch and climb into the dinghy that they had released. Soon, they were picked up by a German minesweeper, taken aboard, given hot soup and dry clothes before spending the rest of the war as prisoners. Geoffrey Garside described one bombing sortie with 59 Squadron against German E-boats near the Dutch coast as

hopeless and a bit gruesome. They had too much firepower and fighter protection. It was a long flight and as you approached there was anti-aircraft fire, lots of different coloured flak. We had to fly straight and steady to drop the bombs at the target from about 1,000 feet. The pilot was a bit nervous, saying, 'For goodness' sake, drop the bombs and let's get out of here.'[45]

The narrative, however, was not one of universal gloom. Ted Rayner of 220 Squadron had more success when he was sent in his Hudson to attack a German convoy carrying iron ore off the Danish coast.

As we came within range of the convoy's guns, I took the Hudson up into cloud and circled about 180 degrees so that when we emerged we approached the ships from the opposite direction to where they had last seen us, gaining those vital few seconds of indecision and adjustment among the gun crews. We dived low as I pushed the airscrew pitch controls into high revs, gave the engines full boost and selected as the target the largest ship, of about 7,000 tons, in the middle of the convoy. The bomb fuses had been set at an eleven-second delay so that we would be clear from a low-level attack by the time the bombs exploded. In the co-ordinated attack which had become second nature, I pressed the Browning gun firing button to let off a few rounds – 'just to let them know we're serious' – then pressed the bomb release. I hauled back on the control column to lift the aircraft over the ship. The rear gun clattered its message for a few seconds, then we came round again on an east–west heading as quickly as possible for a second attack. We dropped two GPs [general purpose bombs] – on target according to the rear gunner – and we were away, up into cloud again, on course for home.[46]

In fact, despite all the setbacks and limited resources, the anti-shipping operations began to show a real improvement towards the end of 1941. As Christina Goulter, the foremost historian of the RAF's anti-shipping offensive, has pointed out, in the third quarter of the year six enemy vessels were sunk and five sustained serious damage, 'But in the last three months of the year, the figures leapt to 17 sunk and ten damaged.'[47] This success, she argues, was not down to any increase in the number of aircraft and sorties, but to the development of intelligence, including the interception of coded traffic, reports from agents and photographic reconnaissance. Between July and October 1941 the resources of the Photographic Reconnaissance Unit (PRU), which was administered by Coastal Command, were rapidly expanded from twelve aircraft to seventy-two, while the number of expert photo interpreters was also increased. Some of the new flight crews were Norwegian, bringing invaluable knowledge of their native coastline.

In response to the higher losses, the Germans put more of their ships in convoys, strengthened their armament and introduced the Sperrbrecher (or 'Barrier-breaker') escort vessel, ninety-three of which were in operation by the end of 1941. As a result of these stronger defences, fifty-four Coastal Command anti-shipping planes were downed in the last quarter of the year compared to thirty-five in the first quarter, causing the decision to abandon the traditional low-level attacks in favour of medium-level ones. Remarkably, at this stage of the war, it was more dangerous to serve in a Coastal Command anti-shipping unit than in a Bomber Command squadron. A bomber tour of duty comprised thirty sorties, giving a crewman a 44 per cent chance of survival, whereas research by Coastal Command in 1942 revealed that a torpedo crew, on its first tour operations lasting 200 hours, had only a 17.5 per cent chance of survival.

This high rate of attrition added to Joubert's despondent mood, already low because of the range of problems he faced. On every front, he struggled with shortages and disputes with other commands. His catalogue of grievances grew longer, covering such problems as delays to the installation of ASV in Catalinas, liaison with the Navy at Gibraltar, deficiencies in operational training and the discipline of crews in flying boats. But by far the biggest remained the need for long-range aircraft in the Atlantic. As he told the First Sea Lord in mid-November, he had been promised twenty Liberators in April, but that total had kept being lowered over subsequent months.

Even 120 Squadron, now established in Northern Ireland, was under threat. Coastal Command had been given, he told Pound, 'just enough aircraft' to form the squadron, but 'there is nothing left for wastage. At the present rate of wastage, the squadron will have disappeared as a useful organization by January unless higher authority, by which I do not mean the Air Ministry, can be persuaded' to allot a 'due proportion' of new Liberators.[48] This mention of 'higher authority' was an obvious reference to Churchill, who, in Joubert's view, had failed to recognize Coastal Command's need. Sir Wilfrid Freeman, to whom a copy of the letter had been sent, was furious at this attempt to dragoon Pound into putting pressure on Downing Street without consulting the Air Ministry. 'I think it is all wrong that you should urge the First Sea Lord, as I think you do, to go behind the Chief of the Air Staff's back to the Prime Minister,' he wrote.[49] Under fire, Joubert responded with a plaintive handwritten letter to Freeman: 'I find the job I'm given to do a difficult one. On one hand the Admiralty bully me daily to get more long-range aircraft; on the other a strong force of people headed by the Prime Minister take away what I've got. Have patience with me!' He again complained about the promised supply of Liberators that had yet to materialize, then expressed his regret at the attitude of Churchill, who had been prejudiced by unfair American claims about his command's failure to use the plane. 'Have a heart old boy. I know what a hell of a time you are having and I try to avoid giving you more trouble but if you and I can have it out frankly, I may save the Air Ministry trouble with the Admiralty.'[50]

But the battle for more resources was only to intensify. Little more than a fortnight after Joubert wrote this letter, the course of the war was transformed by Japan's attack on Pearl Harbor, followed by Germany's declaration of war on the United States. Coastal Command was about to enter its most torrid passage of the war.

6

Endurance

WRITING IN HIS wartime diary, the intelligence officer Hector Bolitho referred to the special character of the men in Coastal Command: 'Flying as crews over immense spaces of sea gives them some of the tranquillity of sailors, with occasional flashes of exuberance.'[1] It was a view that was also held by Joubert, who undertook several sorties to gain an insight into the experiences of the operational personnel in his command.

> These flights brought home forcibly to me the intense boredom of long patrols over a grey and empty sea and the not inconsiderable risks from the weather. Add to that the knowledge that an unsuccessful battle with a U-boat would probably involve a lingering death from exposure in a dinghy 400 miles from shore or a fairly rapid end by drowning and the nervous strain becomes very clear.

Yet Joubert never failed to be impressed by the resilience, fortitude and patience of his men, as he continued: 'Though the Coastal Command crews lacked glamour and public recognition in their important work, they remained unaffected. Slogging along over thousands of miles of patrol, with an average chance of seeing one U-boat in 400 hours of flying, their morale remained high.'[2]

The intensification of the maritime war from the end of 1941 did not diminish the wearisome nature of many of the Command's operations. The mix of long hours and biting cold was remembered by Edward Nichols, who was a rear gunner on a Whitley with 612 Squadron.

> As well as a bit lonely, the rear turret was the coldest place in the aircraft, with draughts coming in from every opening and crack. We

kept our eyes peeled, constantly searching the sea and sky. It was a bit of an art, because without realizing it you could finish up looking at just the Perspex in front of you and not beyond. You had constantly to keep your eyes adjusted.[3]

One pilot, recounting to the Air Ministry in 1942 his recent experiences of flying from the south-west over the Atlantic, commented: 'We are for ever searching for signs of the enemy, but nothing appears. Even the waves are formalised into monotony, each one looking exactly like its predecessor.'[4] Long trips of deep concentration could play havoc with the mind, as another pilot told the ministry, 'I have more than once found myself making a sudden, steep bank when out in the middle of the Atlantic under the impression I was avoiding a mountain.'[5] Malcolm Hamilton, who piloted white-camouflaged Whitleys before switching to Bomber Command, recalled that his tour was 'very boring because we were flying up and down for hours'. On one occasion, over the Bay of Biscay,

we were at 800 feet, just underneath the clouds. We saw this brightness when we came to the end of the southern leg. The bomb aimer, sitting up in the front turret, called out, 'Are those seagulls over towards the land there?' The gunner said, 'My God, I think they're aircraft. And if they are, they'll be Germans.' You have never seen a Whitley do such a steep turn and rush into the clouds where we stayed the rest of the day. They were in fact Messerschmitts.[6]

The duration of each sortie was governed not only by operational needs and the amount of fuel the aircraft could carry, with a safety margin for sudden bursts of higher consumption like in an attack or a dogfight, but also by the length of time a crew could physically tolerate without losing the capacity to perform their duties. This last factor dictated the concept of the prudent limit of endurance (PLE), which in January 1942 Joubert set at fourteen hours, though this could be stretched to eighteen hours on certain missions at the height of the conflict. Leslie Baveystock, while serving in 1942 in 201 Squadron based in Castle Archdale, Northern Ireland, regularly flew 'very tiring' twelve-hour flights to the Bay of Biscay and back. 'We sometimes had to do guard duties when the plane was moored. If this clashed with a couple of operational flights, it was not uncommon to be cooped up in an aircraft for 50 or more hours.'[7] Fatigue was a central feature of life on base. John Appleton, a Catalina navigator with 210 Squadron, recalled that 'if demand for sorties was high and the weather was suitable, we would fly every third day'.[8]

The size of the crew varied greatly according to the type of aircraft. The pugnacious Beaufighter had just two men whereas the Sunderland would often carry a complement of ten: two pilots, one observer navigator, two engineers, two wireless operators and three gunners. In practice, however, most crew members were also trained as gunners in addition to their specialist duties, so were able to man the turrets in an emergency. Before any mission, the crews had to don their flying gear, which for much of the war comprised a flying helmet and the RAF uniform worn beneath the Sidcot suit, the thick, insulating garment designed by aviation pioneer Sir Sidney Cotton. But there were alternatives, as described by Edward Nichols when he was based in Wick with 612 Squadron.

We had Irvin jackets and trousers – sheepskin-lined leather – also knee-high naval type white woollen socks, roll-necked white woollen naval pullovers, silk and wool long-sleeved vests and long johns, plus a battledress with all sorts of convenient pockets. We attached to the collar a whistle, to blow if you were unfortunate enough to find yourself in the sea; further a yellow Mae West, an inflatable life jacket to keep you afloat.[9]

Once kitted out, the crews would be given a briefing by their squadron commanders on the nature of their mission, based on instructions teleprinted to the unit by the group and command headquarters, with the planned track shown in red ribbon on a large wall map in the operations room. Beyond weather reports, the target and code signals, other details were dependent on the task's complexity; a multiple low-level strike, accompanied by fighter escorts, on a German convoy would require more information than a routine, solo patrol over the Atlantic where the captain would bear a large personal

responsibility for decisions. After that, the crews collected their para-
chutes, as well as charts, logbooks, the apparatus for enciphering
messages and the cartridges for the colours of the day, so that if they
were challenged by the Royal Navy they could identify themselves by
firing a Very flare pistol. Long-range aircraft also carried a homing
pigeon for use in an emergency, as Hudson wireless operator George
Bain explained,

> The bird was our third line of communication. If you went down, you
> could write a message, clip it to him and send him off. The alternative
> use was that, if your radio went dead or you were out of range, and
> you suddenly saw an enemy ship – say in a Norwegian fjord – you
> could send the pigeon back to base with a report.[10]

One other important item was the escape kit for each crew
member, which contained amphetamine pills, maps, water purifier,
cash, high-energy food rations and a compass.

Weighed down with their gear, the crew went out to their aircraft,
usually taken there by bus. In the case of flying boats moored on the
water, this part of the journey was more awkward, since it had to be
undertaken by a set of dinghies. Moreover, ropes were not allowed on
any vessel serving the Sunderlands and Catalinas because of fear that
there could be a serious accident if one became entangled in the
propellers. Instead, a long hook was used to pull the dinghy alongside
the plane. As the crew boarded, the final preparations were under
way. On his first mission in the mighty Sunderland, Leslie Baveystock
was struck by the 'frenzied activity going on throughout the entire
aircraft' when he arrived.

> The aircraft rigger and one other member of the crew were up front,
> with the gun turret wound back from its usual position, grappling
> with the complicated strops that kept us attached to the mooring buoy.
> Gunners were fitting guns into the turrets, while the flight engineers
> were up on the main wing, turning over each of the four Bristol
> Pegasus engines with the aid of handles inserted through holes in the
> side panels. This was to make sure that oil or fuel was not trapped in
> the cylinder heads of the lower cylinders, which might cause hydraulic

locking when the engines started. The second pilot was also outside the aircraft, looking over the control surfaces, including the rudder and elevators.[11]

Similar drills were carried out on all operational aircraft. For the New Zealander James Sanders, plagued in his first days as a pilot by the anxiety that he might have overlooked something on his obsolescent Blenheim, this was almost the most nerve-wracking moment of any flight: 'I have known it all – the churning belly, the dry mouth and the nagging, doubt-ridden, double flight check before take-off, fearful that I might have mis-trimmed the elevators.' But he could not hesitate when it came time for his unit to take to the air. He watched the Blenheim in front of him pause 'at the end of the grass runway strip as the pilot went through his mnemonic of HTMPFFG – hydraulics, trim, mixture, pitch, fuel, flaps and gills'. Then the plane rolled forward, gathered speed and became airborne. Sanders was next in line. 'I watched the control tower, got the green Aldis flash and it was my turn to move up for take-off and chant my checklist sacrament like a priest before an altar.' Over the intercom, he asked the two other crew members if they were ready. When they replied in the affirmative, he pushed the throttles forward, pointed the aircraft into the eye of the wind and raced across the grass

as purposefully as any tired Blenheim could and . . . we had lift off . . . Up came the wheels and up came the small amount of flap I had used to get an early release from earth. We climbed higher and I reached behind my left hip and groped for the quaint, plunger-type controls that would change my fine pitch to a cruising coarse setting.[12]

On an early July morning in 1941, Jim Hunter, an observer in 217 Squadron, was part of an operation to attack the *Scharnhorst* in his Beaufort, taking off from his base at St Eval. On entering the plane, he was struck by its smell, 'the all-pervading odour of 100 octane fuel. Add to this the scent of various lubricants and especially at start up, the exhaust gases and one has an environment which, I think, defies description. It is not objectionable, it's almost homely.' With the ground crews having completed their work, the skipper gave the signal and the chocks were removed. 'The port engine started nicely with the usual cloud of exhaust smoke and purple flames from the rich mixture lapping over the wing's leading edge. The engine was set to fast idle while the same procedure was used for the starboard engine.' Once the temperatures and pressures for both had reached normal, the engines were run up, the pitch for the propellers was set and the magnetos checked for serviceability. 'Then back to fast idle once more to await the "green" from the caravan at the end of the field.' Next the Aldis lamp flashed. Hunter said to himself a prayer for a safe return once the plane began to move. 'For take-off, the throttles were advanced with considerable caution in order to avoid any swing occurring as we accelerated across the bumpy field.' As the observer, Hunter sat beside the pilot at take-off with his feet braced against the base of the instrument panel. The Beaufort's airspeed built up to 100 knots and the plane became airborne 'on the second bounce'.[13]

For a flying boat taking off in darkness, a flare path from the harbour was laid out on the surface of the water by a set of dinghies, each of them equipped with a pole attached to which were two lights: a dim one for clear nights and a brighter one for conditions of poorer visibility. A vivid description of the take-off in a Sunderland from Plymouth Sound was left by Leslie Baveystock:

> As soon as we were clear of the other aircraft, the inner engines were started. Leaving the sheltered water . . . we ran into quite a chop, but this did not disturb the Sunderland, now moving comfortably at a speed of about ten knots When the engines reached their correct temperature, each one was run up to 1,200 revs.

Final checks were then carried out on the ignition systems and engine pressures while the pilot also ensured that the propellers were in fully fine pitch. The plane was finally ready for take-off:

> The skipper opened the outer engines first, at the same time hauling the control column back into his stomach. This allowed the nose of the aircraft to rise as high as possible before opening the throttles of the inner engines. The purpose of this was to cut down the amount of spray from the bow wave that would strike the propellers

when the inner engines opened up . . . With the nose at its maximum height, the inner engines were gradually opened up until the props were finally clear of the spray. Full throttle was then given to all four engines. With the aircraft now coming up 'onto the step' (in other words 'planing'), the control column was centralized with the speed reaching about 50 knots. At about 85 to 90 knots the skipper eased back on the stick and the aircraft rose gracefully in the air. Once airborne, the aircraft held straight and level until normal climbing speed was reached at 105 knots.[14]

For a flying boat, the condition of the water made a big difference, with calmness heightening the difficulty. John Appleton recalled that in his Catalina,

if the water surface was moderately rippled, we were soon up on the step and accelerating to take-off speed and then up, up and away. If, however, as sometimes happened, the water was glassy smooth the aircraft would not 'unstick' no matter what speed was attained. If this was likely, a dinghy or tender would run down the take-off path, zigzagging ahead of the aircraft and so breaking up the surface. This enabled the aircraft to unstick and take-off.[15]

On a lengthy anti-submarine or convoy protection mission, once the aircraft was safely airborne and on a steady course in favourable conditions, then the automatic pilot, known as George, could be used. In contrast to Bomber and Fighter commands, most of Coastal Command's sorties took place at comparatively low level. The task of ensuring that the correct track was followed to the patrol area or rendezvous point fell to the navigator, whose calculations, constantly updated, drew on factors like wind direction, drift, barometric pressure and ground speed. Over wide stretches of water without any landmarks, it was a remarkable skill.

Other roles were just as important. After two hours in the air on a typical flight, the second pilot would take over the controls, allowing the first to have some rest. The engineer monitored the instrument panels to check on fuel consumption and the behaviour of the engines, communicating with the pilot by means of a small electric telegraph. In much of Coastal Command, the wireless operator was also responsible for the ASV radar, watching for any blip that appeared on the cathode-ray screen to indicate the potential presence of the enemy. Keeping a visual lookout across the seas were the gunners, one of whom could in some crews double up as a bomb aimer. In fact, due to extensive training in Coastal Command, the demarcation between the various occupations was relatively fluid, as Don Boorman, a Sunderland wireless operator in 201 Squadron, recalled:

I used to work a rota out for the gunners, two hours on the wireless, which was the worst one, then two hours on the radar, which was the easy one, and then they would take turns in the turrets. I often used to go to the rear guns. When we went on an operation, we would fire the guns into the sea to check they were going. Our radios were always tuned into the headquarters that were mapping our routes and if anything was wrong, we would send a message in morse code.

In the turret, he said, 'your job was to keep your eyes open, looking for the water breaker of the submarine. If the periscope came up it would make a line.'[16]

The spacious accommodation on the Catalina and Sunderland enabled each type to have an on-board galley kitchen, where hot food and drinks could be produced. In the view of the Air Ministry, this feature was a necessity rather than a luxury because research found that a proper, balanced diet on lengthy operations significantly reduced fatigue. 'We were out for almost a day, so we had to have a meal while we were flying,' said Boorman.[17] Others, on shorter journeys in smaller planes, had to make do with sandwiches, though according to William Middlemiss of 233 Squadron, a few crews took other refreshments. 'Some pilots flew under the influence. I should not say that, but they were pretty well squiffed.'[18] Nor did the toilet facilities on the aircraft match those of the well-appointed Sunderland with its flushing lavatory. 'Our loo was a tiny funnel on the end of a piece of hosepipe which to use in rough conditions was quite a feat, because if we made a mistake we would have to clean out the aircraft ourselves,' recalled John Davis, who flew Ansons at the start of the war.[19] Those weather conditions in the Atlantic and the North Sea could frequently be appalling. One member of the Canadian 409 Squadron, which flew Beaufighters as part of Coastal Command from June 1941, wrote of his experiences:

> When the clouds were low and rain and sleet reduced visibility to only hundreds of yards, you had to balance the importance of your job against the fact that it was getting dangerous to fly. If you went deeper and deeper into the murk, hoping that it might get better if you carried on a little further, you often ended up squeezed into a couple of hundred feet of space between the grey wispiness of the lowest part of the cloud base and the heaving desolation which could smash you into scrap metal if you hit it.[20]

William Day of 58 Squadron, based at St Eval, had this memory of a sweep over the Bay of Biscay:

> We did our searches at 700 feet or less and on this occasion the cumulonimbus cloud cover was extremely low. When you get it that low, it gets hold of you, throwing you up in the air and down again. I was sure the sea was coming up to me in the rear turret, at least that is what it looked like. Then we dropped out of the cloud with what seemed to be a ripping sound. We had a second pilot who was whipping back on the trimming tab to retrim the aircraft. He was holding on for grim life. We must have pulled up around 200 or 300 feet from the sea. It was a hair-raising experience.[21]

The weather could be an unpredictable factor, but there was nothing undirected about Coastal Command's operations. On the contrary, crews were required to fly according to clear tactical guidelines that had been developed by the planners to maximize air coverage or the chances of a sighting or firepower on a target. Among the approved patterns were: the simple line patrol straight out from a given point and back; the more sophisticated crossover patrol, where a unit of planes flew along a series of diagonals in a shape that resembled two triangles joined at their apexes; a bust patrol, used by heavily armed anti-shipping strike aircraft along the French or Dutch coasts; or a box patrol to search a given area of sea. For convoy protection, the first duty of the Coastal Command crew was to find the flotilla of ships and its naval escorts, though this process was often helped in daylight by the smoke trails, which could be visible 50 miles away. Once the convoy was sighted, signals of mutual recognition were exchanged between the lead destroyer or corvette and the RAF aircraft. This procedure was very necessary because of the Navy's understandable tendency to shoot first and argue later. Arthur Lane of 58 Squadron was in a Wellington on convoy duty near the Channel when

all of a sudden, orange lights came hurtling at us. What had happened was that boys on the coastal boats and the corvette – they could be trigger happy – had heard our aircraft and seen us when we broke cloud. The Wellington at first glance could look a bit like a JU 88, with its two radial engines and single fin. The lads were not going to waste time asking, 'Is it or isn't it?' So they opened up. Luckily we weren't hit but we didn't hang around. We shot straight back in the cloud.[22]

If the recognition signals were successfully exchanged, the convoy patrol began. 'Up and down, round and round, watching and watched,' recorded the Air Ministry's contemporary account, which added that on most sorties there was 'nothing much to report at the end of them, another eighteen hours to add to the hundreds already to the credit of the crew'.[23] Yet when the monotony on a convoy patrol or an anti-submarine sweep was broken by the sighting of a U-boat, then high drama could follow. Senior officers at the Admiralty and Coastal Command, along with Blackett's scientists at the Operational Research Section, devoted a huge amount of their time to analysing the most effective tactics to use against Dönitz's force. The angle of approach, the optimum moment of attack, the height of depth charges' detonation, the spacing of the stick of explosives, the speed of the run to the target, the use of ASV radar, the deployment of searchlights and the assessment of damage; all were examined exhaustively. The extent of this analysis and its influence on tactics is highlighted in a typical report of July 1942 from Coastal Command headquarters, which revealed that in 34 per cent of attacks the U-boats were still partly visible at the moment of release of depth charges, and in another 31 per cent of cases the U-boats had disappeared from view just fifteen seconds previously. It is therefore the policy of this Command to concentrate efforts on sinking those U-boats which are still on or near the surface.

This meant that, for the depth charges, 'pistols will be set at the shallowest setting'. Furthermore, 'aircraft carrying no more than six depth charges, will drop the whole load, spaced at 36 feet, in one stick', while planes with a bigger load were to do the same with the first six, but 'keep the remainder for subsequent attacks'. The report contained a host of other instructions. 'The attack can be carried out from any direction,' read one; 'normal height of release is to be 50 feet' read another. 'The object of the attack must be to make the centre of the stick fall on the centre of the U-boat', a goal that needed to take account of how

> the time from the release of depth charge at 50 feet to detonation at the shallow setting is approximately five seconds. If the U-boat is in the process of crash diving, her speed will be six knots (ten feet per second). Therefore if the U-boat is attacked while some part of the hull is still visible, the centre of the stick should be aimed at 5 x 10 = 50 feet ahead of the conning tower.[24]

Crews were also warned that an oil slick on the surface, often greeted as a sign of a kill, could be misleading, so, in the absence of other evidence, depth charges and flying time should not be wasted on such a target.

> It is considered that in a number of instances, oil slicks arise from oil or oily bilges pumped out, probably days before, by surface ships. Alternatively they might be caused by oil from sunken wrecks which gushes up more freely when depth charged, giving the impression of a damage to a U-boat.[25]

On a more positive note, advice was given to crews in a report of May 1942 about the effect of gunfire on a surfaced U-boat:

Attack by 20-mm cannon and machine guns will not cripple a U-boat but it may seriously impair its fighting efficiency. In one instance machine-gun bullets pierced the fuel tanks, making the U-boat commander reluctant to dive, with the result that the boat was sunk by surface vessels later.[26]

Another paper, in November 1942, stressed the advantages that air patrols had.

The U-boat must spend the larger portion of its time on the surface. Its speed, relative to aircraft, is low. The power of surprise possessed by aircraft is good and given scientific aids for detection and a good lookout, the aircraft can attack the U-boat with a very much greater chance of success and on a greater number of occasions during a U-boat's cruise than can the most elaborate surface craft organization.[27]

There was also praise for Coastal Command from German prisoners of war. A paper of March 1942 recorded that their testimony 'leaves no doubt that the crews of the U-boats live the life of the hunted and that they only feel secure when submerged. It follows that whenever the boat comes to the surface it maintains a constant watch against approaching aircraft.' The report continued, 'Constant diving is a source of irritation to the crew and retards the progress of the boat. The knowledge that there are aircraft in the locality plays on their fears and increases the strain.'[28]

A pamphlet from Coastal Command, produced that same year, set out in clear language official advice for anti-submarine operations, starting with a candid explanation of the skill required.

Accurate anti-submarine bombing is by far the most difficult task that is given to any pilot in the RAF to perform. The problem which is presented to him is to get a straddle with a fairly close-spaced stick of depth charges on an unseen and moving target, using as his aiming mark the fixed and visible swirl. To add to his difficulties he must get down from an operational height to 50 feet and deliver his attack within a matter of one or two minutes if he is to be successful and the lethal range of underwater weapons is so small that an error of only a couple of feet may make all the difference between a kill and only damage. Finally no sight is yet provided but the bombing has to be done by eye.

As well as advocating an average height of 5,000 feet on patrol, the pamphlet went on to emphasize the need for constant, well-drilled practice and an efficient lookout through a rota system to keep eyes fresh. It was also urged that, after an attack, pilots should not remain circling directly over the scene, for that would keep the U-boat submerged. Instead he should fly about 20–30 miles away, then return in about half an hour, by which time the U-boat may have surfaced.

> The aircraft may or may not have expended his depth charges on the first dive. If he didn't, he will get his chance again now. If he did, a dummy attack should be made just the same. The U-boat will have to do another hurried crash dive, using up a lot more battery power.

Moreover,

> every time a dummy attack is made machine guns should always be opened up on the U-boat. A lucky hit may be scored on the periscope or some electric lead or high pressure air line, which is extremely irritating to the U-boat crew who have to repair or plug it. Besides the rattle of bullets on the hull is not a pleasant sound to those inside the boat.[29]

The experience of a U-boat crew under attack was well described by Hans Goebeler in his memoir of the submarine war.

> We heard the unmistakable roar of aircraft engines resonating through the hull of our boat. I unconsciously ducked my head at the sound, instinctively aware of how close the aircraft must be for us to hear its engines over the humming of our diesels. Suddenly a deafening blast, a thousand times louder than a thunderclap, knocked us off our feet. It felt as if a giant fist had slammed the boat down into the water. A split second later three more explosions ripped through the air, even louder than the first . . . Inside the boat was pure pandemonium. The lights had gone out and the air was suddenly filled with thick acrid

smoke . . . Shouts from the aft end of the boat told us that there was a large breach in the hull. A thick jet of seawater was pouring into the boat, filling the diesel bilge and flooding the engine room. Someone reported that the depth meter indicated that the water was weighing the boat down. Translation: we were sinking.

But U-boat crews were astonishingly resilient. The hole was plugged, the water stopped rising, emergency lights were activated and the air supply restored, enabled the submarine to limp back to base.[30] No pilot pursued his prey with more zeal than rugged Ulsterman Terry Bulloch, the son of a staunchly Unionist merchant in the linen industry. A fine rugby player and cricketer who had become obsessed with aviation in his Belfast youth, he had joined the RAF on leaving school in 1936, soon displaying his aerobatic skill, superb eyesight, raw courage, quick temper and dislike of officialdom. 'Windy buggers' and 'useless bastards' were two of his epithets for deskbound officers.[31] In 1942 he even turned down a promotion to the rank of wing commander because he knew that such a position would involve less flying and more administration, so he remained a squadron leader for the rest of the war, dedicated to his vocation of hunting down the enemy at sea. Some complained that, such was his disdain for authority, he acted as if he ran his own independent air force, but others admired his ruthless focus on attack, and his achievements had an influence on Coastal Command's tactics, particularly his belief that a U-boat should be attacked along its track at a slight angle to provide a margin of error. A fellow crewman Michael Layton, when asked who was responsible for most of the U-boat sightings in his squadron, replied: 'Oh, it's always the Bull. Whenever subs are around, his eyes seem to stick out of his head.'[32] One internal Coastal Command report stated that Bulloch 'probably has the best record of any anti-submarine captain in this command', therefore his views should be heeded. 'He makes several statements which are at variance with Coastal Command instructions but the remarks of a really successful, practical man go down with operational aircrews so much better than do official orders.'[33]

The autumn of 1942 saw Bulloch based in Iceland with 120 Squadron, Coastal Command's only Liberator unit, where he enhanced his reputation for tracking more U-boats than any other pilot. At 11.30

a.m. on 8 December he was on patrol, protecting convoy HX217 on its way to Britain when his sharp eyes spotted the wake of a U-boat travelling on the surface. Immediately he sounded the plane's klaxon that told the crew to take up 'Action Stations'. It was now the usual race against time for the Liberator, with its load of eight depth charges, to reach the U-boat before it dived. As Bulloch sped towards the target, the wireless operator flashed a message in morse code back to base to give the plane's location and report the imminence of an attack. Arriving just as the U-boat, which was later confirmed to be U-254, began to disappear beneath the surface, the Liberator managed to release six of its depth charges at just the right angle. The explosions sent a torrent of water gushing into the air, followed by the rapid spread of debris and dirty brown oil. Just four members of the 45-strong crew survived and were picked up by another German submarine.

Bulloch was far from finished. Soon after the wireless operator had transmitted a report of the successful attack, the skipper spotted two more U-boats. He went for the second, trailing one and dropped his two remaining depth charges, though it was not clear if the boat was sunk. He then flew back to convoy HX217 to resume his protection duties, only to spot yet another U-boat. Now without depth charges, he opened up with his cannons, the barrage of sixty rounds forcing the vessel into a hurried dive. As soon as a further report was submitted he spotted a sixth U-boat and then a seventh, both of which were subjected to more fire from his Browning guns before he ran out of ammunition. The mayhem was still not over for the Germans. Bulloch's flight engineer installed another clip of ammunition, just in time for the skipper to make an attack on his eighth U-boat, which he blasted with 100 rounds from the .303 machine guns. On his return to base after being in the air for seventeen hours, near the prudent limit of endurance, Bulloch was far from triumphant. On the contrary, he expressed regret at the insufficiency of depth charges. Nevertheless, through his concentrated aggression and daring, he had thrown a deadly wolf pack into disarray and guarded the convoy from attack. 'He was the supreme Liberator captain' and 'an exceptional pilot', said his station commander Victor McBrateny.[34]

Until the autumn of 1942, when the first strike wing was formed, anti-shipping and coastal bombing operations did not receive the same attention as the U-boat war. In the words of Roy Conyers Nesbit, who flew in 217 Squadron, such efforts were 'ill-defined' and marked by 'poor tactics, inadequate aircraft and lack of fighter escorts'.[35] Even so, they could be just as demanding and often even more dangerous because of German anti-aircraft defences. Serving that year in Malta, which was under constant aerial bombardment, Tony Spooner had the job of searching for enemy shipping, and then, with the help of ASV, guiding the Royal Navy or RAF bombers or Fleet Air Arm Swordfish on to the targets.

> Our main duty was to look for Axis convoys going to North Africa. We were called the Special Duties Squadron and we were supposed to act as reconnaissance at night, using our own codes and radio frequency to communicate. ASV worked much better in the Mediterranean with the calm sea and dry air; our planes were a mass of aerials because of radar. I once did fourteen hours in a Wellington which must be some sort of record. Because we were loaded to the eyebrows with fuel, I had no means of carrying bombs.[36]

Patrick Gibbs was another senior Coastal Command officer who fought over the Mediterranean at this time, flying Beauforts from Alexandria to disrupt the Axis supply lines. Strikes against enemy shipping, he recalled, were rare, but on one occasion he went on the attack against an Italian convoy made up of two battleships and lined on either side by destroyers whose guns formed a defensive screen.

> The sky was filled not with individual smoke puffs but with great areas of exploding shells; vast expanses of water were churned up around our aircraft and innumerable lines were drawn across the sky by tracer ammunition . . . Sweat poured down my face as I roused myself to throw my faithful Mark II around the sky, turning first one way, then another, climbing and diving but always heading towards the target.

Even in the face of this barrage, Gibbs found a way through and saw the Italian battleship *Littorio* steaming majestically across his line of sight. 'Hardly able to believe that I was actually within range of such a prized target, I ceased weaving for a split second, steadied my aircraft to take aim and dropped my torpedo.' Unfortunately little damage was caused and soon the *Littorio*'s guns had opened up.

> The whole side of the battleship seemed to go off like a firework and become a line of jets spurting flame; the water beneath me became a cauldron of foam seething under the explosions of shells burst near the surface and the sky around my aircraft was filled with flashes and smoke of others exploding in the air. Opening the engines to full throttle I attempted my escape from the furnace but my aircraft, rocking drunkenly from nearby explosions, seemed to be standing still, and when finally there was a deafening explosion underneath the fuselage and a sickening sound of rending metal, I thought for a bitter moment that the flight had come to an end.

Oil from the broken hydraulic pipe sprayed over the cockpit, which also began to fill with blue smoke. Yet somehow the Beaufort stayed in the air and Gibbs was able to coax it on the journey back through the destroyer screen until, to his relief, he reached open sea and flew on to Luqa aerodrome on Malta, where, with the hydraulics gone, he had to do a belly landing, tobogganing 'down the runway to the accompaniment of a shower of sparks' before the 'inglorious wreck' came to rest.[37]

In contrast to that ferocious defensive response, Ray Loveitt, flying a Beaufort in 42 Squadron, met surprisingly little opposition when he was on a mission to attack the German pocket battleship *Lützow* off the Norwegian coast on the night of 12 June 1941. The enemy vessel, escorted by four destroyers, had been sighted by a Blenheim of Coastal Command's 114 Squadron, but the conditions were not in the RAF's favour as Loveitt approached his PLE, with his vision impeded by thick rain clouds. Just as he thought he would have to return home, he saw the *Lützow* around 3 miles away, bathed in moonlight. Loveitt dived down, then hurtled over the water at a height of just 20 feet, having to rise briefly to avoid crashing into one of the destroyer escorts. To his amazement, there was no reaction from the enemy as the front of the *Lützow* came into view. Not a single shell was fired in his direction, no lines of tracer arced towards his aircraft. He steadied the Beaufort, pressed the drop button, slammed his throttles open, sped over the ship's bows and then began his climb to safety. Still no shot followed him. Suddenly there was an explosion as the torpedo hit the *Lützow*'s hull and a giant plume of water gushed into the air. But Loveitt did not remain at the scene to savour the destruction. Still concerned about the possibility of flak, he now began the journey back across the North Sea. According to the historian Chaz Bowyer, 'his torpedo had crippled the *Lützow*, damaging its port propeller shaft and causing the ship to list heavily to port with part of the upper deck already awash'.[38] The ship had to return to Kiel for major repairs in dry dock. A fortnight later Loveitt was awarded the Distinguished Flying Medal (DFM), the citation for which read,

> After maintaining close formation for over two hours in most difficult conditions, Flight Sergeant Loveitt came out of low rain cloud against the enemy force. He skilfully manoeuvred his aircraft and dropped his torpedo inside the destroyer screen, scoring a direct hit on the battle-ship. The execution of this brilliant attack was so sudden that the enemy was taken completely by surprise.[39]

The asset of surprise in the darkness also began to be enjoyed by anti-submarine crews from mid-1942, thanks to a technological breakthrough that was to transform Coastal Command's capacity. But before that happened, the force was to endure its most humiliating episode of the war.

7

Dash

CHURCHILL WAS OVERWHELMED with relief after the Japanese attack on Pearl Harbor, believing that America's entry into the war would be the decisive factor in the struggle against the Axis. 'Being saturated and satiated with emotion and sensation, I went to bed and slept the sleep of the saved and thankful,' he wrote in his war memoirs.[1] But for Coastal Command and the Admiralty, the immediate prospects were forbidding. As the scope for enemy action widened dramatically across the oceans, Britain's resources would be stretched even further. In a paper at the end of the year, Sir Albert Durston, the director of naval co-operation at the Air Staff, warned

> Now that Japan has entered the war against us and the margin of our naval supremacy has been so greatly reduced, long-range squadrons will become more essential than ever in the Battle of the Atlantic, more especially since the supply of flying boats from America has fallen so far short of expectations.[2]

That sense of foreboding was justified. From January 1942 Dönitz's U-boat fleet embarked on a deadly new phase of the battle. The admiral sent six of his largest submarines to patrol the eastern seaboard of the USA, where their operations were supported by fuel supplies from Type XIV U-boat tankers known as Milch Cows. For the German crews, this became their second 'Happy Time' of the war, since they were able to attack America's ships almost with impunity. Ill-prepared for the fight, the US government failed to adopt even basic defensive measures like a blackout along the shore or the introduction of a convoy system. In the first three weeks of German operations off the east coast 200,000 tons of shipping were sunk. January 1942 saw sixty-six Allied ships hit by U-boats, compared to twenty-eight in December 1941. The monthly total climbed to eighty-two in February.

In the face of this worsening threat, the Admiralty stepped up its demands for both more aircraft and more bombing of the Biscay ports, warning that 'the Germans are building U-boats at the rate of 20 per month, and this figure is expected to reach 24 per month shortly. The importance of strengthening our offensive against the U-boats is very great.'[3] In response, the Air Staff said that these requests could not be met because of the needs of the enhanced heavy bomber assault on Germany, led by ever greater numbers of four-engined Halifaxes and Lancasters, which were now coming into service. But as a substitute, the American four-engined Boeing B-17, known as the Flying Fortress, was available, having proved unsuitable for night bombing due its limited loading capacity and its visibility caused by flames from its exhausts. On the other hand, the Flying Fortress had strong defensive armament and a top speed of 287 mph. The Air Staff therefore proposed that 'all Fortress aircraft allocated to this country throughout 1942 should be earmarked for Coastal Command' with the aim of building five squadrons by the end of the year. In addition, they promised another Bomber Command Whitley squadron, fitted with ASV, would be allotted to Coastal Command and 'to be returned later in the year'.[4]

This was not nearly enough for Joubert, who believed that Churchill and the air chiefs were not facing up to the realities of the war at sea, as he complained that month. 'The prospect of Coastal Command being able to work at reasonable efficiency appears to be becoming more and more remote.' The one Liberator squadron was being allowed to die out without any reliable alternatives.

Neither the Sunderland nor the Fortress, still less the Wellington or the Whitley, are long-range aircraft by Atlantic War standards. While fully aware of the importance of a sustained bomber offensive, it appears to me that if England is to survive this year, in which we are already losing shipping at a rate considerably in excess of American and British building, some part of the bomber offensive would have to be sacrificed and a long-range type such as the Lancaster diverted to our sea communications.[5]

The diligent Dudley Peyton-Ward recognized how difficult Joubert's job was at this time, writing, 'there is no doubt that on occasions during this depressing period, the Air Officer Commanding was metaphorically kicked by the Admiralty for not asking enough and blamed by the Air Ministry for demanding impossibilities'.[6] But others felt that the Admiralty was at fault for not pressing its case hard enough or in challenging Churchill's focus on the bombing offensive. 'I have heard Alexander time and time again give in to Winston without a fight,' recalled Sir William Davis, the Navy's deputy director of plans.[7]

As the losses mounted in the Atlantic, the Allies suffered another heavy blow in early February when the Germans added a fourth wheel to the Enigma machine, making it twenty-six times harder for Bletchley Park to break. Through this innovation, the Kriegsmarine effectively imposed a blackout on its communications with its submarines. The problem was compounded when B-Dienst acquired a new copy of the British merchant navy's own code book, leaving British traffic even more exposed. This was part of a pattern of setbacks in early 1942 that badly eroded confidence in the Allied campaign. On top of the massacre of American shipping, the Russians were faltering against the German invader, British troops in North Africa had failed to advance, and Singapore was about to fall to the Japanese. The situation would have been even worse in the North Atlantic if Hitler had not made a serious misjudgement about Allied intentions. Unsettled by British Commando activity on the Norwegian coast, the Führer became convinced that the Allies were planning to mount a full-scale invasion of Norway. Much to Dönitz's regret, he instructed that that part of the U-boat fleet should return to protect the North Sea while also giving orders that the battleships *Scharnhorst*, *Gneisenau* and *Prinz Eugen* leave their French base for Germany by taking the direct route through the English Channel. The German naval chiefs, led by Erich Raeder, agreed that the ships were vulnerable to Allied bombing of the French ports but were aghast at Hitler's instruction to sail up the Channel, which seemed to them a suicidal gamble given the strength of Britain's maritime forces in home waters. Nevertheless, with their habitual thoroughness they drew up plans for the daring operation, known as Operation Cerberus, under the command of Vice Admiral Otto Ciliax, in which the capital ships would set sail at high speed from France, protected by a powerful force of surface escorts and fighter aircraft.

For months the Allies had been concerned about a possible break-out by the Kriegsmarine's capital ships, and had consequently drawn up their own response, Operation Fuller. Their plan was hampered, however, both by excessive secrecy, which meant that most officers were kept in complete ignorance about it, and by the autonomy of the three branches of the RAF, which undermined co-operation. Fuller featured stronger patrols by Coastal Command Hudsons of 224 and 237 squadrons off Brittany and the Channel, as well as prepara-tions to use the Command's three Beaufort torpedo squadrons, 42, 86 and 217, backed up by Swordfish of the Fleet Air Arm's 825 Squadron. In addition, Spitfires from Fighter Command and 250 aircraft from Bomber Command were to be put on two hours' readiness, while the Royal Navy agreed to send reinforcements of motor torpedo boats, destroyers and mine-layers to the Straits of Dover, plus three submar-ines to patrol the sea off Brest. But crucially, in the wake of the sink-ing of the *Repulse* and *Prince of Wales* in the Pacific in December 1941 by Japanese torpedo bombers, Sir Dudley Pound refused to despatch any capital ships further south, driven by fear that they would be too vulnerable so close to enemy-occupied coastlines. It was to be the first mistake in a disastrous catalogue of errors and ill-luck that at times descended into farce.

On the basis of military and naval intelligence, backed by his own instincts, Joubert gave a remarkably accurate warning on 8 February 1942 of the Germans' imminent breakout within the next week. Far less accurate was the unanimous belief within the Admiralty, the Air Ministry and Coastal Command that the German flotilla would leave Brest by day in order to use the cover of darkness at night once they reached the Straits of Dover, by far the most dangerous part of the journey. In fact, in another example of German audacity and faith in the battleships' protective screens, Ciliax planned to leave on the evening of 11 February and sail through the Channel in daylight, the very opposite of the British military chiefs' conjecture. By 7.30 that evening, having held a conference with his senior officers aboard the *Scharnhorst*, Ciliax was ready to depart, only to be delayed for a couple of hours by an ineffectual RAF bombing raid on Brest. No damage was inflicted and at 9.30 p.m. the *Scharnhorst* steamed out to the open sea, followed by *Gneisenau* and *Prinz Eugen*.

By then, the British string of bungles had already begun. Two Hudsons from 224 Squadron that had taken off from St Eval that evening to carry out reconnaissance over Brest both developed radar problems and returned to base. A third Hudson only went on patrol at 10.40 p.m., by which time Ciliax's formation, travelling at 27 knots, had already made rapid progress along the French coast. Despite its size, it still remained unseen, even when two successive Hudsons of 223 Squadron completed extensive circuits over the Channel between 12.30 a.m. and 7.15 a.m. on the morning of 12 February before going back to their base at Thorney Island near Portsmouth. In their defence, the weather had become increasingly foggy, but that could not explain the next blunder. As dawn broke, ground radar stations near Dover had picked up from the German fighter cover unusual aircraft activity in the Channel, but initially this was dismissed as an air-sea rescue operation. By 10.10 it was clear that something much bigger was happening and Spitfires from Fighter Command's No. 11 Group were sent to investigate. By coincidence another pair of Spitfires were out on a training flight over the Channel, one of them flown by Victor Beamish, who later recalled:

> We were about five miles off the French Coast near Le Touquet. I saw two ships roughly in line astern, surrounded by twelve destroyers and circled again by an outer ring of E-boats. When we arrived over the ships, we saw in the air around nine to twelve Me-109s. They immediately attacked us.[8]

The Spitfire pilots took evasive action and returned fire, then headed home, keeping radio silence until they landed at Hawkinge near Folkstone at 11.07. In doing so, they were following RAF standing orders, which were designed to prevent aircraft from revealing their locations, but in this case such a precaution was both unnecessary, given that they had been seen by the Germans, and misguided, since it meant a vital delay in making their report on the advance of the German convoy.

Almost fourteen hours after the Germans had weighed anchor, the British had confirmation of the Channel Dash. Finally, Operation Fuller was put into action. But the enormity of the task and the impact of the delays appeared to overwhelm their forces, as co-ordination and communication between the units broke down completely. In place of a concentrated attack on the ships, there was disorganized mayhem, slowness and tragedy. Mishaps continued to occur. Seven Beauforts at Thorney Island were ordered into the attack, but only four had been fitted with torpedoes. Once this quartet took to the air, they failed to find their fighter escort, then discovered their briefing about the target had been wrong. Two of them eventually found the ships and managed to launch their torpedoes through heavy flak, but without inflicting any damage. Nor did the other three Beauforts achieve anything better once they had been rearmed and taken to the air. A far worse fate was suffered by the six Swordfish of 825 Squadron, based at Manston and led by Lieutenant Commander Eugene Esmonde, a veteran of the sinking of the *Bismarck*. When the fighter escort failed to materialize in the numbers expected, Esmonde knew the mission was as doomed as the Charge of the Light Brigade, given that it would be undertaken by obsolete biplanes flying straight into heavy enemy gunfire in broad daylight. The station commander at RAF Manston Tom Gleave recalled Esmonde's mood at take-off:

> Although his mouth twitched automatically into the semblance of a grin and his arm lifted in vague salute, he barely recognized me. He knew what he was going into. But it was his duty. His face was tense and white. It was the face of a man already dead. It shocked me as nothing has ever done since.[9]

As the Swordfishes pressed on with their attack at a height of just 50 feet through a merciless barrage from the guns of the battleships, carnage was inevitable. All six planes and thirteen men were lost, including Esmonde, who won a posthumous VC. The Luftwaffe's own diary for that day paid tribute to how the Swordfish were 'piloted by men whose bravery surpasses any other action by either side that day'.[10]

But even the Fleet Air Arm's unparalleled heroics could not disguise the incompetence and dilatoriness of the RAF and Royal Navy. The fourteen Beauforts of 42 Squadron, based at Leuchars in Scotland, had been ordered south on 10 February to RAF Coltishall, in line with Joubert's original directive, though, because of poor weather in the north, they did not actually arrive until late in the morning of the 12th. Even worse, just nine of them had been armed at Leuchars, so five were without weapons, but the Mobile Torpedo Unit had failed to turn up at Coltishall as arranged, leading the Beaufort crews to name it 'the Immobile Unit'.[11] In the desperate circumstances, the torpedo-equipped nine were instructed to fly for the convoy via Manston where they were supposed to rendezvous over the airfield with Hudsons and fighters, but there was more confusion because of both the incompatibility in radio equipment and poor visibility which meant that the formation lost its cohesion.

The chaos was recalled by Arthur Beech of 42 Squadron, who said that the briefing at Coltishall was 'the most fantastic I ever had in my life. It was in a Fighter Command drome and they hadn't got a black-board, so they put a table on its side and laid it against two chairs so we could see it. That sounds funny now but at the time it was dread-ful.' The mission continued to be difficult.

> We got to Manston and circled it. There was no sign of any Spitfires. We had been there five minutes when two squadrons of them turned up but they were no good – their radios were on a different wave-length to ours, so we couldn't speak to them. Then we were ordered to go. Everyone followed except the Spitfires. We went to Texel with no fighters.

There was heavy rain and cloud when Beech's squadron found the convoy, his own plane dropping its torpedo at the *Gneisenau*. 'The ships were firing at us as we went in but we did not get in too close. We dropped at maximum range. The sea was calm. Flying back we were pursued by an Me 110 but I saw in the distance two lines of destroyers.' Beech flashed the colours of the day; his signal was recognized by the first destroyer astern. 'Suddenly I heard a loud bang. The destroyer had got our plane. Thank God for the Navy. We managed to land at Lowestoft.'[12]

There was no evidence that the Beauforts scored any direct hits, and nor did the Hudsons that eventually managed to reach the scene using their ASV radar. The planes of Bomber Command fared no better. Out of 242 despatched, only 39 were reported to have attacked the ships, but none scored any hits. Headed by the destroyer HMS *Worcester*, the light forces of the Royal Navy proved equally ineffective. The last hope lay in the twelve Beauforts of 86 Squadron, which took off from St Eval, refuelled at Thorney Island and then flew to the Dutch coast in the late afternoon to intercept the enemy ships. Yet again, the effort was plagued by misfortune. In rapidly fading light, the crews failed both to meet their fighter escort or find the German convoy. Two Beauforts were shot down in the futile quest. Edward Shackleton, then an intelligence officer at St Eval, remembered: 'We were awfully slow to respond. *Scharnhorst* and *Gneisenau* were halfway up the Channel before we went on the attack, which was never really pressed home. It was a failure.'[13]

During the dash up the Channel the most serious damage to the convoy came, not from an attacking aircraft or naval vessel but from Allied mines laid by No. 5 Group, Bomber Command. Both the *Gneisenau* and *Scharnhorst* were badly rocked by explosions, forcing them to undergo lengthy repairs when they limped into port in Germany on the morning of 13 February. In addition, the Luftwaffe had seventeen aircraft shot down, while two torpedo boats of the Kriegsmarine were damaged. Just a fortnight after the Dash, *Gneisenau*, while in dry dock at Kiel, took such a severe direct hit during another Bomber Command raid that she was never able to put to sea again. In the longer term, paradoxically, Britain's tactical defeat therefore turned into a strategic victory because the threat of the Kriegsmarine's surface fleet in the Atlantic had been drastically reduced. But none of that could detract from the scale of Hitler's triumph. Once again his boldness had been vindicated. Even if the threat of the *Scharnhorst* and the *Gneisenau* had been temporarily removed, the outcome of the Channel Dash was a humiliation for Britain.

The public was dismayed, the press in uproar. 'Nothing more mortifying to the pride of our sea power has happened since the seventeenth century,' thundered the *Times*.[14] Followed just days later by the surrender of Singapore, the fiasco sparked a political crisis that led to outrage in Parliament, a Board of Inquiry and a major reshuffle in the Cabinet, with Beaverbrook out and Attlee elevated to the post of deputy prime minister. Already seriously ill and exhausted, Sir Dudley Pound saw his reputation take another blow. Having lost a total of forty-two aircraft, all three RAF commands came out of the saga badly, but it was Coastal Command that was most discomfited. Amid 'the shambles and self-sacrifice', to use a phrase of Roy Conyers Nesbit,[15] the weakness of its anti-shipping operations had been brutally exposed. Heavily criticized for his complacency, Joubert blamed 'lack of co-ordination and inadequate equipment', on top of 'a vast deal of confusion, in particular at Manston airfield between Fighter Command's controllers, and the coastal and naval commanders'.[16] Sholto Douglas, who was head of Fighter Command at the time, admitted to an 'extraordinary chain of blunders and misunderstandings on our part' but wrote that Coastal Command 'should have done much better'. He added that 'the few Coastal Command aircraft that were available were late in getting off, were wrongly armed, and it appeared did not even know, through a misunderstanding in communications, what they were to do'.[17]

That verdict was largely upheld by the Board of Inquiry, headed by the experienced judge Sir Thomas Bucknill. Its report was delivered in March and debated in two secret sessions in Parliament, though it was not published until after the war because of its condemnation of the absence of unity between the services and within the RAF, reflected in the fact that there was no clear line of authority for the execution of Fuller. The report also pointed to the failure of Coastal Command and the Admiralty to achieve a high level of integration, echoing the row about operational control that had raged towards the end of 1940 and never been fully resolved. Indeed, in a debate in the Lords, some peers complained that the oversight of Coastal Command was an awkward compromise which had produced 'alarming' results such as the poor reconnaissance of Brest.[18] Predictably Lord Trenchard, the founding father of the RAF, heaped all the blame on the Admiralty, whose operational control meant that it was 'responsible for the disposition of machines' and the 'construction of torpedoes'.[19] According to the RAF historian Wing Commander Alistair Byford, part of the difficulty lay in the personality of Joubert, who lacked the weight to impose 'a satisfactory inter-command arrangement' and 'was unable to maintain the generally harmonious relationship with the Navy that had been established by his predecessor'.[20]

One immediate consequence of Fuller worked in Joubert's favour. He had complained that 'if the Air Ministry in its wisdom deprives the Command of the tools necessary to do its work, then that work will be badly done'.[21] Immediately after the fiasco, Joubert wrote to Freeman to ask for 'fast, well-armed aircraft with which to do visual reconnaissance'. He understood 'there is a grave shortage of Mosquitoes and Beaufighters but it seems to me that here is a role for either of these aircraft of such importance that Fighter and Bomber Command could well afford to part with ten or a dozen of this type'.[22] Freeman told him again there was no chance of any Mosquitoes. 'You are wrong in supposing that either Bomber or Fighter Command have a considerable number of these', though he was more hopeful about Beaufighters or, as a substitute, long-range Spitfires.[23]

Furthermore, recognizing that Coastal Command's anti-shipping forces were too meagre, the Air Staff finally agreed to Joubert's long-standing demand for Handley Page Hampdens to be used as torpedo bombers. The move was enacted by the direct transfer of squadrons 144 and 455 from Bomber Command and the modification of the planes by the deepening of the bomb bay and the installation of 500-pound bomb racks under each wing. By the summer of 1942 there were four Hampden squadrons in Coastal Command. But there was to be little improvement in the effectiveness of anti-shipping strikes, not least because the arrival of Hampdens was soon diluted by the departure of more Beaufort and Beaufighter crews for the Middle East.

The continuing weakness of the force was reflected in results: in March and April just two enemy vessels, totalling 1,994 tons, were sunk by Coastal Command. In May a further attempt to sink the *Prinz Eugen* off the Norwegian coast by 42 and 86 squadrons ended in another failure. Soon afterwards, the two squadrons joined the exodus to the Middle East. The Hampden, slow and lacking agility, proved a disappointment as a torpedo bomber, its inadequacy compounded by the German decision to strengthen their anti-aircraft defences at sea by the addition of more guns on their minesweepers and flak vessels. Their well-organized convoys featured not only heavily armed Sperrbrecher merchant ships but also Vorpostenboot auxiliary patrol boats that carried anti-aircraft artillery and machine guns. This array of weaponry exacted a heavy toll on Coastal Command's anti-shipping forces. Losses from anti-shipping operations remained disturbingly high, particularly for the Command's dangerous Rover patrols, in which formations of usually three aircraft undertook low-level searches off the German and Dutch coasts. May saw forty-three anti-shipping planes shot down by flak or fighters in return for just twelve vessels sunk. The following month Joubert had to order a temporary halt in low-level attacks after a quarter of his aircraft sent on such missions failed to return. At the same time, operations over Norway were radically curtailed.

Two lessons were obvious from this experience: first, a dedicated, well-equipped, highly trained strike force was necessary; second, such a force would have to be made up of Beaufighters, faster, more manoeuvrable, and better armed aircraft than most other types.

The crisis in anti-shipping was mirrored in Coastal Command's anti-submarine arm, as Dönitz's fleet, emboldened by its success off the US eastern seaboard, grew in size and confidence; by March 1942 there were ninety U-boats at sea. Yet the demands of the bomber offensive meant that the Air Staff still resisted giving any priority to Joubert and Pound, despite the First Sea Lord's warning that 'if we lose the war at sea we lose the war'.[24] The explanation for this resistance was set out in a memorandum for the War Cabinet by the Air Secretary Sir Archibald Sinclair on 8 March:

Squadrons of Bomber Command could best contribute to the weakening of the U-boat offensive by offensive action against the principal industrial areas of Germany within our range, including the main naval industries and dockyards. To divert them to an uneconomical defensive role would be unsound at any time. It would be doubly so now when we are about to launch a bombing offensive with the aid of new techniques of which we have high expectations and which will enable us to deliver a heavy and concentrated blow against Germany at a moment when German morale is low.[25]

Churchill agreed, arguing that 'the bombing offensive against Germany is our main effort, and, at present, apart from munitions, our sole means of helping Russia'.[26] In the quest to prioritize strategic bombing, Portal and Churchill now had a formidable ally in the form of Arthur Harris, who took over as head of Bomber Command in February and immediately gave it a destructive new sense of purpose. Brave, unsentimental, blunt and ruthless, Harris had spent much of his early life in Rhodesia before serving in the Royal Flying Corps in the First World War. That conflict convinced him that there must be no repeat of the savage, blood-soaked stalemate on the western front. In place of vast armies bogged down in trenches, he adhered with a passionate intensity to the belief that sustained aerial bombardment was the path to victory. His method to achieve that goal was simple: 'kill the Boche and terrify the Boche'.[27] To him, the Navy, the Army and the rest of the RAF were of secondary importance to the bomber force. In particular, he was dismissive of Coastal Command and resented its demands for aircraft and crews. Portal shared his faith in the bomber, but on a personal level found Harris uncouth and difficult. 'The trouble with Harris – off the record – was that he was a cad and would not hesitate to go behind your back to get something he wanted,' Portal told a journalist after the war.[28]

At a pivotal conference of the Chiefs of Staff Committee on 27 March called by Churchill to discuss the Bay of Biscay, the Admiralty set out its demand for six squadrons of Whitleys or Wellingtons and three squadrons of Lancasters. Sir Max Horton, the Navy's head of submarines, argued that the ability to attack the U-boats by day or night during their passage through the Bay would increase the chances of kills and limit the length of their operations by forcing them to spend more time travelling below the surface, thereby using more fuel and power. In response, Portal revealed his doubts about the entire Bay offensive, after a study of Coastal Command's operational statistics over the last year. There had been a total of 281 sightings in the year, resulting in three U-boats known to be sunk and five badly damaged, which Portal calculated was 1,150 hours for each hit. 'In the same amount of flying time 2,625 mines could have been laid from the air,' he said triumphantly. Neither Horton nor Pound had much time for this theory since there was no evidence 'of a single submarine casualty from magnetic mines'.[29] Again, no final decision was reached, Churchill having ordered further analysis by the two staffs.

The next day Portal repeated to Churchill his hostility to any transfer of Lancasters or Liberators from Bomber Command to Coastal Command. 'The Lancaster is our best "heavy" and can carry 8,000 pounds to Berlin.' Any attempt to shift some of them to Coastal Command, he continued, 'will seriously weaken our hitting power'.[30] In addition, Liberators were badly needed for the North African campaign. Yet some kind of compromise had to be reached. With Alexander pressing Churchill over the 'frightful' losses in the Atlantic,[31] the War Cabinet eventually agreed that Coastal Command should be supplied with an additional two squadrons of Whitleys and two of Wellingtons, while eight Liberators 'previously destined for the Middle East' would be lent to Joubert's force.[32] It was a decision that would do little to quell the burgeoning discord over the maritime war.

Many outside the top ranks of the Air Staff and Bomber Command felt that the obsession with area bombing was not just ill-conceived but undermined Britain's war effort by squandering resources that should have been deployed elsewhere. That was the view of Admiral John Tovey, the commander of the Home Fleet, who said that 'whatever the results of bombing cities might be, it could not of itself win the war, whereas the failure of our sea communications would assuredly lose it'.[33] Tovey was so infuriated by the primacy of the bombing campaign that, at one stage, he even urged the Admiralty chiefs to resign if they did not win more support for the aerial defence of the convoys. 'A stand has to be made,' Tovey told Pound, because 'the aircraft of Coastal Command were quite inadequate'.[34] Although their Lordships did not take such a drastic step, the agitation continued. Sir Henry Tizard, one of the government's chief scientists, heavily influenced by data from Patrick Blackett, warned that the present policy of bombing Germany is wrong; we must put our maximum effort first into destroying the enemy's sea communications and preserving our own. That we can only do by operating over the sea on a very much larger scale than we have done hitherto and we shall be forced to use much longer-range aircraft . . . everything is lost by concentrating on this bombing offensive instead of concentrating on the sea problem.[35]

Informed by his research, Blackett was even more sceptical. When Frederick Lindemann, Churchill's scientific adviser, produced a paper that extolled the potential urban devastation that could be caused by an expanded Bomber Command, Blackett issued a riposte based on his own modelling: 'If a quarter of the 4,000 bomber sorties which could be flown each month by the summer of 1942 were diverted to anti-submarine operations, it would save a million tons of Allied shipping a year.'[36] The passage of time only strengthened his opinion. In 1961 he wrote:

If the Allied war effort had been used more intelligently, if more aircraft had been supplied to the Battle of the Atlantic and to support the land-fighting in Africa and later in France, if the bombing of Germany had been carried out with the attrition of enemy defences in mind rather than the razing of cities to the ground, I believe that the war could have been won half a year or even a year earlier.[37]

In early 1942, however, the momentum was with Arthur Harris. With his flair for publicity, Harris began soon after his arrival to plan a sensational operation that, if successful, would dramatically bolster his command's reputation as a potent instrument of war. In doing so, he had to reverse the usual practice whereby Coastal Command begged for aircraft from Bomber Command, instead asking Coastal Command for support. His headline-grabbing scheme was to launch a vast armada of over 1,000 planes at the city of Cologne on the night of 30/31 May under the code name Millennium. Because Bomber Command had little more than 400 front-line operational aircraft, Harris had to build up his force from other sources, such as training units, reserves and other commands. Crucially, Coastal Command was asked to supply 250, but on the eve of the raid the Admiralty refused the request, fearing that the losses would be too high. Despite this decision, Harris managed to scrape together his proposed number of aircraft and the raid went ahead.

It turned out to be more of a public relations triumph than a military one. The British press gloried in its scale, but the damage inflicted on the city, though severe, was less than Harris had hoped. In June, he held two more thousand-bomber raids, the first on Essen, the second on the port of Bremen. The latter, held on the night of 25/26 June, saw the participation of Coastal Command after Churchill, whose dramatic side was captivated by the show-manship of Millennium, had leant heavily on Pound and Alexander to co-operate. 'I must definitely ask for compliance with this request,' he wrote.[38] Following the Admiralty's reluctant approval, Joubert supplied 102 Wellingtons and Hudsons, which targeted the Deschimag shipyard.

The Millennium raids had enhanced Harris's reputation as a commander of ambition and resolve, but the loss rate over Bremen, at 5 per cent, was too high to be sustained. Nor had the initiative done anything to lessen the friction between the Navy and the Establishment over competing priorities. 'Coastal Command at the moment is not sufficiently strong to bear its proper share of the war effort,' Pound complained to Portal in May.[39] Against this backdrop, the deadliness of U-boat attacks was becoming alarming. In May, 607,000 tons of Allied shipping were sunk by Dönitz's submarines, easily a monthly record for the war until then, though the total was surpassed in June when 700,000 tons were lost. At a liaison committee meeting in May, when disquiet was expressed at the low number of Coastal Command sightings of U-boats given the escalation in enemy activity, Captain Peyton-Ward explained 'that this was almost entirely a question of the lack of aircraft available', adding that Coastal Command had 'very few' long-range, heavy aircraft.

> He said a very strong case could be made to show that they would be
> of the greatest value in attacking the U-boats entering and leaving the
> French ports and in extending the air support to our shipping a greater
> distance from the coast. The number of U-boats within 300 miles of

the coast was fully as great as within 300 to 500 miles but the number of ships sunk at the greater range was much larger. This was due to the air support being inadequate to a range of 300 miles and most inadequate beyond this range.[40]

However, Coastal Command was about to make a far-reaching breakthrough, not in the size of its force but in its technology.

8

Light

DAYLIGHT WAS FADING over the horizon as the four Wellingtons taxied to the end of the runway, ready for take-off. It was late in the evening on 3 June 1942 and the crews of 172 Squadron were gripped by nervous anticipation ahead of their experimental flight from their base at RAF Chivenor in Devon. Once airborne, they climbed slowly out to sea, then took a gradual turn southwards to strike a track for the Bay of Biscay. Soon the sky had turned pitch black, except for the occasional glint of a star. Suddenly a remarkable sight filled their vision, almost as if it were a harbinger of their mission into the darkness. One crewman, Canadian Donald Fraser, recalled, 'A sporadic shower of meteors burned itself up in the earth's atmosphere, momentarily frightening us with its unexpectedness.'[1]

The trip continued towards the Spanish coast. Its leader was Jeff Greswell, a Coastal Command veteran described by Fraser as a 'thin wiry man' with a small moustache, a crop of black hair and an enviable flying record.[2] Greswell's experience and authority were essential for this trial of the practicality of the new searchlight designed by Humphrey de Verd Leigh. With his aeronautical expertise, Squadron Leader Greswell had been intimately involved with Leigh's project. Now the moment had come to put theory into practice. If the Leigh Light worked, it could radically alter the balance of the submarine war by leaving the U-boats no hiding place at night near their French bases.

Approaching the Bay, the Wellingtons fanned out and began the search for the enemy. A frisson of excitement ran through Fraser's plane as the radar operator picked up a blip on his ASV screen, indicating a vessel 5 miles ahead. Immediately the skipper sounded the klaxon for action stations.

The searchlight had been lowered and the navigator had scrambled up beside the pilot. I put the searchlight through a practice run with the light off, adjusting the controls up and down and from side to side as shown on the indicators in front of me; the index finger of my right hand toyed with the on/off switch for the search-light beam.[3]

At 2 miles from the target, amid mounting tension, the bomb doors were opened. Then, at a distance of three-quarters of a mile from the target, Fraser switched on the light and started to swing it across the path of the Wellington's flight. But to the crew's disappointment, once it was illuminated, the object of their search turned out to be only a fishing vessel. Fraser's account continued, 'The captain ordered, "light off – light up – bomb doors closed". The engines whined as he opened the throttle and the Wimpy [Wellington] climbed slowly to its patrol height of 1,000 feet.'[4] Just after the searchlight had been retracted through a laborious process of hand-pumping, a second blip was spotted, and the attack operation repeated, only for the crew to find that the target was another fishing boat. Two of the other Wellingtons had similar encounters.

But Greswell and his second pilot Allan Triggs had more luck when at 2 a.m. they picked up a contact 70 miles off the Spanish coast. 'Using the standard attack procedure, the Leigh Light was lit at three-quarters-mile range at 250 feet, but failed to pick up the target ahead in the beam as we had hoped.'[5] Greswell soon realized what had happened. 'The barometric pressure set on the altimeter some 400 miles away in Chivenor was such that, when indicating 250 feet, we were actually flying nearer 400 feet when the light was switched on – the beam overshot the target.' Greswell reset the altimeter and climbed away, only to catch sight of a submarine still on the surface, firing coloured flares into the sky to give its position. The crew knew that these were not the signals of a British submarine, so Greswell came in for a second approach.

This time the homing process worked perfectly. I opened the bomb doors, the Leigh Light illuminated the U-boat and I attacked from the starboard beam, dropping a stick of four depth charges. The tail gunner saw the depth charge plumes, saying they had straddled the U-boat, and he opened fire on the conning tower as we flew over.[6]

It turned out that the submarine was not a German one but an Italian, the *Luigi Torelli*, which had sustained such severe damage, including fires in two battery chambers and the complete loss of electrical power, that it only just reached the nearest Spanish port. On his return leg, Greswell spotted another submarine and, having expended all his four depth charges, used the Leigh Light to make a machine-gun attack, scoring hits on its hull and conning tower.

A mood of elation swept through Coastal Command's headquarters at the news of Greswell's success. The force now had a valuable new aid in its arsenal. Just a day after his historic trip to the Bay, Greswell had an interview with Joubert, where they agreed on the need to put more Leigh Light Wellingtons into production and to demand that the Air Ministry step up the supply of more accurate, American altimeters. Joubert later wrote that the impact of the Leigh Light was

> instantaneous. Up till that moment the U-boats had been diving by day and proceeding at high speed on the surface at night, thus escaping our air patrols. But the searchlight aircraft completely changed the scene. Terrified at the chance of being caught fully surfaced by an aircraft they could not see until it was upon them, the U-boats returned to the practice of proceeding on the surface by day and submerging by night when in the searchlight area. From this moment, the sightings and attacks rose sharply.[7]

That was spelt out in an Air Ministry report of January 1944, which stated that in the period from Greswell's attack on 4 June 1942 to the end of 1943, '151 sightings have been made during the hours of darkness with the aid of this light, resulting in 108 attacks'.[8]

Yet for all his enthusiasm to Greswell, Joubert bore some responsibility for delays in putting the Leigh Light into service. If he had fully backed the project from the start of his time in charge, instead of encouraging another, less practicable innovation, then this equipment might have been available sooner. It was as early as October 1940 that

Humphrey de Verd Leigh, known as Sammy, had written to Coastal Command headquarters, when Bowhill was the chief, with his proposal for a searchlight to be installed in a Wellington for 'locating and attacking enemy submarines at night'. Leigh noted that, while ASV radar could detect the presence of surface craft, it had two huge drawbacks: first it could not identify whether these craft were submarines or not; and second, ASV went blind about a mile from the target. The purpose of his searchlight, therefore, would be 'to bridge this gap and allow proper identification'.[9] It was an idea that reflected both his inquisitive mind and his grasp of engineering. The son of a Hampshire vicar, he had been an apprentice with the Vickers company before joining the Royal Naval Air Service in the First World War. Hunting German U-boats had been one of his duties in the conflict. After demobilization he worked for many years on a cotton plantation in the Sudan, then went into Coastal Command in September 1939, serving in its personnel department. A year later, with the German U-boat crews enjoying their first 'Happy Time', Bowhill was intrigued by the idea of the searchlight and took it up with the Air Ministry, which approved a contract with Vickers to begin experiments. Once the device had been built, trials with an ASV Wellington in March and April 1941 proved 'beyond doubt that the direct illumination of a sea target from an aircraft using ASV was an entirely practicable proposition'.[10] Bowhill was delighted, writing to the Air Ministry that 'the results are so encouraging that I feel we are on the verge of producing a very effective instrument'.[11] He urged that Leigh be given a research post so that he could work exclusively on the searchlight, a suggestion backed by the Command's senior Air Staff officer Geoffrey Bromet:

> Development of this idea and improvements to the equipment should be regarded as a full-time job for Squadron Leader Leigh. Without his technical knowledge and drive, an experiment which may well lead to important results is in danger of going slow – might even fall by the wayside – through lack of a champion who is undeterred by obstacles.[12]

But that was precisely the outcome that almost occurred. On becoming commander-in-chief in June 1941, Joubert favoured a very different concept: the Turbinlite. Developed by the Air Staff's chief scientist William Helmore and the General Electric Company initially for use against enemy night intruders, this was a far more powerful searchlight and Joubert decided to adopt it for Coastal Command's anti-U-boat operations.

With his own light now apparently shelved, Leigh returned to his personnel duties. But he was not finished. Against Joubert's instructions, he carried on with his scheme in private, even asking the engineering firm of Savage & Parsons, which had worked on the Wellington, to build him a full prototype. Leigh recorded that the company, which was headed by the inventor and skywriting pioneer Major Jack Savage, 'had no official order to produce such a Light and it was purely out of faith in my invention and as a result of my persuasion that they did so'.[13] It was fortunate that they proceeded, for the Turbinlite turned out to be a flop. What seemed to be its greatest asset, namely its tremendous power, actually brought a host of problems. Its batteries were so heavy that the plane could neither carry depth charges nor an operational load of fuel; the light burned through its carbon rods at a phenomenal rate; and at low level in damp conditions over the sea, its watery glare dazzled the pilot rather than increased his field of vision.

Joubert changed his mind and told Leigh to resume the development of his light. According to Donald Fraser, when Leigh explained that he had already had a prototype built, Joubert was angered: 'Who gave you permission to go on with this work?' 'Nobody, sir,' replied Leigh. In his own memoir, Joubert admitted that he 'took Leigh to task' over his freelance work.[14] Yet the needs of the Command were more important than Leigh's disobedience. 'Nothing more was said,' recalled Fraser.[15]

Weighing only about 1,000 pounds, Leigh's device for the Wellington consisted of a 24-inch lamp mounted in a retractable under-turret controlled by a hydraulic motor. For other planes like the Catalina he also came up with a lighter, detachable 32-inch nacelle version that fitted under a wing and had electric controls. A special Coastal Command flight was set up to conduct trials at Chivenor, which proved 'completely satisfactory'.[16] With the zeal of a repenting sinner, Joubert became a passionate advocate for the Leigh Light,

pressing the Air Staff for more production versions even before 172's
sortie in June. 'I hope you will do what you can to have the necessary
orders placed at once,' he wrote in February.[17] The ministry waited
until the outcome of Greswell's mission before approving production
orders from Vickers for sufficient Leigh Lights to equip two Wellington
squadrons and all Catalinas, as well as enough to conduct trials on
Fortresses and Liberators. To Joubert's frustration, the promised
schedule of deliveries by Savage & Parsons was not met, prompting
him to write to Stafford Cripps, the minister of aircraft production. 'I
am very dissatisfied with the position in regard to manufacture,' he
told Cripps as he stressed 'the real urgency' of the programme and
requested that the company be given 'additional labour'.[18] Cripps
gave Joubert an alarming but credible explanation for the delays:
'Towards the end of the month Major Savage had what is practically
a nervous breakdown' and before this episode 'had planned his
production so ineffectively that he omitted to manufacture a number
of parts'. Cripps assured Joubert that the General Electric Company
were now helping Savage & Parsons to make progress on the fulfilment of the orders.[19] De Verd Leigh had his own source of annoyance
when he learnt that Air Commodore Helmore was being given the
credit in parts of Whitehall and the press for the searchlight's invention. 'He had no part in the Leigh Light any more than I had in the
Helmore Turbinlite . . . I was responsible for carrying this idea into
practical effect.'[20]

Due to his invention, the waters of the Bay became more treacher-
ous for the U-boats. On 6 July 1942 the Leigh Light system claimed
its first definite kill of a German vessel when a Wellington of 172
Squadron, piloted by American volunteer Wiley Howell, sank U-boat
502 off La Rochelle with a perfect straddle of depth charges. All fifty-
two German crew members lost their lives. Dönitz was perturbed by
the change, writing in his diary, 'The aircraft has suddenly become a
very dangerous opponent.'[21]

But huge risks also continued for Coastal Command crews. Allan
Triggs, who had flown alongside Greswell on the first successful Leigh
Light mission, experienced an engine failure on 12 August while on
a sortie over the Bay and had to ditch in the sea. He and the rest of
the Wellington crew made it to their dinghy but spent the next six

days at sea before they were picked up by the Royal Navy after a
succession of rescue attempts had failed due to poor weather and
enemy action. One Sunderland despatched to the scene came down
awkwardly in the heavy swell, whipped up by a 25-knot wind, and
was badly damaged, with the result that its own crew also had to take
to a dinghy. Tragedy struck when that dinghy burst, drowning five of
the Sunderland crew. The only survivor, navigator John Watson,
managed to swim to another tiny craft that had been dropped earlier
by a Whitley. On the second day, another Whitley spotted the men in
the water, only to be shot down by a Luftwaffe fighter. More air-sea
rescue planes were sent but struggled to find the dinghies until at last,
on 17 August, a Hudson with rescue gear appeared above them,
followed at dawn the next morning by a high-speed launch (HSL),
protected by three more Hudsons, two Beaufighters and three other
naval launches. Altogether in this draining episode, fifty-seven RAF
aircraft had been involved, two were destroyed and seventeen crewmen lost. There were almost more casualties on the journey back to
Britain when the convoy was targeted by a pair of Fw 190s, but these
enemy planes were chased off by the Beaufighters.

Greswell's success with the Leigh Light was immediately followed
by another morale booster provided by one of Coastal Command's
most daring feats of the war. Code-named Operation Squabble, the
plan was hatched after British intelligence reported that the Germans
were to hold a military parade along the Champs-Elysées in Paris in
early June. Armed with this information, Joubert decided that a single
Beaufighter should make an uninvited appearance at the event to the
accompaniment of heavy machine-gun fire. Many on the Air Staff
had grave doubts, thinking the risks were too great, but Joubert was
adamant. The men he chose for this mission were Ken Gatward, a
former journalist now in 236 Squadron, and his navigator George
Fern, who were briefed on their task by Joubert at Coastal Command
HQ; in summary they had to 'fly at low level down the Champs-
Elysées, strafe the musicians and soldiers, and if that fails, attack the
Gestapo Headquarters in the Ministry of Marine'.[22] Subsequently, an
additional duty was added: to drop the two largest tricolours possessed
by the Royal Navy, one on the Arc de Triomphe, the other on the
Marine Ministry. After some intensive low-level practice and tests

with the French flags, Gatward and Fern were ready for action by the scheduled date of 12 June. Taking off from Thorney Island near Portsmouth and having crossed the Channel, they raced over northern France at tree-top level towards Paris without being detected by the Luftwaffe despite sunny weather. Soon the unmistakable silhouette of the Eiffel Tower came into view. They could not resist looping the structure before releasing the first tricolour, carefully folded and fitted with weights in its corners so it spread out as it fell. Gatward recalled in a post-war interview,

> I said to Sergeant Fern, 'Are you ready for the first flag?' and he said, 'Yes, I'm all ready but the slipstream is almost breaking my arm!' He was pushing this furled flag down a flare chute into the slipstream of the propellers and at the right moment, he let it go. We couldn't stop to see exactly where the first dropped but Vichy said it fell right on the Tomb of the Unknown Warrior, which of course was where we wanted it to be.[23]

But as they carried on down the Champs-Elysées, they saw neither a band nor a military parade. The event had been cancelled. Gatward and Fern now turned their attention to the Ministry of Marine, completing one circuit over the building, then coming in for a second run. According to Gatward's account,

> we came in as low as we dared, in case they had any light Ack-Ack on the rooftops . . . We came square up to the Ministry of Marine and we were right in line at a range of about 500 yards before we let fly with our four cannons and saw the sparks flying off the building. We hadn't any time to see whether the shells burst inside but a good deal went through the windows. We sprayed the place from base to apex and only cleared the roof by about five feet. While I was doing this, Fern was shouting out encouragement and pushing out the second flag, which we hoped would fall slap across the front door.

They saw 'a number of German military cars stop in the street with Huns standing around them and others dodging around the street and the avenue. But we couldn't let fly at them because there were too many civilians about.'[24] Then they started for home, flying back at a height of just 30 feet over France before landing at RAF Northolt where they were personally greeted by Joubert. They had only been over central Paris for six minutes, but their exploit, eagerly reported by the BBC and the press, raised national spirits at a time when the North African campaign was going badly. 'As these men were struggling desperately against powerful enemy forces, the RAF Coastal Command Beaufighter tourist excursion was a balm for hurt pride,' stated *Tatler* magazine.[25] For their bravery on this mission, Gatward received the DFC and Fern the DFM.

Despite its uplifting nature, Operation Squabble was a sideshow compared to the wider picture of the unfolding war in the summer of 1942. In almost every theatre the Allies continued to struggle. On 21 June the vital port of Tobruk, in Libya, fell, raising fears that the Germans could soon take Egypt. Further north, the Russians were fighting heroically but were desperate for supplies from Britain and the United States. To provide these, the Allies had established regular convoys from August 1941 through the Arctic to Russia's northern ports, but because of the huge distances, aerial cover was limited, while the German naval forces in Norway had been greatly strengthened from the beginning of 1942. To provide more protection, Joubert came up with a number of suggestions. One was to establish a flying boat base on the strategically important Norwegian island of Spitsbergen, which was ruled out because of its remoteness, poor weather and the presence of German forces in the area, revealed by Coastal Command's long-range reconnaissance. Equally impractical was Joubert's idea that the German surface ships should be countered by sending a detachment of torpedo bombers to Vayenga in Russia; the Admiralty rejected this on the grounds that there were insufficient trained crews at home. There was a more favourable reception for his third idea, that eight Catalinas should operate from the Kola Inlet on the Barents Sea and Lake Lakhta, near St Petersburg, when the next convoy sailed. Yet this force proved hopelessly inadequate after PQ17 had begun its journey from Iceland on 27 June. Under sustained attack from German aircraft, ships and U-boats, only eleven of the thirty-five vessels in the convoy made it to their destination. After this disaster, Joubert pressed again for the use of torpedo bombers to guard the Russian convoys. Shaken by the experience of PQ17, the Air and Naval staffs now agreed to send a stronger Coastal Command force to north Russia, comprising a full squadron of Catalinas, four photo reconnaissance Spitfires and thirty-two Hampden torpedo bombers. Undertaken on 4 September, the lengthy journey, at the limit of the Hampden's range, exacted a ferocious toll. One Hampden was shot down by a Russian fighter, two others had to make forced landings in Russia after running out of fuel, and six crashed in Norway and Sweden. Nevertheless, the surviving aircraft enhanced PQ18's cover when it sailed on at the beginning of September. The losses were still high at eleven out of forty ships, but this was nothing like the scale of the PQ17 catastrophe. Moreover the Germans lost three U-boats and thirty-five aircraft.

One of the RAF casualties was Catalina pilot Dennis Healy of 210 Squadron, a man of astonishing bravery and skill, who had won the DSO after undertaking a series of reconnaissance sorties in May and early June to the island of Spitsbergen. In a period of just nine days, he carried out four long sorties, covering a total distance of almost 10,000 miles, in a Catalina fitted with long-range ASV and fuel tanks, often flying through thick fog, headwinds of up to 100 knots, heavy ice formations and magnetic storms that paralysed many of his instruments. Not content with his reconnaissance duties, he also dropped food supplies by parachute to the Norwegian survivors of a previous military expedition to the island. True to his valiant, selfless character, he was killed 200 miles from Murmansk on 25 September when his Catalina came under attack from a Junkers Ju 88, the German cannon shells and bullets smashing through his cockpit windscreen.

The other Catalinas of 210 Squadron returned to Britain once PQ18 had arrived in Russia, but the Coastal Command Spitfires and Hampdens were handed over to the Soviet Union, with their crews travelling back home on the Royal Navy cruiser HMS *Argonaut*. According to the official RAF history, the requirements of PQ18 and its predecessor 'had occupied 111 aircraft from 14 different squadrons of Coastal Command. Between them these aircraft had put in 279 sorties in 2,290 flying hours. By far the greater part of this time had been taken up with getting to and from the area of operations.'[26] PQ18 was to be the last convoy of its kind, partly because of the naval and air demands of the African campaign, partly because of the onset of winter and partly because the land route to Russia through Persia became increasingly accessible.

The war in the Atlantic remained as fierce as ever. Although the Americans had instituted a convoy system of their own, which drastically improved protection, losses to the U-boats remained fearsome. In the three months from July to September the U-boats sank 311 ships for 1.76 million tons. The USA's predicament led Coastal Command to send twenty Hudsons of 53 Squadron to Rhode Island to bolster anti-submarine patrols on the eastern seaboard. When that crisis had eased, the Hudsons were moved further south to Trinidad to counter U-boats and their refuelling tankers in the Gulf of Mexico, with a detachment also sent to British Guiana, though they saw little activity as the Bay and the mid-Atlantic were the real focus of conflict. For all the setbacks and obstructionism he had endured, Joubert now enjoyed two significant political victories, one on weaponry, the other on the supply of aircraft.

He had been complaining for months about the inadequate explosive power of Coastal Command's depth charges, which were filled with Amatol. What he sought instead were charges packed with the far more potent Torpex, comprising 42 per cent RDX, 40 per cent TNT and 18 per cent aluminium powder. They would be, he told the Air Ministry, 'weight for weight 50 per cent better than our present explosives and volume for volume 75 per cent better' so they would 'greatly increase our chances of getting kills'.[27] The Air Ministry rejected his request on the grounds that RDX was only available in small quantities, a stance that infuriated Blackett, who believed that Coastal Command was again being given a lower priority than Bomber Command. 'I feel very strongly that the Air Ministry ought to be pressed again and again to release some of their supply destined for their big, beautiful bombs,' he told Joubert sarcastically.[28] Blackett was backed up by the Command's senior Air Staff officer George Baker, who told the ministry, 'Other targets remain to be bombed another day. We have to get ours when the chance occurs. If we miss, it may cause the loss of 1,000s of tons of shipping.'[29]

In early 1942 the Air Ministry had not budged and Joubert was becoming impatient, warning that the feebleness of the depth charges 'is seriously impeding the effort of our anti-submarine warfare as a whole' and adding that the supply of Torpex was needed as 'the highest priority'.[30] Finally in April, as RDX production expanded in America, a batch of Torpex was assigned to Coastal Command for its depth charges. Still concerned about shortages, Baker again took up the case for greater provision: 'I hope you will not think I am flogging a dead horse; indeed I know it is a live one, although it is not galloping fast enough.'[31] In response, the Air Ministry pointed out that the Admiralty now had the lion's share of the coming supplies; out of 260 tons, 210 were to go to the Navy, 30 to the RAF and 20 to the Army. 'Thus all your troubles with shortages of Torpex airborne depth charges should cease shortly,' Baker was told.[32] There was no room for complacency in the Battle of the Atlantic, but Torpex, like the Leigh Light – whose maiden sorties by Greswell coincided with the first successful use of the weapon – undoubtedly augmented Coastal Command's lethality. As the force's own in-house review stated in August 1942, 'The use of Torpex-filled, shallow-set depth charges has greatly increased the power of our attacks.'[33] Calculations by the Operational Research Section put the figure for this increased deadliness at 30 per cent by 1943.

Coastal Command's second triumph was perhaps even more surprising, given the intransigence of Harris. Exasperated by the continual demands for more aircraft to cover the Atlantic and the Bay, the bomber chief wrote to Churchill on 17 June to warn against allowing Britain's aerial power 'to become inextricably implicated as a subsidiary weapon in the prosecution of vastly protracted and avoidable land and sea campaigns'. Pouring out his disdain for Joubert's force, he told the prime minister that it would be wrong

> to bolster further the already swollen establishment of the purely defensive Coastal Command which achieves nothing essential, either to our survival or the defeat of the enemy. Coastal Command is therefore an obstacle to victory. Why nibble at the fringes of the enemy's submarine and air power when we can obliterate with comparative ease the very sources of that power?[34]

But against the backdrop of the shipping losses, Portal and the Air Staff were less hostile, when, in early July, the Admiralty made another request for the loan of two Lancaster squadrons for three months to cover the outer part of the Bay until more Liberator or Fortress units had been established in Coastal Command. Portal could not resist claiming that the planes would be better used by Bomber Command; he estimated that in those three months they 'might be expected to drop 800 tons of bombs and in addition 600 mines', many of which destroy submarines or ships. 'I am so strongly convinced of this that I regard the loss of these two squadrons to Bomber Command as unacceptable,' he wrote. 'Nevertheless, I fully recognize the value of anti-submarine patrols in the outer zone and I am anxious to do all I can to improve their efficiency.' He therefore proposed that additional planes would come from two sources: first, Mark V Whitleys, fitted with long-range fuel tanks, from Operational Training Units (OTUs), with long-range flights over the Bay forming part of the crews' instruction; and second, Harris would be required to 'arrange for a certain number of Lancasters in operational squadrons to be taken off their normal operations and used for long-range anti-submarine patrol. This would be done in general at the expense of the mining effort.' Portal said he could not give 'the exact number of aircraft that would be available each week' but he hoped to 'work up to a maximum of 30 sorties a week'.[35] Pound welcomed the proposal, particularly its recognition of the principle that 'the RAF and the Navy bear the responsibility for the security of our sea communications within the range of shore-based aircraft', though he hoped that the number of OTU Whitleys 'will not be high. I have been frequently told that they are difficult aircraft for anti-submarine work during a long flight and furthermore the Lancaster has a most important tactical advantage in its combination of long range and heavy depth charge load.'[36]

By August 1942 Coastal Command was finally making real progress after almost three years of setbacks and neglect. Despite the regrettable absence of substantial numbers of Liberators, of which there still just two squadrons, Joubert's force now had fifty Catalinas and Sunderlands as well as almost three hundred other aircraft, including eight Beaufighter squadrons to tackle German heavy fighter defences over the Bay of Biscay, plus specialist photo reconnaissance, air-sea rescue and meteorological units. Just as their equipment was improving, crews were becoming more experienced on operations, more skilled in the use of radar, and more adept in attack. Joubert wrote to Norman Anderson, head of Eastern Command in the Royal Canadian Air Force:

> We are putting up a tremendous effort ... and have had a certain amount of success. There is no doubt that the combined day and night offensive (in the Bay) is causing the Germans a great deal of trouble ... the Torpex charges continue to show that we have discovered the right way to damage and sink submarines.[37]

In late August 1942 Dudley Peyton-Ward reported eagerly to one of Coastal Command's committees that in the previous month forty-four U-boats were sighted by anti-submarine aircraft, resulting in thirty-four attacks. 'These figures exceed those for any previous month of the war,' he declared.[38] The following month there was even better news. Professor E. J. Williams of the Operational Research Section revealed that each U-boat sighting now took an average of 75 flying hours, compared to 170 hours earlier in the year. Of 135 sightings made from the beginning of August to mid-September, '91 were followed by attacks,' said the professor.[39] That new effectiveness was mirrored in U-boat losses. Of the ten U-boats sunk in August, aircraft were responsible for half these kills. September saw another ten sinkings, with aircraft claiming three kills and one shared with the Navy, while in October Allied air power accounted for nine and a half of the sixteen U-boat losses. 'From a small force defensively employed and achieving negligible results, Coastal Command has become a most important unit in the anti-submarine campaign. It may prove to be the deciding factor', wrote Peyton-Ward towards the end of 1942.[40] Dönitz admitted that he was becoming anxious about 'the increase in enemy air cover' that now threatened 'our whole method of conducting submarine warfare, which was based on mobility and operations on the surface'.[41] At a naval conference in September with the Führer and the Kriegsmarine chief Erich Raeder, Dönitz warned 'how very great the dangers were to U-boats from aircraft'.[42] Among several steps such as the provision of more fighter support in the Bay and the acceleration of the use of aircraft detection technology, the conference also agreed to strengthen the defensive armament of the submarines by mounting additional anti-aircraft machine guns on a second platform behind the conning tower.

Dönitz, however, misread the political mood within the British government when he wrote that 'In the conflict between the demands of Bomber Command for its offensive against Germany and Coastal Command for its defensive operations against the U-boat arm, the British gave precedence to combatting the U-boats.'[43] The Admiralty would have argued that just the opposite was true, as highlighted by their struggles to increase the strength of Coastal Command, often in the face of opposition not just from the Air Staff but also from Downing Street. As early as May 1941 the Second Sea Lord Admiral Whitworth had written that 'our fight with the Air Ministry becomes more and more fierce as the war proceeds. It is much more savage than our war with the Hun, which is unsatisfactory and such a waste of effort.'[44] Now in 1942, against the reality of ever more deadly aggression from the Kriegsmarine, conflict arose with a new intensity over the central issue of the priority given to Bomber Command above the needs of the maritime struggle. Only bombing could win the war, asserted the RAF strategists, so the resources for this mission should not be dissipated. 'The bomber offensive has been repeatedly put forward by the Chiefs of Staff and accepted by the War Cabinet as a cardinal factor in our programme for victory,' wrote Portal to Churchill, adding that Bomber Command's targets for expansion had not been met because of 'shrinkage mainly due to diversions to Coastal Command and maritime work overseas'. The destruction of Germany's war capacity, he warned, would not occur 'if Bomber Command continues to be milked for each and every desirable but not vital purpose'.[45] That outlook was challenged by the Admiralty, which pointed out that Bomber Command would have neither fuel nor equipment if Britain's supply lines were cut. National survival was at stake, argued the naval chiefs, so strengthening the maritime effort was of overriding importance.

One of Churchill's many extraordinary attributes as prime minister was his ability to take a detailed, penetrating interest in all aspects of the war's conduct. The Battle of the Air prompted his enquiring mind to focus on the operational efficiency of Coastal Command, fuelled by the recurrent belief that the RAF's maritime arm was not making the best use of its resources. His doubts were reinforced by his former scientific adviser Frederick Lindemann, now elevated to the government as Paymaster General and to the peerage as Lord Cherwell, who argued that Coastal Command was not putting enough aircraft in the sky in proportion to its size. On 4 June Cherwell suggested to Churchill that it would be feasible for Coastal Command to 'increase the number of sorties' without 'augmenting the number of machines' since its heavier types of aircraft only 'make rather more than one sortie a week on average'.[46] Churchill immediately asked Portal to look into Cherwell's idea, telling him in a handwritten note that 'it is very much in the RAF's interest to avoid further inroads, as are constantly threatened'.[47] Portal's preliminary inquiry, reported to Churchill on 15 June, confirmed Cherwell's claim that Coastal Command's long-range aircraft each made approximately one sortie per week. 'This is too low an average and it should be possible to increase it substantially,' wrote Portal, explaining that Coastal Command's Operational Research Section would now conduct a full, urgent investigation.[48]

By this stage of the war Professor Blackett's renown had led to his promotion as head of operational research at the Admiralty, with E. J. Williams taking his place at Coastal Command. Williams quickly began work, aided by Dr Cecil Gordon whose ideological outlook was displayed in his membership of the Communist Party. Together Williams and Gordon identified a number of problems in Coastal Command's management of maintenance. One was the poor allocation of labour, with the result that in some squadrons ground crews were overworked and in others they had little to do. Another was the stringent rules on serviceability, which required that 70 per cent of aircraft should be ready for operational duty at all times. The Operational Research Section's imaginative, counterintuitive solution was a system called Planned Maintenance Flying, whereby serviceability rates were to be lowered dramatically to increase overall flying hours while a centralized team of technicians and inspectors would be created at each command station, in place of detached, separate crews for every unit.

Churchill's backing heightened the pressure for the scheme to be implemented swiftly. Influenced by Cherwell's research, he told Sinclair and Alexander,

I understand that Coastal Command squadrons with an initial estab-lishment of 20 machines are flying only about 20 hours a day, and that a substantial increase in the number of sorties per squadron could be obtained if the maintenance organization were expanded and improved. Until everything possible had been done in this direction there can be no case for transferring additional squadrons from Bomber to Coastal Command.[49]

Alexander struck a note of caution, telling the prime minister that 'by reducing the percentage of serviceable aircraft . . . we shall wear out the aircraft more quickly'. Nor did Alexander feel it was fair to judge efficiency simply by 'the numbers of operational sorties' since 'the duties confronting Coastal Command are often of an urgent nature, brooking no delay'.[50] By now, Churchill was becoming frus-trated with the Admiralty. 'You must not trench so heavily upon the resources of the RAF. I do not sustain the impression that the costly Biscay patrols have justified the inroads into our bombing resources,' he told Pound.[51] In reply the First Sea Lord denied that the Bay offensive had been a failure, claiming that 44 per cent of recent attacks on U-boats had 'led to serious damage'. But the U-boat war was so serious 'that it should be tackled with all the means we possess' through

aircraft properly trained and equipped and used permanently on the work. The present scheme of temporarily loaned aircraft from Bomber Command, though producing results which we cannot afford to forgo, should be replaced by a permanent transfer of bombers to Coastal Command.[52]

Pound also made a powerful riposte to Harris, who was agitating at this time for the RAF to concentrate on razing forty German cities to the ground. 'Unless we get at least as great an effort from the air force over the sea as do our enemies, there will be a grave danger of our losing the war at sea and then, amongst other things, there will be no petrol for your bombers.'[53]

The position of Joubert was ambivalent. Having complained in the past of feeling under siege from the conflicting demands of the Admiralty and the Air Ministry, his support now for Pound and Alexander was only lukewarm, partly because he believed that the Royal Navy was not giving the necessary assistance to Coastal Command in the anti-U-boat campaign. Joubert was happy to implement the Planned Maintenance Flying scheme, beginning with 502 Squadron, flying Whitleys, the Leigh Light Wellington Squadron and the Liberators of 120 Squadron. Referring to 502, he informed Portal 'that the effect on serviceability has been very marked and that I can shortly expect to get an increased number of sorties, certainly up to six a day. This is very encouraging.'[54]

The Battle of the Air rumbled on in the autumn. More ammunition was provided to the devotees of the bombing campaign in a secret Air Ministry report which revealed that the risk to pilots per sortie in Bomber Command was four times greater than those in Coastal Command, while the risk to aircraft was three times as great. These lower casualty rates, wrote Cherwell to Churchill on 15 September, 'confirm my view that it would be better to get Coastal Command to increase their rate of effort rather than take away bomber squadrons'.[55] Churchill agreed, telling Sinclair the next day, 'We must have bomber squadrons. You must arm me to get them.'[56] But the Admiralty fiercely continued to oppose the return of the bombers that had been lent to Coastal Command, Pound urging that 'our policy should surely be to redouble our efforts and not reduce them'. Portal used the row to set out for Churchill a renewed case for the bombing campaign, just as the prime minister wanted. In a ten-page memorandum, he complained that progress towards meeting the strategic offensive's objectives would never be met 'if Bomber Command continues to be milked for each and every desirable but not vital purpose'. Portal told Churchill that the RAF was facing up to this duty, but it meant that 'Bomber Command has been, and still is being, depleted by constant demands for heavy bombers to do anything except that for which they were primarily designed and produced – namely bombing Germany.'[57]

A climactic point in the war had been reached. The fate of the Allied campaign in North Africa and the Russian struggle on the eastern front hung in the balance. In the Atlantic, the epic conflict was about to be waged with a new ferocity, deepening the pressure on Britain's supply lines. If disaster was to be averted, it was now more urgent than ever for Coastal Command to be given the resources it needed for the fight. Yet even in the face of that reality, the Air Staff were still focused on the absolute priority for the strategic offensive. 'Spent the afternoon in the office battling with Portal's latest ideas for the policy of the conduct of this war. Needless to say it is based on bombing Germany at the expense of everything else,' wrote Alan Brooke, the chief of the Imperial General Staff, in his diary in September 1942.[58] The stage was set for further draining rounds in the Battle of the Air, whose outcome would help to settle the destiny, not just of Coastal Command but of the entire war in the west.

9
Gap

B Y THE AUTUMN of 1942, the anti-U-boat war had escalated into a crisis due to the continuing expansion of Dönitz's fleet, a reflection of Hitler's growing faith in his submarine commander inspired by the spectacular losses inflicted by his wolf packs. Dönitz had said in 1939, 'I will show that the U-boat can win this war. Nothing is impossible for me.'[1] Now that boast looked as though it could be realized. From August he had been able to put more than 100 U-boats to sea, finally attaining the striking power he had demanded since the start of the conflict. This growth in capacity was devastating for the Allies, who now seemed in danger of losing the tonnage war, by which the Reich was sinking ships faster than they could be built. Dönitz's fleet was suffering nothing like this attrition. 'We are not destroying more than a third of the monthly output of new U-boats,' complained Alexander.[2] In November, 808,000 tons were sunk, with the U-boats responsible for 729,000 of the total, up from 619,400 tons in October. The British supply lines were being slowly strangled. Food rationing, already stringent, had to be tightened again, while oil stocks for non-military use were down to their last three months at the end of the year. Sir John Tovey, the commander of the Home Fleet, told Joubert in September that he was 'fearfully disturbed, and have been for some time, at the large number of U-boats that are passing between here and Iceland at the rate of about 30 a month'. Warning that it was 'madness to allow these U-boats such an easy passage', Tovey expressed his concern that, having just met Sinclair,

> some of the powers-that-be get a false impression and merely regard a U-boat, not in contact with a convoy, as a small naval vessel with a

Sir Frederick Bowhill,
the first wartime chief of
Coastal Command.

The outdated Vickers Wildebeest
biplane symbolised the inadequacy
of Coastal Command's resources at
the outbreak of war.

A Short Sunderland of 210 Squadron escorting a convoy of Canadian troopships.

Sir Philip Joubert de la Ferté took charge of Coastal Command in June 1941. The lack of priority given to his command was a constant issue.

Sir John Slessor, who became commander in early 1943, was widely regarded by politicians and RAF chiefs as Coastal Command's best leader.

The operations room at Derby House, Liverpool, from where the Battle of the Atlantic was planned.

Members of the Women's Auxiliary
Air Force loading equipment into a
Short Sunderland.

Homing pigeons were used
by Coastal Command to send
emergency messages from
stricken planes.

The interior of a Short Sunderland, with navigator and wireless operator in
the foreground. One crewman recalled: 'I loved the Sunderland. You went
on board and felt at home.'

Lockheed Hudsons of 233 Squadron flying in formation over Northern Ireland, May 1941.

A Mark I Consolidated Catalina flying boat of 202 Squadron, based in Gibraltar, carries out an anti-submarine patrol.

The Consolidated Liberator, whose colossal range transformed Coastal Command's fortunes in the Battle of the Atlantic.

Flying over the North Sea, a Bristol Beaufighter of 455 Squadron fires a salvo of eight rocket projectiles.

Ground crew preparing to load a torpedo into a Bristol Beaufort of 42 Squadron, July 1941.

In the absence of shipborne degaussing equipment, giant electro-magnetic rings were installed beneath the airframes of Vickers Wellingtons to destroy enemy mines.

Coastal Command had a vast reach across the western theatre at its wartime peak. Liberators line up on a frozen airfield near Reykjavik after a heavy blizzard in February 1945.

Against the dramatic backdrop of the Rock of Gibraltar, ground crew sit beneath a Vickers Wellington of 458 Squadron.

The establishment of a base in the Azores in 1943 greatly strengthened Coastal Command's cover of the Atlantic. An airman guards a tented encampment at Lagens, with a Wellington of 172 Squadron in the background.

U-boat U-625 under attack by a Sunderland of 422 Squadron in the Atlantic, west of Ireland, 10 March 1944. The vessel was sunk and none of the crew survived.

A Liberator lit up by a Leigh Light at St Eval, Cornwall. The light 'completely changed the scene' for Coastal Command, by providing them with the capacity to illuminate enemy targets at night.

The German Sperrbrecher *Magdeburg* was sunk in August 1944 after coming under deadly fire from Beaufighters of 236 and 404 squadrons off the coast of France.

Sholto Douglas, the last wartime chief of Coastal Command. Despite his distinguished record, he was regarded with suspicion by his colleagues because of his attachment to socialism and his exuberant social life.

An airborne lifeboat is prepared for attachment to a Vickers Warwick of Coastal Command's highly efficient air–sea rescue wing.

Coastal Command's last mission was undertaken on 4 June 1945 by a Sunderland of 201 Squadron, based at Castle Archdale on Lough Erne.

crew of about 50 and therefore not worth much effort whereas one of these blighters that gets out represents a potential loss of anything from 50,000 to 150,000 tons or more of shipping.[3]

The expansion of the U-boat fleet was compounded by a major technological setback for the Allies, which nullified some of the gains made through the introduction of the Leigh Light. Confronted with the new threat of exposure by RAF searchlights, Dönitz had initially ordered his U-boats to remain submerged when transiting the Bay, but German naval engineers came up with a better solution that seized back the advantage from Coastal Command. What they devised was the Metox radar receiver, which gave the U-boat crews advance warning of the approach of enemy aircraft. Named after the French company based in occupied Paris that manufactured the equipment, the Metox receiver was tuned to pick up the 1.5-metre signals emitted by the RAF's ASV radar sets, rendering the British pulses as audible beeps in an operator's headphones that doubled in frequency when the attacking aircraft had made contact. Despite its primitive construction, Metox was an invaluable defensive tool. If it was working properly in an encounter at sea, it enabled the U-boat to dive below the surface before a Coastal Command plane could draw close enough to switch on the Leigh Light. It was not just effective at night. During the day, it had the capacity to survey the sky further than the visual range of a U-boat's lookouts armed with even the most powerful binoculars. Coastal Command was frank about the problems that Metox caused. A report by Joubert in October admitted, 'We now have conclusive evidence as a result of certain experiments carried out in the Bay and elsewhere that the Germans are employing a listening device which enables them to detect our ASV and dive before they can be spotted visually.'[4] As an indicator of the seriousness of Metox's impact, Coastal Command issued urgent instructions to all its anti-submarine (A/S) squadrons that made patrols with ASV, codenamed in this instance as S/E for special equipment:

In good visibility by day S/E not, repeat not, to be used. By night or when good cloud cover available S/E to be switched on for a period of ten seconds every five minutes . . . If contact is obtained, distance and approximate direction to be noted and S/E switched off. Aircraft should fly to within two or three miles of estimated position of U-boat when S/E should be switched on and used in the normal manner. In conditions of bad visibility, S/E may be used in the normal manner. These instructions apply only to aircraft on A/S patrol. Aircraft on convoy escort may use S/E when approaching and in company with the convoy.[5]

Yet, for all their rationale, such orders hampered the use of ASV. A better answer was needed for Coastal Command and it lay in a different sort of radar that could not be detected by Metox. Development of such a model was already under way. A team at the Air Ministry's Telecommunications Research Establishment (TRE), led by the brilliant physicist Robert Hanbury Brown, were working on an airborne, ground-scanning radar, called H2S, that would vastly improve the accuracy of bombing missions to Germany, though Hanbury Brown was sure the equipment could be adapted for maritime work by changing the aircraft's antenna. At the same time, the Admiralty and Coastal Command were pushing for the introduction of a more advanced version of ASV, known as the Mark III, which operated on a shorter 10-cm wavelength and had a greater range than the previous 1.5-metre types. Early success with an experimental model in January 1942 led to a production contract being placed with Ferranti, the electrical engineering company, followed by further rewarding trials in the spring. 'It is considered that the fundamental principles of 10-cm ASV offer such tremendous benefit for this Command over 1.5-metre equipment that it can definitely be stated at this early stage that it is a very definite operational requirement,' Joubert wrote to the Air Ministry.[6] Despite this official enthusiasm, Ferranti warned that operational Mark III sets would probably not start to be delivered until early 1943. That elongated timescale switched attention back to Hanbury Brown's H2S, the maritime version of which was almost identical and could be available sooner.

Then the Battle of the Air reared its fractious head again. Focused on the bomber offensive and backed by Harris, Churchill wanted priority to be given to the H2S, as he had set out at a meeting in Downing Street on 3 July. When he demanded 200 sets for Bomber

Command by October, he was told that such a schedule was impossible. But Churchill was in no mood for any delays. According to the account left by Bernard Lovell, another TRE scientist present, 'the first of many unsmoked but chewed cigars was ejected over his shoulder to impact on the surrounds of the fireplace behind him. "We don't have any objections in this room. I must have 200 sets by October."'[7]

The pressure from the top to concentrate on the immediate needs of Bomber Command had adverse consequences for Coastal Command, as Ferranti, much to Joubert's dismay, was instructed to suspend its work on the ASV Mark III and progress on the maritime H2S project slowed. During this saga, Harris was as negative as ever, claiming that the new radar system might be vital for bombers but would be far less useful in the hands of anti-submarine aircraft crews: 'I feel that the provision of aircraft equipped with this apparatus will mark the beginning rather than the end of difficulties involved with sinking U-boats.'[8] When Professor Blackett read of Harris's opinion, he scribbled 'nonsense' next to it on the written record.[9] In fact, 10-cm radar was more effective as an anti-submarine weapon than as a high-altitude bombing aid because a U-boat's conning tower usually generated a strong signal. Dudley Pound added his voice in support of Coastal Command, telling Portal in late September,

> the 10-centimetre ASV or similar equipment is understood to be already in production but it is being allocated first to Bomber Command. This will mean that Coastal Command will not receive this equipment until the spring or the summer of next year. I think it is of great importance that sufficient equipment should be allocated to Coastal Command.[10]

In reply, Portal stressed that the new system was 'designed to assist our bombers finding their targets in Germany', though he had given instruction for a trial installation to be held 'forthwith' in a Wellington.[11] In the longer term there was the promise of a steady supply of sets from the USA, where production had started on an American version, known as the SCR-517.

The needs of Coastal Command were addressed at a high-level meeting chaired by Stafford Cripps and called in November to investigate 'whether the production of ASV had been put back by the priority given to H2S'. Trying to lessen anxieties about long delays, Dr Philip Dee of the TRE reported that, despite some prototype difficulties, it has been 'found possible to make the two sets interchangeable except for a few minor details'. The meeting therefore agreed that H2S and ASV Mark III 'should be regarded as identical and suitable for either purpose'. Furthermore, Joubert was promised that, given the projected output of ASV, there would be 'sufficient sets to equip all the new aircraft coming forward for Coastal Command in the planned expansion programme next year'.[12] Even with such assurances, Harris still emerged in front. By the end of 1942 twenty-four of his four-engined heavy bombers were equipped with H2S, while 65 per cent of future deliveries went to his command. The Mark III, as the maritime version was called, did not go into operational service with Coastal Command until March 1943, beginning with a Wellington of 172 Squadron. Once again, the Admiralty had been outmanoeuvred. 'Alexander and Pound were simply not a strong enough team to cope with Churchill himself, obsessed as he was with the concept of offensive measures,' wrote Stephen Roskill, the naval historian and former officer.[13]

The strain on Coastal Command was compounded in the autumn of 1942 by the need to provide cover for the Allied landings in French Morocco and Algeria, code-named Operation Torch, which aimed to break the Vichy regime, pave the way for the defeat of the Axis in North Africa and regain supremacy in the southern Mediterranean. Led by Dwight Eisenhower, the Allied invasion comprised 107,000 troops and 850 naval vessels in seven convoys and one naval task force, against which the Germans were expected to send sixty U-boats 'within 10 days of becoming aware of this Operation', in the words of the Admiralty.[14] Coastal Command was central to the plans to negate this threat. As well as flying the usual patrols over the Bay and the Atlantic, Joubert was instructed to escort the convoys in the hours of daylight, with Gibraltar reinforced by Catalinas of 210 Squadron, Hudsons of 500 Squadron and long-range Beaufighters of 235 Squadron. Further support was provided by the loan of a Halifax squadron from Bomber Command, to be based at RAF Beaulieu in Hampshire, as well as Liberators from the US Army Air Forces, mounting four sorties a day, and Catalinas from the US Navy.

A few more B-24 Liberators had gone into Coastal Command's service by the time of Torch, as two Hudson squadrons were converted to the Mark III version of the long-range bomber. Shortly before the landings one of them, piloted by David Sleep of 224 Squadron, was involved in an incident that revealed the crew's astounding perspicacity and gallantry. Flying over the Bay on 20 October, Sleep came across a U-boat on the surface and immediately went on the attack, dropping his depth charges in a perfect straddle from just 30 feet. The subsequent blast not only sank the vessel, later confirmed as U-216, but also caused severe damage to Sleep's aircraft, with both elevators destroyed in the explosions. Having struggled to climb, the plane began to drop. But the crew did not panic. With remarkable coolness they started to jettison equipment from the plane while Sleep and his co-pilot fought with the control column. The toughest, most dangerous task was to release the remaining depth charges through the open bomb doors; after one and a half hours of struggle, this was finally accomplished by a brave flight sergeant who had to balance himself precariously on the plane's narrow catwalk that ran through the bomb bay. By instructing the rest of the crew to move into the Liberator's nose and by strapping the control column into a forward position, Sleep finally managed to get his aircraft on an even keel. After a nerveshredding flight over water, the battered Liberator made it to Cornwall, where Sleep made a crash landing at Predannack airfield on the Lizard peninsula. The plane burst into flames on impact, yet all the crew escaped without serious injury, the navigator having been pulled out by his comrades after he had become trapped in the burning wreckage.

The Germans were aware of the heavy concentrations of shipping in British and American ports, but believed that these were preparations for an invasion of either Norway or Dakar in West Africa. Operation Torch, which began on 8 November, therefore achieved a high degree of surprise. When the Germans realized the scale of North African landings and bolstered their submarine forces in the Mediterranean, they encountered powerful Allied resistance, particularly from the air. Between 23 October and 30 November, when the last Torch convoy arrived in Africa, Coastal Command's aircraft based in Britain sighted twenty-nine enemy submarines and launched sixteen attacks, while its planes based in Gibraltar and North Africa made 113 sightings and sixty attacks. It was a tribute to this effort that not a single Allied ship in the operation was lost, though seventeen aircraft were shot down, some by friendly fire from the Allied navies.

One daring, politically significant mission that Coastal Command undertook at the start of Torch was to bring the Free French General Henri Giraud to Gibraltar, from where it was planned he would fly to Algiers to command the pro-Allied forces of his native land. Having escaped from a prisoner of war camp in Germany, Giraud had made it to Vichy France via Switzerland, before being smuggled out of Toulon in an Allied submarine. Because the vessel would not have reached Africa in time for the landings, he and his party had then been picked up at a rendezvous point in the Mediterranean by a Coastal Command Catalina flown by James Louw, a South African RAF volunteer who had won the DFC in 1941. In his contemporary report of the adventure, Louw wrote that the commanding officer at Gibraltar, Sturley Simpson, 'stressed the great importance of bringing these passengers back and that they must be brought back safely'. After taking off at midnight, Louw arrived at the location as dawn broke, and after searching for forty-five minutes sighted the submarine. 'The sea conditions were very bad and although I thought the chances of landing and taking off again were very small, I decided to make the attempt. The landing was successful but the sea was so rough that I thought the aircraft would break up or be seriously damaged.' Yet Louw managed to bring the Catalina within 30 feet of the submarine, ready for the transfer of passengers by collapsible dinghy. Then an apparent new threat suddenly emerged as an unidentified plane appeared overhead, only to fly away northwards after circling Louw's Catalina. The transfer proceeded, taking almost an hour and a half. By its completion, the sea was even choppier, but Louw took off and brought the group to Gibraltar without further incident.[15]

Vichy was routed as the Allies established a second front in North Africa to accompany General Bernard Montgomery's victory at El Alamein, the first defeat of German land forces in the west. The tide had now turned decisively against the Axis Powers in this theatre. But the same was not true of the Atlantic campaign. Paradoxically, the very diversion of RAF and naval resources that ensured the landings were a triumph also weakened the usual convoy protection and enabled Dönitz's wolf packs to roam more freely, leading to the loss of 123 ships in mid-ocean during November alone. Despite poor weather in December, a total of sixty ships of 330,000 tons were sunk in the Atlantic. Alarm and frustration spread through parts of the government towards the end of 1942 as the U-boat threat loomed larger than ever. Even when Bletchley Park cracked the four-rotor Enigma naval code, following the capture of more material, the gloom did not lift. In the House of Lords one peer, Lord Clark, demanded assurances that 'the Royal Navy is receiving all the aircraft in numbers, type, armament and equipment that the various naval commanders consider essential'.[16] In a report produced in 1943, the Admiralty admitted that at the turn of the year 'there seemed a real danger that the enemy would achieve his aim of severing the routes which united Britain with the North American continent'.[17]

To the Admiralty, the remedy seemed obvious. The crisis would ease, argued ministers and the Naval Staff, once sufficient long-range aircraft were provided to cover the whole Atlantic and mount intensive patrols over the Bay of Biscay. That case was set out in a paper of 13 November 1942 by Dudley Pound, who maintained that 'the key to the whole problem is to get at least 40 long-range aircraft to re-equip selected squadrons in Coastal Command and to persuade the Canadians to increase their air cover'. To achieve this, he suggested 'as an emergency and temporary measure', the government should 'comb out all resources of the United Nations [i.e. the Allies] for Liberator I and Liberator IIs'. In addition, 10-cm ASV should be fitted for all long- and medium-range aircraft operating in the Bay.[18] These arguments were reiterated by A. V. Alexander in a memorandum to the prime minister that stressed the central role of Coastal Command in the fight against the U-boat. 'I have recommended devoting our attention to the part played by aircraft because it is this which can have the most effect in the anti-submarine campaign and because the situation is so urgent in the North Atlantic that no delay should be accepted.' Turning to other demands on the RAF, particularly the strategic offensive against the Reich, he said frankly that an immediate priority for the maritime campaign would involve 'sacrifices elsewhere', though he argued that, in reference to the bombers, this would be 'a very small proportion of Allied production'. Furthermore, 'it is no exaggeration to say that unless this sacrifice is made now – with regard to aircraft equipment and personnel – the build-up will not take place'. Echoing Pound, he said that the most dangerous area of the Atlantic lay between Iceland and Newfoundland. 'The vital need at the moment is that we should have sufficient long-range aircraft to bridge the gap.' Justice was piled on necessity, he claimed, since under previously agreed expansion plans 'Coastal Command should have 72 very long range aircraft of the Liberator III type'.[19]

The logic of the Admiralty's demand for Coastal Command to be given greater priority was demonstrated in the experience of two convoys that sailed one day apart in December, HX217 and SC111, which were harassed by twenty submarines from Dönitz's force but without the devastating impact of previous clashes. That was largely because of the cover provided by 120 Squadron based in Iceland, of which Terry Bulloch was the outstanding pilot, epitomized by his performance on 8 December when he attacked seven U-boats during a nine-hour patrol alongside the convoy (see chapter 6). With his unrivalled eyesight, ferocity of purpose and tactical awareness, Bulloch was an exception, yet he showed what could be achieved with air escorts in skilled, determined hands. During parts of the voyage, support was also provided by Sunderlands, Catalinas and Flying Fortresses, one of which on 11 December sighted three U-boats and attacked two. Although Dönitz put out one of his strongest packs yet in the Battle, just two ships out of seventy in the convoy were lost, while sixteen Allied attacks were made on the submarines, with two probable sinkings. The German commander, often inclined to pessimism, commented ruefully, 'By increasing the range of their air cover, the English have succeeded in gaining air control over a great part of the North Atlantic with land-based planes, and narrowing the area in which U-boats can operate without threat from the air.'[20] Coastal Command's own Operational Research Section came to the startling conclusion that regular, long-range air escorts would reduce convoy losses by no less than 64 per cent.

Yet Churchill, most of the Cabinet and the Air Staff were still not entirely convinced. They knew that something had to be done. In the event, the main changes related, not to the supply of aircraft, but to organizational structure. One was to replace the Battle of the Atlantic Committee, set up in February 1941 by Churchill, with an Anti-U-boat Warfare Committee, which had a new emphasis on the technological and aerial side of the campaign, as reflected in the appointment of the minister of aircraft production as deputy chairman. Announcing the change in the Commons, Churchill told MPs that

> it must not be supposed that this Committee in any way supersedes or replaces the regular and systematic control of anti-U-boat warfare by the Admiralty. There is no question of appointing a naval super-commander-in-chief under the Admiralty or a special Minister to deal with the U-boat campaign. The war at sea is all one and the Admiralty organization has been adapted by continual improvement and refinement to deal with it as a whole.[21]

More importantly, in mid-November the spirited, self-confident head of submarines Max Horton was promoted to take command of the Western Approaches in place of Sir Percy Noble. A natural leader often compared to Montgomery, Horton had been at sea since he was thirteen and in addition to the vast range of his expertise he had an uncanny ability to intuit the enemy's manoeuvres. His magisterial competence was matched by a streak of hardness, as one of his officers, Denys Rayner recalled:

> His own staff regarded him as something less than a God but more than a man. If they had not they would have found themselves relieved. He had more personal charm than any man I have ever met, but he could be unbelievably cruel to those who fell by the wayside.[22]

From his new base in Derby House, Liverpool, where he followed the Battle of the Atlantic on the giant wall chart in its operations room, Horton decided it was time to go on the offensive against the U-boat. To this end he introduced a number of tactical developments, such as the creation of well-armed support groups of destroyers, frigates and sloops, which travelled alongside the convoy escorts but had the freedom to hunt down and kill enemy submarines. Under the innovative leadership of Captain Johnnie Walker, the first such support group quickly gained a reputation as a deadly foe of the wolf packs. Horton was also a passionate believer in intensive training, while, unlike some others in the Navy, he recognized the importance of aerial power; to deepen his understanding of Coastal Command's work, he regularly joined lengthy patrols.

Just as Horton was embarking on his new role, Joubert's chequered spell at Coastal Command was coming to an end. Neither the Air Staff nor the Admiralty saw him as the figure to lead the next stage of the maritime campaign. In mid-October 1942 Alexander had written to Sinclair,

> The First Sea Lord has suggested to me that a change in the command of Coastal Command would be desirable. We fully recognize and are grateful for the excellent work which Joubert has done in the technical development of Coastal Command aircraft, but the First Sea Lord feels that Joubert lacks the operational grip which was evident in Bowhill's time.[23]

The verdict of Sir Wilfrid Freeman, who as vice chief of the Air Staff had regularly clashed with Joubert, was that he was 'insufficiently attached to the doctrines of the Air Staff'. In addition, said Freeman, Joubert was 'always lacking in judgement and most people who knew him well were astonished he ever got as far as he did'.[24] Appointed to the less demanding post of RAF inspector general, Joubert was bitter about the way he had been treated. 'The move was a great disappointment to me,' he wrote later.[25] Yet for all the criticism he endured, he had presided over a transformation in Coastal Command since he had taken over in June 1941, with the number of flying boats having doubled and the total of long-range squadrons having increased threefold. Altogether, the Command's establishment had gone up from thirty-two squadrons of 568 planes, many of them obsolescent Ansons, Blenheims and Beauforts, to fifty-four squadrons of 880 aircraft, including Liberators, Beaufighters, Spitfires and Fortresses. In the same vein, the Command had shared in just two U-boat kills when he was appointed. In conjunction with US and Canadian forces, it had destroyed another 27 and damaged 120 by the time he left.

His departure was announced in December, and at a final Coastal Command committee meeting of the year Joubert was showered with valedictory messages, typified by the words of Commander Harold Fawcett, of the Admiralty's directorate in anti-submarine warfare. The growing success against the U-boat, said Fawcett, was due to 'the personal inspiration and direction of the Commander-in-Chief', as was 'the close co-operation and excellent relations existing between the Command and his directorate'.[26] Clearly moved, Joubert expressed his deep thanks 'for the help you have given me and the good team-work that has gone on at this headquarters. It couldn't have been a better time, nor could the help have been better. I think we have given the Boche a good deal to think about.'[27]

10

Convoy

SIR JOHN SLESSOR, Joubert's successor, should never have been an airman. As a child, he had contracted polio and was left lame in both legs. When he tried to enlist at the outbreak of the First World War, he was rejected by an army medical board as 'totally unfit for any form of military service'.[1] But a combination of his own tenacity and a family connection in the upper ranks of the Royal Flying Corps enabled him to circumvent this decision. On his eighteenth birthday, he became a commissioned officer, serving first at home in an anti-Zeppelin fighter squadron, then in the Middle East, where he won the Military Cross for his bombing attacks on Turks and Sudanese rebels. Wounded in action, he spent the rest of the war as an instructor in both France and England.

Slessor's streak of iron-willed determination that won him a place in the Royal Flying Corps was evident throughout his long career, which culminated in his being made chief of the Air Staff in the early 1950s. For decades, his was a clear, authoritative voice on the development of military strategy and relations with Britain's allies. Of all the wartime heads of Coastal Command, he was the most distinguished: vigorous in policy, articulate in exposition, strong in purpose. When Harold Macmillan, the future Tory prime minister, spent time alongside him in talks with the USA on the unfolding Mediterranean campaign after Torch, he wrote in his diary, 'Slessor is concise, firm, hitting every nail on the head, the most impressive of the lot.'[2] The exceptional Coastal Command pilot Mike Ensor described him as 'the most approachable very, very senior officer I ever knew'.[3]

Born in India in 1897, Slessor had military service in his blood for his father was a major in the Sherwood Foresters. Most of his own adulthood was spent in uniform except for a brief spell after the First

World War, when he became disillusioned with the RAF and resigned his commission, only to find that civilian life did not appeal. On rejoining the RAF, he quickly moved up its hierarchy, proving a success both as a squadron commander and staff officer. During his journey upwards, particularly during his spell as the RAF's director of plans between 1937 and 1940, he grew into one of the foremost advocates of the bomber doctrine, in which victory could be achieved by aerial assault against the enemy's infrastructure. 'Our belief in the bomber was in fact intuitive, a matter of faith,' he wrote later.[4] The fervour of his attachment to the official creed fed a number of delusions. One was his misapprehension in the early years of the war that Germany was crumbling under the RAF bombardment, reflected in his statement in June 1941 that 'the Boche is really feeling it' when in truth most attacks were wildly inaccurate; only one in five RAF bombs fell within 5 miles of their target.[5] Another was the failure in the late 1930s to recognize the importance of air power over the sea or to give sufficient attention to naval co-operation. Indeed, from an RAF viewpoint, Slessor had actually welcomed the decision in 1937 to transfer the Fleet Air Arm to the Navy because this removed a distraction from the Air Force's central goal.

But it would be far too simplistic to regard Slessor as another bomber evangelist in the mould of Arthur Harris. A big man in both stature and vision, he knew not only that the war had to be waged on many fronts, but also that the defence of maritime supply lines was crucial to the rest of the Allied effort. 'It was obviously no good indulging in praiseworthy persistence in winning the war in the long-term over Germany if meanwhile we were losing it at sea,' he wrote.[6] Slessor was also a pragmatist. Part of his objection to the Admiralty's persistent pleas for more Coastal Command planes before 1943 was that sheer quantity would achieve little, arguing, 'you do not defeat the U-boat offensive by piling up against it quite unsuitable aircraft that lack any of the essential specialized equipment'.[7]

Slessor was appointed commander-in-chief in late 1942 but did not formally take up his position until February 1943. The delay was caused by the seriousness and urgency of his duties as assistant chief of the Air Staff, in which role he was helping to formulate the Allies' strategy and conduct high-level negotiations with the USA. Despite the hiatus at the top of Coastal Command, these responsibilities had the tremendous advantage of providing Slessor with a profound grasp of the problems facing the RAF and the Navy. By far the greatest was, inevitably, the Battle of the Atlantic, where the wolf packs were reaching new levels of deadliness. Dönitz himself, with over 120 U-boats at his disposal for the campaign, had also reached a new height of importance within the Reich's war machine. In January he became head of the entire Kriegsmarine on the resignation of Erich Raeder after Hitler had lost all faith in Germany's surface fleet, whose perceived failures and lack of offensive spirit he contrasted with the lethal success of the U-boats. So deep was the Führer's anger that he even spoke of his determination to scrap the Reich's capital ships and use their guns for coastal defence, though on taking command, Dönitz dissuaded him from this course. But the reprieve did nothing to lessen Dönitz's resolve to step up his campaign against the Allied supply lines. One of his first actions was to shift many of his submarines from Norway and the western Mediterranean back to the Atlantic. Even in appalling weather across the ocean in January 1943, thirty Allied ships of 189,000 tons were sunk, a figure that rose to fifty ships of 310,000 tons in February; particular punishment was suffered by the convoy SC18 that set out from New York on 24 January and, despite a strong naval escort, was targeted by twenty U-boats. In total, eight of the sixty-four freighters in the convoy were lost. Many of the attacks were made at night, which emphasized the need for cover from long-range aircraft fitted with Leigh Lights. Still in office if not in power because of the drawn-out succession, Joubert told a meeting of the Anti-U-boat Warfare Committee in January,

> To put it quite bluntly, the Navy and ourselves had completely failed to arrest the development of the U-boat war. The numbers had increased to astronomical proportions and the number of U-boats at sea made it practically impossible now to carry out effective evasion with convoys. We were faced with the need to fight our convoys through the U-boat packs and to put it again quite bluntly we had neither the number of escort vessels nor the number of aircraft to do the job effectively. So taking it by and large the outlook was extremely depressing.[8]

As had been apparent for months, the most pressing need was for Liberators, the only aircraft with the reach, bomb load and speed for the task of providing cover across the Atlantic and disrupting the U-boats' transit across the Bay. Not everyone admired the huge American bomber. One pilot, Stuart Weir, went so far as to claim, 'The Liberator is not an aircraft. It might have been produced by the bus designer of the London Passenger Transport Board.'[9] But that disparagement was very much a minority view. 'It was our first real aeroplane', was the view of Terry Bulloch of 120 Squadron,[10] an opinion shared by Joe Collins of 59 Squadron, who called it 'the greatest aircraft in anti-submarine warfare', though he admitted that it was 'not a forgiving aircraft' or 'easy' to fly because of its tendency to wallow 'most unstably' and 'the poor view from its cockpit'.[11] With a patrol radius of 1,000 miles to and from its base, it could scan far wider stretches of the ocean that even the Sunderland, which had a radius of 600 miles, or the Catalina at 800 miles. Stafford Cripps, the perspicacious minister for aircraft production, was right when he said that 'very long range aircraft are the true solution to the U-boat menace'.[12]

Yet, though the case was obvious, the realization of that goal was beset with complications, not least because of American inter-service rivalries and political priorities. On one hand, Admiral Ernest King, the obstinate, irascible commander of the US Navy who had little of President Roosevelt's admiration for Britain, believed anti-submarine patrols were futile, and wanted to focus more on the Pacific rather than the European war. Of King's notorious temper, Roosevelt himself once said that 'he shaves every morning with a blow torch'.[13] On the other, General Henry 'Hap' Arnold, the head of the US Army Air Forces (USAAF), harboured his own ambition to create an independent service similar to the RAF and saw strategic bombing in Europe as a means to achieve that. He therefore wanted as many heavy bombers as possible, and, until the arrival of the Boeing Superfortress, the Liberator was the finest American type. Furthermore, the highly advanced nature of the plane meant that early output at Consolidated's huge plant in San Diego was not as rapid as hoped, while in Britain the demand for modifications, combined with the lack of spare parts, also created bottlenecks. Looking back on the initial supply of Liberators to the RAF, Joe Collins wrote that 'speed was definitely not of the essence in this rather sorry tale'.[14]

In the autumn of 1942, according to the Air Ministry, Coastal Command had thirty-nine Liberators in three squadrons, 59, 120 and 224, but by the end of the year the picture, far from improving, had deteriorated. Part of this was due to wastage, part due to the work needed to convert the planes for anti-submarine operations. The first two versions, the Mark I and Mark II, were now outdated and the former was even out of production. But deliveries of the newer Mark III, which featured extra armament, were slow, and further hold-ups came as a result of modifications to create the Mark V with 10-cm radar and auxiliary fuel tanks to extend its range even further, accommodated by the removal of some armour as well as the rear guns and the mid-upper turret. Indeed No. 59 Squadron at Chivenor had its Liberator IIIs withdrawn, even though they had only arrived in August, in order that the unit could undergo a later conversion to the Mark V. In the temporary absence of any Liberators, the squadron was given Flying Fortresses, significantly reducing its radius of action. 'It is all a little bit of a mess,' confessed Slessor after a visit to Chivenor in February.[15] Nor was there much optimism about imminent progress, given that the conversion programme to the Mark V, to be carried out by the engineering firm of Scottish Aviation based at Prestwick, was expected to take at least three months. 'Until January, the strength is bound to fall,' the Air Ministry warned Joubert in early November,[16] a lament followed up a fortnight later at a meeting of the Ministry of Aircraft Production: 'There is very little hope of an increased supply of Liberator IIIs or Vs in the near future.'[17]

Against the backdrop of the U-boats' potency, the meagreness of the RAF Liberator force could not be easily accepted by the government. Churchill wrote to Harry Hopkins, Roosevelt's most trusted aide, asking urgently for thirty Very Long Range (VLR) Liberators equipped with 10-cm radar, only to be told that the USA could not spare any for the RAF. However, Hopkins said that twenty of them would be sent to England as part of the USAAF 'to operate under the control of General Eisenhower' in undertaking anti-submarine work, with the proviso that they could be transferred to the Mediterranean at any time.[18] By January 1943 the USAAF unit, based at St Eval, was ready for operations, though the American airmen were unimpressed by the primitive conditions at Coastal Command's Cornwall airfield. Poor food, gloomy weather and an absence of maintenance hangars were among their complaints. Despite these problems, the Americans soon proved their worth, reaching far into the Bay of Biscay and sinking U-519 at the end of January. But their spell at St Eval was short-lived. In March the detachment, now numbering two squadrons, was transferred to Morocco to take part in the Mediterranean campaign. That decision again illustrated how the RAF needed its own substantial Liberator force.

Political pressure had to be cranked up and it was: by Slessor during a visit to the USA at the end of 1942. By then, Allied losses of shipping had reached nearly 8 million gross tons for the year. The main purpose of his high-level diplomacy was to cement the USAAF into an alliance for the sustained bombing of Germany in 1943, but he also stressed the need for long-range maritime aircraft. His intervention seemed to bear fruit at the historic Allied summit in Casablanca held in January 1943, presided over by Churchill and Roosevelt. Held in an atmosphere of crisis about the Atlantic campaign, it was agreed at the final plenary meeting that 'the defeat of the U-boat remains the first charge on the resources of the United Nations [i.e. the Allies]'.[19] From this resounding declaration stemmed several crucial subsidiary decisions: first, the Allies would mount an intensive bombing campaign against the U-boat bases on the French coast; second, convoy protection would be enhanced by escort carriers; and third, the USA would supply Coastal Command with at least eighty VLR Liberators. At last there seemed a real chance of closing the Atlantic gap. The needs of the maritime air wing had finally received recognition at the highest level.

The apparent success of Casablanca left Slessor eager to take charge of his command. 'I was instantly gripped by the fascination of a struggle in which we felt we were pitting our wits and skill against a ruthless and formidable enemy, for stakes which we all know to be of literally vital importance,' he wrote.[20] Slessor was highly conscientious, writing all his memoranda, speeches and articles in his own scholarly hand. In fact, according to Hector Bolitho, the flood of material from Slessor's office sometimes drew a whispered protest:

'My God, another note from the Old Man!'[21] On his arrival at Coastal Command headquarters, Slessor was impressed with the insight and diligence of Captain Peyton-Ward, the naval liaison officer, who never seemed to take any leave and had a deep understanding of the RAF crews' mindset, partly because he conducted extensive debriefings with them. He also regarded Peyton-Ward as a man of physical courage: his arthritic hip 'gave him constant pain' but he 'never allowed it to affect his devotion to duty or his quiet good humour'.[22] The new commander-in-chief had far less time for Professor Patrick Blackett, the head of the Admiralty's Operational Research, whom he regarded 'as emotionally and temperamentally incapable of taking a really objective view of strategic problems', preferring to indulge in some of 'the most bogus, pseudo-scientific analyses I have ever seen'.[23] Having been in charge of a Bomber Command group himself from 1941 to 1942, Slessor further felt that, as well as Joubert's lack of clout, another legacy of his leadership had been excessive circumspection. In a note to his group commanders, he wrote that 'we are not really making use of the endurance inherent in our aircraft because we are being too prudent about our PLE'. Even accounting for weather and the need to keep a reserve in hand, 'I have no doubt that nine times out of ten our aircraft come back with far more than the scheduled proportion of fuel in their tanks. We obviously cannot afford this.' He estimated that such an approach

> added up to a monthly loss of something of the order of the whole planned effort of one complete squadron . . . I think this is partly due to the fact that we in Coastal Command and Group Headquarters are too cautious and conservative. As a Group Commander in Bomber Command, I used, for instance, to send the old Hampden to Berlin. Provided the meteorological conditions were as forecast, he would have one hour's petrol left on his ETA at home. This was cutting it pretty fine (finer than anything I have seen at Coastal) and every now and then we lost an aircraft. But that is a chance we must take in war.

He concluded, 'I want you to go into this personally and take immediate steps to impress upon all your station and squadron commanders the essential need for sucking the last drop of endurance out of aircraft.

PLE means Prudent Limit of Endurance, not a 100 per cent margin of safety.'[24]

Slessor soon experienced other problems. Predictably, not much of the fine rhetoric of Casablanca translated into reality. Given instructions by the US president and the British prime minister, Harris could not disobey the order to mount a bombing offensive against the French submarine bases, but, as he had warned, the effort was futile because the U-boat pens were now so well protected by layers of concrete 16-feet thick in some places. Joubert had claimed in October 1942 that 'the destruction of these ports as U-boat bases and the starting point for many of the tankers that refuel the U-boats at sea would cut down the operational efficiency of the U-boats by not less than 50 per cent'.[25] But that was wishful thinking. 'It was a great mistake of the British not to have attacked these pens from the air when they were under construction,' wrote Dönitz.[26] For five months the Allies carried out attacks on the Biscay ports, the RAF bombing by night, the USAAF by day. In over 7,000 sorties, their aircraft released 18,000 tons of explosive and incendiaries, yet, despite widespread devastation to civilian life along the French coast, not a single shelter was penetrated or U-boat destroyed. In return, the Allies had lost ninety-nine aircraft. Harris, having 'protested repeatedly against this hopeless misuse of air power which could not possibly achieve the object that was intended', had seen all his doubts vindicated.[27] Paradoxically, this failure worked to his advantage, as it strengthened his hand in his fight with the Admiralty to stop the drain of Bomber Command's resources to the maritime campaign, since he could argue that diversions from the strategic offensive against Germany were counterproductive.

The other aspect of the war on the Biscay coast was the assault on the U-boat traffic through the Bay, long viewed by Coastal Command as the arena offering the richest potential for submarine kills. Aiming to exploit the growing strength of the Command, a new tactical plan was devised to flood the Bay with heavy patrols. In theory, according to a paper by Command staff, this intensification would 'make it impracticable for the U-boats in that area to dive each time an ASV signal is heard. Under such conditions, the U-boats would either have to remain submerged during the flooding period or ignore the ASV signals and run the risk of being attacked.'[28] The scheme was put into action on 4 February, the day before Slessor formally took charge, and was code-named Operation Gondola. Organized by Geoffrey Bromet, the dependable commander of No. 19 Group headquartered in Plymouth, Gondola involved more than 300 sorties over the next twelve days, but the results of the high-density patrols were disappointing, with just one U-boat sunk from nineteen sightings and eight attacks. The problems were that, despite the increase in aircraft numbers, too few of them were equipped with Leigh Lights or 10-cm radar sets and there were too few Liberators.

In early 1943 Coastal Command still had only two Liberator squadrons, amounting to just seventeen operational aircraft and none west of Iceland. Against a backdrop of American wrangling and possessiveness, the promise of eighty new planes seemed as distant as ever. Nevertheless, the savage losses in the Atlantic had the effect of concentrating minds, even that of the obdurate, Anglophobic Admiral King. At the beginning of March, as the wolf packs continued to wreak havoc, he convened a conference of the Allies in Washington to discuss the deepening crisis over the Atlantic convoys. Representing Coastal Command was Albert Durston, now the senior Air Staff officer at Coastal Command's headquarters.

After lengthy discussions, the Americans agreed to provide more air support for the campaign, as reflected in two decisions. The first was to pledge over the long term 255 Liberators for the Atlantic, made up of 75 from the USAAF, 60 from the US Navy and 120 from the RAF. The second was to reinforce the bases of the Royal Canadian Air Force in Newfoundland with VLR aircraft, with the result that Britain and Canada would finally be able to close the Atlantic Gap once the planes were delivered. As for Britain, Portal told the Anti-U-boat Warfare Committee that, due to the Washington conference, 'increased deliveries' from America meant 'that by August 90 Liberators would be available to Coastal Command and in addition 30 Halifaxes and 30 Fortresses for Very Long Range and Long Range duties'.[29] Inevitably, however, Harris grumbled about the concentration on Liberators for the Atlantic, believing that heavy bombers should be used 'in the immediate future for striking directly at Germany' instead of being 'deployed mainly for defensive purposes'.[30]

The Washington agreement was badly needed, for March 1943 was one of the darkest months for the Allies in the submarine war, made all the worse by the Kriegsmarine's introduction of a new weather code-book that imposed a temporary blackout on Bletchley Park's ability to read the Enigma traffic. In contrast, armed with B-Dienst's decrypts of the Royal Navy's signals, Dönitz was often able to target the convoy routes with over fifty U-boats. The carnage was brutal. In the first twenty days of March, ninety-five ships were lost. Altogether that month, 693,000 tons of Allied shipping was sunk, 627,000 by U-boats, of which 476,000 went down in the North Atlantic. The Allies' vulnerability was epitomized by the damage inflicted on two convoys, HX229 and SC122. Between them, they lost twenty-one ships of 141,000 tons, as the U-boats exploited the air gap that still existed. The convoy system itself now appeared to be in danger of collapse.

Yet the picture of German supremacy was deceptive. For all its devastation, March was the climax of the U-boat war, not a precursor to victory. The very success of the wolf packs that month galvanized the USA to expedite the decisions of Washington and Casablanca as far as Liberator production allowed. After Churchill told Roosevelt that the sinkings in the Atlantic had become 'intolerable' and more air support was needed, the president wrote directly to King and George Marshall, the US Army's chief of staff, instructing them to give immediate priority to anti-submarine operations in the north Atlantic by enabling 'an increase in the number of long-range bombers operating from Newfoundland, Greenland, Iceland and Great Britain'.[31] King could not stonewall any longer, and sixty Liberators were at once transferred from other theatres to duties in the Atlantic, where they had an immediate impact. With protection established right across the northern part of the ocean, the Germans lost their advantage. At the same time, more of Max Horton's destroyer support groups came into service in April, adding to the arsenal of the escorts which also included high-frequency direction-finding Huff-Duff equipment, to locate U-boats, and the deadly Hedgehog projector, which fired twenty-four spigot mortars when attacking a submarine. With remarkable prescience, Admiral Horton sensed that, even amid the huge convoy losses in March, Allied fortunes were turning due to the increase in aerial cover. He wrote:

The air of course is a tremendous factor and it is only recently that the many promises that have been made show signs of fulfilment so far as shore-based air is concerned, after three and a half years of war. All these things are coming to a head just now and although the last week has been one of the blackest on the sea, so far as I am concerned I am really hopeful.[32]

Horton was right. As long-range aircraft became available so the destructiveness of the Allies grew. A joint report from the Admiralty and Air Ministry read:

We are killing U-boats round the convoys, and confidently expect to kill more as our combined VLR and escort vessel programmes in the North Atlantic come to fruition. We regard it as vital that nothing should be done to interfere with those programmes; on the British side they have already been accelerated.[33]

Results soon vindicated the champions of air cover. German sinkings began to mount dramatically. In March fifteen U-boats were lost, seven to aircraft, rising to seenteen in April, with aircraft responsible for eight of the kills. In May the total leapt to forty-four, of which twenty-five were accounted for by aircraft. One German prisoner of war, captured in the summer of 1943, complained, 'It is no longer any fun to sail in a U-boat. We don't really mind even a cruiser and we can face destroyers without turning a hair. But if an aircraft is there, we've had it. It directs surface craft to the spot even if it does not attack itself.'[34] Another U-boat crewman, Hans Goebeler, recalled how

the entire tide of the war had turned decisively against the U-boats. First of all the build-up of enemy forces had made our previous tactics totally ineffective. Gone were the days when we could manoeuvre primarily on the surface and dive only when conducting an attack or escaping. The Metox device still warned us in time to avoid most air attacks but once we were forced underwater our speed was insufficient to catch all but the slowest ships. By forcing us to remain submerged, the Allies turned our U-boats into little more than slow-moving minefields, dangerous to their ships only if they happened to blunder across our path.

Under these conditions, Metox itself became a 'mixed blessing' to Goebeler's crew:

> It protected us from surprise but because the mechanism was unable to measure the distance of the enemy's signals, we could not distinguish between attacking aircraft and those merely passing by at a long range. As a result, every enemy radar contact forced us to an emergency dive. The constant alarms jangled our nerves, exhausted our bodies and prevented our boat from fully replenishing our air supply and recharging our battery power.[35]

In fact, Dönitz had to issue an order for his men to stand firm, telling them, 'The sailor must know his job and be steadfast. There must be no vacillating. He must not give way to the mood of the moment.'[36]

Coastal Command crews could sense the change in fortunes, as an intelligence report stated:

> The battle still goes on but very much more profitably on the side of the Allies. In spite of an increased drive by the German High Command, sinkings in April and May have been much smaller. It is clear from German broadcasts and newspaper articles that U-boat losses are becoming very high.

The Command's in-house journal claimed that 'no service could stand a continued rate of loss as was suffered by the U-boat fleet in May', adding gleefully that one German radio presenter, Heinrich Schweich, had admitted on air that 'the enemy defences in the Atlantic have got the better of us'.[37] Harry Platt, who flew Liberators from St Eval in 1943, wrote in his private memoir that 'more squadrons were engaged in the task – also more modern aircraft – and with all other types of considerations by late summer the U-boats were suffering'.[38] The growing challenge to the U-boats was epitomized by 120 Squadron based in Iceland, one of whose pilots, Jack Colman, left this account of an incident when his radar operator picked up a contact

8 miles ahead on the port side. 'We increased revs and boost – a rich mixture – opened the bomb doors and the depth charges were set for a stick of six at 36-foot spacing. It was six miles away and we were still at 1,000 feet, skimming cloud.' The crew now took up action stations as the Liberator pressed on towards the target. Then, as he lowered height, Colman saw the U-boat on the surface, 2 miles away.

> We subscribed an arc to bring us diagonally across its track. It was going to dive or shoot back as we screamed down, trimming a bit tail heavy to help us pull out. As it was diving, we hurtled 50 feet above the waves, heading to cross its track some way ahead of the conning tower. We kept low for a few seconds, then Joe (one of the gunners) shouted in glee from the turret, 'Jesus Christ, the bloody sea is blowing up, and again, again, again, again. What a bloody sight, went hundreds of feet in the air – it's still coming down.'[39]

The water churned between further eruptions, and oil could be seen on the surface, though for all the graphic imagery this was not proof that a kill had been achieved. Even so, the episode illustrated the strain that the U-boats now faced.

Mounting confidence was also encapsulated in an attack on U-boat U-563, skippered by Oberleutnant Gustav Borchardt, that left Brest on 29 May to take part in the Atlantic operations. Two days later, as the vessel sailed westwards on the surface at 12 knots, it was spotted by a Halifax of 58 Squadron, flown by the distinguished pilot Wilfrid Oulton, who exploited cloud cover to stalk his prey. Oulton already had two U-boat kills to his credit that month, though the second had not been confirmed. Now he was on the trail again. Within 4 miles of the target, Oulton flew down from 3,000 feet and launched his attack. At a distance of just 1,000 yards, the navigator opened fire with the Halifax's nose guns, followed by a second burst from 600 yards which penetrated the conning tower. With practised skill, Oulton swung the Halifax to starboard, then came in for the bombing run at an angle of 30 degrees to the U-boat's track. Having dropped six depth charges in a straddle across Borchardt's submarine, he then came in again from dead astern, releasing three more depth charges as the navigator sprayed the stricken U-boat with more machine-gun fire. Several German crew manning a flak cannon managed to hit back as their boat moved awkwardly round in circles. Yet, despite the clear damage, the vessel refused to sink. With his depth charges expended, Oulton had to break off the assault, only for another Halifax from 58 Squadron to take over. Its depth charges fell short, but it was joined soon afterwards by two Sunderlands. Such reinforcements were an indicator of both the RAF's strength and the effectiveness of its communications. One of the Sunderland pilots, Flight Lieutenant Maxwell Mainprize, recalled the final moments of the encounter.

> The U-boat, which had been trailing oil and manoeuvring freely, stopped. I circled and made a second attack with four depth charges, two minutes later, from the starboard beam. After the second attack the U-boat was down by the bows, stern clear of the water. It appeared to be sinking slowly.

The entire crew of forty-nine was lost, with Oulton's Halifax and the two Sunderlands sharing the kill.[40] Oulton himself was awarded the DSO. On the return of the planes to England, the crews were congratulated on making what was regarded as a model attack in terms of tactics and co-ordination. In the words of Geoffrey Bromet, the sinking was 'an example of good co-operation and successful homing'.[41]

Portal was even more effusive about the growing power of Coastal Command. On the day of the exploit, he sent a message to the squadrons, full of praise for their perseverance and courage: 'Now that you have gained this remarkable advantage over the U-boats, I know you will press it home with ever increasing vigour and determination until, in conjunction with the Royal Navy, you have broken the enemy's morale.'[42] It was a theme relayed in the press and Parliament. 'Substantial progress has been made in providing air cover for convoys coming to Britain from across the Atlantic. Specially adapted Liberator bombers, capable of flying more than 1,000 miles from their bases, now protect our ships almost from port to port,' reported the *Daily Telegraph* on 18 May.[43] The junior Admiralty minister Lord Bruntsfield told the Upper House that the decline in merchant ship losses 'has resulted in large increases in the tonnage available to the United Nations. This improved situation in the Battle of the Atlantic reflects the growing size of our escort forces, both ships and aircraft, and the growing deadliness of our new weapons and devices.' May, he added triumphantly, 'is the best month of the war for kills so far'.[44]

Dönitz had seen an astoundingly swift reversal in his position. By May his total U-boat force was 425, including vessels on trial and in crew training, but the scope for action was becoming drastically restricted. That harsh new reality was highlighted when all thirty-five ships in convoy SC130, sailing from Newfoundland on 18 May, managed to reach Britain without any losses, in contrast to the sinking of three U-boats. Just as big a failure was the attempt to ambush convoy HX239, beginning on 22 May. Again the balance sheet decisively favoured the Allies. No ships were sunk, but two U-boats were lost, both to aircraft. Dönitz wrote:

> The overwhelming superiority achieved by the enemy defence was finally proved beyond dispute in the operations and the next two convoys, SC130 and HX239. The convoy escorts worked in exemplary harmony with specially trained support groups. To that must be added the continuous air cover, which was provided by carrier-borne and long-range, shore-based aircraft, most of them equipped with new radar. There were also the new, heavier depth charges and improved means of throwing them. With all this against us, it became impossible to carry on the fight against the convoys.[45]

He still had high hopes of new types of U-boat and stronger defensive armament, but for the present he could not sustain the losses in the Atlantic. On 24 May he called a halt to operations in the ocean.

II

Bay

THE SHORT SUNDERLAND may have been superseded by the Liberator in the Battle of the Atlantic, but even after almost four years of war, the majestic flying boat was still invaluable to Coastal Command for reconnaissance, hunting U-boats or anti-shipping duties. Admired by crews for its ease of flying and spacious comfort, it could carry eight depth charges and 2,000 pounds of bombs on movable racks, as well as 2,550 gallons of fuel in ten self-sealing fuel tanks in its high wings. It was also highly reliable, able to remain airborne even if two of its four engines failed. What was perhaps even more impressive was its defensive armament, with four .303 Browning machine guns in its power-operated tail turret, two manually operated sets of Brownings on either side of the fuselage, and two more Brownings in the nose, bolstered in several versions by four fixed guns that were fired by the pilot. Later in the war a dorsal turret was added, giving the plane a total of sixteen guns.

Never was its nickname of the Flying Porcupine more justified than in an incident at seven o'clock in the evening on 2 June 1943, when a Sunderland of 461 Squadron, piloted by Australian Flight Lieutenant Colin Walker, was on anti-submarine patrol over the Bay of Biscay, having taken off from its base at Pembroke Dock. As the plane continued on its mission, the gunner in the tail turret sighted enemy aircraft to port. Immediately, Walker tried to climb to the safety of cloud cover, but the Germans were gaining on him. Combat was inevitable. The crewmen took up their positions behind the nose, side and dorsal guns, ready to fire back at the attackers once they came within range. To make his aircraft more manoeuvrable in the imminent dogfight, Walker took the Pegasus engines to full power and ordered that the bombs and depth charges be jettisoned. Now drawing near, the enemy planes could be clearly identified as eight Junkers Ju 88 C twin-engined heavy fighters, one of the most versatile, effective types in the Luftwaffe. The first two Ju 88s made simultaneous passes on either side of the Sunderland, their hits with incendiary rounds starting blazes in both the cockpit and the port outer engine. As Walker put the plane into a corkscrew manoeuvre to evade the attackers, his second pilot managed to put out the flames with an extinguisher. Another Ju 88 came in for a third attack, only to be shot down from 50 yards by the dorsal turret gunner. The same fate was suffered by the next Ju 88, which plunged into the sea after bursts from the Sunderland's dorsal and nose guns. The rear gunner joined the fray, striking a Ju 88 that tried to attack from the rear.

By now the Sunderland and its crew had sustained heavy blows: all the men had been wounded, the starboard gunner mortally; wires to the elevator and rudder trims had been shot away; the hull was riddled with hundreds of holes; the hydraulic lead to the rear turret was cut; a second engine was put out of action; and vital instruments, including the airspeed indicator and fuel gauges, were damaged. But the Sunderland was still flying and fighting. Having regrouped, the Germans then launched a further series of assaults, yet they were the ones who experienced the most wreckage, with one Junkers Ju 88 shot down and another suffering a hit to its port engine. Just two German fighters remained; they decided that retreat was the sensible option. The remarkable encounter had lasted three-quarters of an hour, involved twenty attacks and resulted in six Luftwaffe fighters being lost or damaged. After the Sunderland crew had dumped more equipment, Walker and his co-pilot managed to nurse the plane back on a journey of 350 miles to the Cornish coast, where they landed in Penzance bay and ran the plane up to the beach using their two functioning engines.[1] Walker subsequently received the DSO. The heroism of him and his crew moved Portal so much that he sent them a personal message of congratulations:

I should like Flight Lieutenant Walker and the surviving members of his gallant crew to be told of the admiration and pride I felt on learn-ing the details of this epic battle which will go down in history as one of the finest instances in this war of the triumph of coolness, skill and determination against overwhelming odds.[2]

The episode reflected not just the courage of the RAF but also the ferocity of the conflict in the summer of 1943 over the Bay of Biscay, which had by now become the key arena in the anti-submarine war after Dönitz suspended operations in the Atlantic. Aerial support had been essential to the Allies' growing success there, and the Luftwaffe should have been a vital ingredient of the Reich's defence of the U-boat fleet off the French coast. But in the opening years of the war the Germans were badly hampered by the profound antipathy between their air and naval forces. The discord that regularly arose between the Air Ministry and the Admiralty in Britain paled beside the friction on the German side, much of it caused by the Luftwaffe chief Hermann Goering, who jealously guarded his force's autonomy, had no interest in naval aviation, despised the Kriegsmarine and loathed Raeder. His disdain meant that the Luftwaffe did not have enough Condors for the Battle of the Atlantic or fighters to ward off the RAF in the protection of shipping and U-boat traffic. Even when, much to Goering's fury, Hitler agreed to the establishment of a naval air command, the Fliegerführer Atlantik, in early 1941, it had barely 100 aircraft. The numbers grew over the following year, particularly in the supply of Ju 88s, though this was not enough to deny the RAF air superiority over the Bay in 1943.

Slessor was determined to use that advantage. Now that the tide had turned in the Atlantic, his belief was that the Bay was 'the decisive point on which we should concentrate' in order to bring about the final defeat of the submarine menace, like felling 'a tree by cutting through its trunk'. For Coastal Command, 'this was the one place where we could be absolutely certain there would be U-boats to be found and killed'.[3] But it was a stance that brought him into conflict with the US Navy commander Admiral King, who thought he was demanding too much, and the British Admiralty, who felt he was demanding too little. At the end of March the Admiralty suddenly came forward with a dramatic call for no fewer than 190 more long-range aircraft for the Bay offensive. This demand was set out in a paper by Patrick Blackett, the Admiralty's head of operational research, who argued for saturation coverage of the Bay through 100 sorties a day and 40 a night by long-range aircraft equipped with ASV. The prospect of a vast enhancement of Coastal Command's fleet, however, did not appeal to Slessor. He believed that a far better approach would be to push the Americans to move more of their aircraft from the Caribbean and the American west coast, where there was no longer any real threat, to southern England to operate in the eastern Atlantic theatre. His view was reinforced by private information from Bob Lovett, the US assistant secretary of war for air, who told him that '70 of our VLR Liberators were sitting doing nothing on the Pacific Coast', which to Slessor 'amply illustrated the ridiculous state of affairs now prevailing'.[4] With the support of Harris and Portal, Slessor persuaded the Defence Committee to reject Blackett's paper, concluding, 'if ever there was an example of the unwisdom of letting sailors try to run air operations, that was one'. Then on 4 April he wrote a lengthy memorandum to Pound setting out his objections and suggesting the alternative of US redeployment. In the immediate term another thirty to forty long- and medium-range aircraft could be reassigned to the Bay from within Coastal Command's resources, though these would not have ASV. In the longer-term, from July 1943, the real answer was to convince the American Chiefs of Staff 'that the Bay is a productive area for U-boat kills and I suggest we should ask them to assign six squadrons (72 planes), including a proportion of VLR anti-submarine aircraft'. It was 'not worth asking for more,' he warned Pound, because 'this is the maximum force which could in practice be made available, maintained and accommodated in south-west England this summer'.[5]

Pound, increasingly dogged by ill health, did not fight Slessor but joined him in making the request to the Americans, which was put forward in a paper on 21 April. But Admiral King, the head of the US Navy, who had already baulked at the demands of the Atlantic campaign, was not receptive to the idea. Still focused on the needs of the Pacific, he denied there was any surplus of US Liberators and described the search for U-boats from the air as like 'looking for a needle in a haystack'.[6] Discussions between London and Washington dragged on, until eventually the Americans agreed to transfer two Liberator squadrons of twenty-four aircraft to the United Kingdom, though they would not arrive until mid-July. 'This was very far short of the 72 aircraft for which we had asked, and towards the end of June I flew to Washington to discover whether it was intended to send any more US squadrons to this country,' recalled Slessor.[7] His visit yielded an apparently welcome result, with one further naval and two more army Liberator squadrons promised for the Bay. Yet these pledges were never fulfilled due largely to more obstructionism and arbitrary policy-making by King. By the end of the year there were still only three US Navy Liberator squadrons. It turned out that Coastal Command had largely to fight the Bay offensive on its own. After his visit in June, Slessor wrote to Trenchard, 'there is a tendency in Washington to want air cover for every ship that sails. The old Hun has only got to send one U-boat to the Caribbean and the local Admiral there is screaming for more aircraft.' He felt that if 'anyone wants a living argument for the folly of not having an autonomous air force, let him go to Washington now. I have never known relations as bitter between the US Army and Navy as they are now over anti-submarine squadrons.'[8]

The long dispute both with the USA and within the American military in 1943 led to calls for a unified Allied command to take charge of the whole Atlantic campaign, thereby improving co-ordination. But by May it was clear that the plan had gained no traction. Instead, the British and Americans created a much more low-key body, the Allied Anti-Submarine Survey Board, but with limited powers it achieved little. Slessor was not sad at the demise of the scheme, as he wrote to Patrick Brind, the assistant chief of the Naval Staff:

> The idea, which appeals to people who don't really know what the system is and how it works, of great Combined headquarters in which a High panjandrum (or two high panjandrums in different coloured coats) sit looking at a great chart and moving flags about and making weighty decisions is I think in reality not only unnecessary but unworkable.[9]

In fact, Slessor thought there was already too much bureaucracy in Coastal Command without adding more layers. To Blackett he wrote in April, there are a darned sight too many committees about this war . . . frankly, I think there are altogether too many people commanding Coastal Command, while the one chap who ought to be doing it – me – spends half his time writing papers or briefs on somebody else's papers for yet another committee.[10]

Even in the face of these difficulties, Slessor had tremendous faith in the Bay offensive, telling Trenchard: 'Every U-boat that operates in the whole Atlantic has to go out from and come back to a Bay port – and that's where we can kill the U-boat menace. Kill him at sea – don't waste bombs on his base ports.'[11] He had started the offensive with Operation Gondola in February, followed by Operation Enclose in the last week of March, which involved 182 sorties and fifteen U-boat attacks, though only one sinking was achieved. At this stage, the Germans still tended to crash dive when they were sighted on the surface, but the increasing number of Coastal Command aircraft with Leigh Lights and ASV Mark III 10-cm radar, undetectable by the Metox receivers, made that tactic far more difficult. As the RAF stepped up the assault with Operation Enclose II in April, Dönitz ordered his U-boats to remain submerged at night and surface during the day, when their crews could keep a visual lookout. Moreover, instead of invariably diving once spotted, they were instructed to fight back against the enemy if possible, helped by the introduction of extra armament. Many submarines were now fitted with additional platforms to accommodate fully automatic 37-mm anti-aircraft cannon or twin 20-mm flak guns.

The disconcerting experience of coming under fire was described by Donald Fraser of 172 Squadron while diving towards a U-boat in the Bay:

I saw machine-gun tracers and rapid fire, probably from 20-mm guns, spurting up towards me. I felt very lonely and naked sitting in the greenhouse at the front of the plane. I had not started to shake, that would come later. The shells appeared to be bursting to starboard. Were they hitting the wing?[12]

Despite the German resistance, the Wellington carried on towards the target. 'We swept over the conning tower at what seemed like zero feet, although it was actually 10 or 20.' As they flew over the submarine, the skipper shouted that the starboard engine was on fire. 'I knew at our low altitude that we would be smashed into mincemeat if we crashed into the sea. Luckily, we did not appear to be losing height. The fire seemed to go out. Perhaps the skipper had imagined it, or I had misheard him.' Then Fraser realized that the bomb doors had not opened, so the plane went round, preparing for a second attack. But by now the submarine had disappeared. Despite searching for more than an hour, the Wellington crew found no sign of it. With petrol running low, the skipper began the long journey back to Chivenor. Altogether the flight had lasted thirteen hours.

More fruitful, but still fraught, was a sortie by Squadron Leader Peter Cundy in a Liberator over the Bay of Biscay in 1943:

> The U-boat captain saw us coming. He opened fire with all armament, including a 37-mm cannon while the aircraft was still a mile away and, as the range closed, he scored hits on us. My gunners were not idle. They returned hot fire and one of the U-boat crew was seen to fall overboard. We had stopped a few bullets; there was a hole in a tank and petrol was flowing over the engine exhaust. I thought there might be a fire at any moment but we carried on and dropped our depth charges, one of which hit the U-boat abaft of the conning tower and bounced off into the sea. As we circled for a second attack we saw the depth charges go off. There was a sudden spurt of water close to the enemy's guns which abruptly ceased firing . . . The enemy started evasive action but was very low in the water and only a little way on. Once again we flew over and our second stick of depth charges straddled it, hiding the U-boat in the huge plumes of the explosions which merged into a single gigantic fountain of water. I circled round again and we saw the U-boat. All that we could see was a dark brown patch of oil. Several bodies rose to the surface.

Despite the damage to the Liberator, Cundy managed to nurse it back to St Eval on three engines.[13]

By April Coastal Command had 150 aircraft in the Bay for the offensive, seventy-five of them long-range planes with ASV III. But some of the early scepticism proved justified; the overall results of operations to the end of that month, which concluded with Operation Derange, did not match the effort. Coastal Command had flown 80,443 hours but sunk only ten U-boats and damaged twenty-four, in return for the loss of 170 aircraft. Some crewmen, like D. M. Gall of 201 Squadron, recalled the tedium of much of the work over the Bay:

> I should say that we disliked anti-submarine patrols, compared with convoy escort work. With the latter, at least we had something to look at, but on patrols we had to suffer the extreme boredom of flying mile after mile with nothing to see but the sea for something like 15 hours at a time.[14]

Yet even if they saw nothing, the presence of Coastal Command planes was putting pressure on the U-boats, as the commander Teddy Suhren wrote,

> the last test awaiting us was the Bay of Biscay. Although we had got through it previously at full speed and on the surface, I was not much in favour of this tactic. The accuracy with which the planes had flown at us made me assume that the enemy had radar now fitted to their planes in spite of all expectations to the contrary and that they could pinpoint us on the surface; not all aircraft perhaps but certainly in those squadrons which were involved with anti-submarine pursuit. It would only take a plane like that to appear suddenly through the cloud above us and not even prayer or evasive tactics would do any good. We'd be bombed before we knew anything about it.[15]

In response to the fightback policy, Slessor stepped up daylight patrols in May and also stressed to crews that they should press on with attacks even under anti-aircraft fire. In an official instruction on 5 May 1943, he wrote that the aircraft captain

> must remember that the primary reason for his existence, for the time being, is to kill U-boats and a U-boat on the surface presents a better chance of a kill than one submerged. It is no coincidence that, of the six certain or probable kills in the past fortnight, all have been U-boats that stayed on the surface and fought back. It should also be borne in

mind that even a big aircraft, properly handled and using its guns well, is a fleeting and difficult target for the gunners in the necessarily cramped gun positions of a U-boat. A U-boat in any sort of sea is a poor gun platform, especially when the boat is steaming beam-on to a sea.[16]

Coastal Command knew that the Germans were exacting a heavier toll, as its anti-submarine committee reported in early June. 'Of the aircraft attacked by return fire from the U-boat, approximately 30 per cent were hit but this figure is increasing as the U-boat armament is improved. From September to March, the percentage was 13, in April it was 19 and in May 23.'[17] To counter this attrition, Coastal Command sought to introduce new, more lethal weapons. One was a 600-pound depth charge, of which Joubert had been a passionate advocate, though Blackett and Williams had been far more doubtful about its value because it had to be dropped from a higher altitude and there-fore accuracy, so essential to the fight against the U-boats, was lost. The 600-pounder finally went into action in 1943, only to confirm the scepticism by accounting for just one U-boat. It never proved a success. In total just ninety-seven of these heavy charges were dropped in twenty-eight attacks by the end of the war, compared to 5,790 traditional 250-pound Torpex charges in 1,170 attacks. Of the latter, Slessor wrote that 'if the depth-setting was right, if the distance between the depth charges making up the stick was properly spaced, above all if crews were well trained and laid their sticks accurately, it was an exceedingly effective weapon'.[18]

Far more effective than the 600-pound depth charge was the rocket projectile, whose development owed much to the pioneering govern-ment scientist Sir Henry Tizard. Initially used by the RAF as a tank-busting weapon in the desert campaign, it had obvious potential in both anti-shipping and anti-submarine operations and had success-fully completed its trials with Coastal Command by February 1943. In the maritime war, the projectile, which travelled at 1,800 feet per second when fired, came with two types of head: a 60-pound one filled with high explosive and a 25-pound armour-piercing one made of solid steel. From the early summer, aircraft equipped with this weapon went into action against the U-boats, scoring their first kill off the Azores on 23 May when a solid-head projectile fired by a carrier-borne Fleet Air Arm Swordfish tore through the pressure hull of U-752, the large holes preventing the submarine from diving and leaving the vessel easy prey for the British naval craft that arrived swiftly on the scene. This was followed by a successful rocket attack on 28 May by a Coastal Command Hudson of 608 Squadron on U-755, which was spotted on the surface near Mallorca in the western Mediterranean. In the spirit of Dönitz's new tactical instructions, the U-boat skipper Walter Göing decided to fight it out against the RAF attacker, but the encounter turned out to be calamitously one-sided for him and his crew. Flown by G. A. K. Ogilvy, the Hudson came in from a low height and fired a two-rocket salvo. One missile failed to release but the other hit the underside of the hull right in the centre. After he had circled the stricken boat, Ogilvy came in for a second attack, which proved even more devastating as three of the four rockets made direct hits. On orders from Göing, the crew tried to abandon ship, only to find the Hudson spraying them with 7,000 rounds from its machine guns. The vessel went down in nine minutes, with the loss of thirty-nine lives.

Confidence in the rockets led to Coastal Command's decision in April to install them on all the Beaufighters of 236 Squadron, which was now to be a new element in the Bay offensive. Once intensive training had been completed, 236 went to Predannack in Cornwall for its anti-submarine duties. On 1 June, soon after the squadron had arrived, Mark Bateman took off in his Beaufighter armed with four rockets under each wing, to patrol the Bay. After almost three hours in the air flying at 3,500 feet, the navigator sighted a U-boat about 10 miles away. Immediately Bateman went on the attack. He was just 5,000 yards from the target when his Beaufighter was seen by the U-boat's two lookouts in the conning tower. They sounded the alarm with the vessel's electric bell and the captain gave orders to dive, but it was too late. The conning tower was still visible above the surface when Bateman fired his first two salvos at the boat, aiming not directly at the hull but, as he had been trained, at the sea 25 yards in front of the target. In his account of the incident based on eyewitness testimony, Roy Conyers Nesbit described how 'three seconds after firing, the projectiles hit the sea by the side of the U-boat and their trajectories curved upwards as density changed from air to water'. They then struck the German vessel 'with tremendous force, puncturing holes in the pressure hull. The warheads broke off and smashed through the other side of the U-boat, leaving the motor tubes flaming and spinning inside the hull. Great jets of sea-water spurted uncontrollably into the perforated and stricken U-boat.' Soon the submarine was at the bottom of the sea, and the 236 Beaufighter was on its way back to Predannack.[19]

The rocket projectiles had turned out to be a valuable addition to Coastal Command's armoury; their qualities were praised by the ace Terry Bulloch, who perfected his own technique for their use on Liberators in 224 Squadron. His method was to fire two rockets from each side in the dive at 800 feet, another salvo of four at 600 feet and finally two pairs at 500 feet before he pulled out of the dive. Describing the solid 25-pound rocket as 'a great weapon', he said that 'when released at the correct dive angle and speed' it had 'remarkable ballistic qualities. On entering the water they would descend to approximately 25 to 30 feet deep, then level off, travel horizontally for a distance, then re-emerge from the sea. The head would penetrate the pressure hull of a U-boat and come out the other side.'[20]

A compelling description of a slightly different approach to the use of these projectiles was given by Peter Burden who flew in Hudsons with 206 Squadron:

Tactics were evolved which radically changed the aircraft attack. Hitherto, an attack with depth charges was made at a dive from the patrol height of 600 feet with the bomb doors open to about 50 feet for releasing the depth charges. This gave the maximum probability of getting the depth charges in the right place and the least chance of them fracturing on impact with the sea. Rocket projectiles required that an attack be started from 1,500 feet in a steep dive which took the airspeed up to about 350 knots, very fast for an aircraft whose cruising speed was usually about 130 knots. Two rockets were fired at about 1,000 feet, another pair at 600 feet and the final four at 300 feet. The first two pairs burnt out before reaching the target but the smoke and noise were alleged to give the screaming habdabs to any gun crew on the sub and that and the rapid closing with the target gave a much better chance for the aircraft to escape damage. The end of the attack dive was a heave back on the control column and a sincere hope that the aircraft was at least levelled out and hopefully even climbing before reaching sea level. It was a nice judgement when to pull out of the dive, leaving it as long as possible to get the best chance of hits on the target but not too late so that the aircraft became the missile that hit the sub.[21]

The depth charge, however, remained the prime anti-submarine weapon of Coastal Command, partly because, as Burden pointed out, the projectiles could be dangerous in less capable hands. In contrast to this tale of success on weaponry, one problem that Coastal Command never fully resolved was the creation of a trusted bombsight. The Mark XIV, widely used in Bomber Command, proved erratic at low level. To overcome this difficulty, the Operational Research Section devised the Mark III, which on the insistence of Joubert entered service in late 1942 and utilized a primitive form of mechanical computer to guide the bomb release. Also known as the Angular Velocity Sight, it was said to increase the chances of destroying a U-boat by 35 per cent, but it was not universally popular with crews, who often preferred to rely on the judgement of their own eyes.

Due to Coastal Command's aggressive response, Dönitz's fightback policy failed to give the protection he had hoped as the offensive escalated. From June, Slessor divided the Bay into two operational zones, an outer western area code-named Sea Slug, which was covered by aircraft from 15 Group, and an inner, eastern area code-named Musketry, where the regular patrols along parallel tracks were co-ordinated by 19 Group and backed up by the Royal Navy's support units. The aim was to create what was called the Unclimbable Fence, trapping the enemy in the Bay. A signal from Albert Durston, the senior staff officer, to Coastal Command's groups emphasized the priority of this task.

It is of the utmost importance to follow up and intensify our recent successes against the U-boats. Until further orders, the maximum possible effort of both 19 and 15 Groups is to be directed to the Bay

offensive after the minimum, repeat minimum, requirements of air
cover for threatened convoys has been satisfied.[22]

The growing vigour had its impact. In the period from 1 July to 2
August, 368 aircraft in twenty-five squadrons of Coastal Command
flew 9,689 hours, making over ninety sightings and sixty-three attacks,
which resulted in the loss of sixteen U-boats and severe damage to
another six. But the Germans were endlessly resourceful. Now under
even more pressure, Dönitz instructed his U-boats transiting the Bay
to move in groups of up to five, thereby concentrating their firepower
and providing mutual protection. Furthermore, in August he
suspended the use of Metox receivers, recognizing that the Allies'
Mark III ASV radar could pick up their signals, while he instructed
his U-boats to hug the Spanish coast on their journeys where possible, taking advantage of the pro-Axis neutrality of General Franco's
regime, which the Allies could not violate. He also was finally given
more support by the Luftwaffe, with twin-engined Dornier Do 17s
and Henschel Hs 293 radio-controlled glide bombs joining the Ju 88s
in the coastal defences. In fact, the Luftwaffe's force for the Bay
increased significantly during the summer. In May there had been just
forty-nine fighters and sixty-four bombers available for such duties,
but these totals rose to: sixty fighters and 120 bombers in July; and
eighty fighters and 132 bombers in August. This combination of
strong defensive measures resulted in heavy losses and fewer sightings
for the Allies, with Coastal Command having a plane a day shot down
in August. Liberator wireless operator Eddie Cheek later said, 'When
the enemy pitched fast, heavily armed fighter aircraft against lumbering submarine bombers, we soon realized that the rules of the game
had changed and the change was certainly not in our favour.'[23]

The new fierceness of the conflict in the Bay was epitomized by an
extraordinary clash on 30 July, which revealed the highest levels of
courage and chivalry in the maritime war. That day, a convoy of three
U-boats, escorted by destroyers, minesweepers and six Ju 88s, was
crossing the Bay when it was spotted by a number of Allied planes,
including a Catalina of 210 Squadron, a Liberator of 53 Squadron, a
Halifax of 502 Squadron and a Sunderland of 461 Squadron, which
was flown by Australian Dudley Marrows, who was coming to the

end of a gruelling fourteen-hour flight. The U-boat formation had tremendous firepower, with their combined twenty-seven anti-aircraft guns forcing a couple of the planes to bomb from high altitude. Yet even faced with this barrage of fire, Marrows and his crew decided to dive in for a standard attack on the submarines. 'The only thing to do was to go in as low as I possibly could, hoping that there would be some trouble when the submarines were broadside onto the swell for them adequately to depress their guns at all times.'[24] As the Sunderland came in, it was hit in the wing spar by flak and had to break off the attack. The damage was superficial so Marrows dived in again, almost skimming the wave-top as the three U-boats' guns opened up. But he could not be deterred and managed to drop seven 450-pound depth charges on one of the submarines, U-461, skippered by Wolf Steibler. As Marrows's Sunderland climbed away, the navigator saw some of the sinking U-boat's 68-strong crew in the water, clinging to debris. The Sunderland's crew then unanimously made a bold, generous decision: they resolved to drop their plane's own inflatable dinghy for the German survivors, among them Wolf Steibler. 'You could see these poor blokes, about 15 of them, struggling in the water. That turns you round to saying, "OK, they're human." Not a single one of our crew of twelve disagreed,' Marrows later recalled.[25]

Now low on fuel, Marrows and his crew began the journey back to Pembroke Dock, only to spot another U-boat on the way. Despite the damage to their plane's wing spar, they dived down again and attacked the submarine from a low level in the face of more anti-aircraft fire, suffering a direct hit with a cannon shell that started a fire and knocked out the plane's electrical system before they had the chance to release their remaining depth charges. Yet they still were able to strafe the boat with their machine guns before Marrows managed to haul the Sunderland back to the port of St Mary's in the Scilly Isles.

Although the crew's action in dropping the dinghy for the Germans had been against RAF regulations, Marrows was awarded the DFC for his 'devotion to duty, disregard for personal safety and fine fighting spirit'.[26] Along with his destruction of U-461, the other two U-boats in the formation were sunk, one by aircraft, the other by surface craft from the Royal Navy. Forty years later, Marrows's wife Silvia attended a reunion in Germany of Sunderland and U-boat crew members. She was approached by a German woman who said, 'Please thank your husband for giving me the many happy years of marriage I have had.' Her husband was Wolf Steibler, the skipper.[27]

Despite all Slessor's efforts, the Germans had not been broken in the Bay. The trunk of the tree had not been severed as autumn approached. Operations Sea Slug and Musketry were replaced by a new, wide-ranging effort called Percussion focused nearer the Spanish coast, but that was no more effective. In May, after the successes in the Atlantic, Slessor had told Portal that Coastal Command was 'having a phenomenal month'.[28] Even in July, Patrick Brind, the assistant chief of the Naval Staff, told a committee meeting that 'he considered Coastal Command had made a great contribution in the Bay offensive towards the defeat of the U-boat'.[29] But now, at the end of August, there was deepening anxiety about the resilience of Dönitz's fleet, as reflected in a secret Coastal Command paper:

> The enemy is not defeated in the U-boat, traffic through the Bay of Biscay has not diminished recently. Nevertheless, since the 5th of August, only occasional sightings have been made, attacks by our aircraft have been few and no kills have resulted. Meanwhile our aircraft losses during this period have increased by 150 per cent . . . the situation is grave. In three weeks we have lost the initiative which cost us so much effort and which we enjoyed for a few brief months. In this period, by a change of policy, the enemy has regained the offensive.

The paper outlined the perceived reasons for the reversal, including the heavy German aerial escorts 'operating at the extreme range of our long-range fighters' and the rerouting of U-boats along the Spanish coast in disregard of 'territorial waters'. According to the paper, the latter tactic also undermined the effectiveness of Coastal Command's Leigh Light planes: 'The work of Leigh Light aircraft is difficult in all parts of this area and virtually impossible inshore.'[30] The suggested answers were perseverance, greater use of naval support groups, an increase of patrols from the Gibraltar–Morocco area, deployment of heavily armed Flying Fortresses and bombing the aerodromes in occupied France. But the atmosphere also bred an incendiary accusation from Wing Commander Lionel Cohen, an RAF liaison officer at the Admiralty's Operations Division, about Coastal Command's fighting spirit against the Luftwaffe: 'The morale of the squadrons is deteriorating . . . If any of our aircraft sight another aircraft during patrol, they immediately take evasive action by steering west and rarely make an attempt to investigate the contact. This is a defeatist measure.' To re-establish 'the fine morale which existed in the squadrons', Cohen suggested more protection from Spitfire, Mosquito and Beaufighter units, as well as better training in formation flying for anti-submarine patrols.[31]

Slessor himself, the prime evangelist for the Bay offensive, was alarmed at the change in fortunes, writing to Douglas Evill, vice chief of the Air Staff, at the end of August:

> Operations in the Bay have taken a turn seriously unfavourable to us . . . The enemy fighters are making our task very difficult and the enemy bombers may make the position of the surface ships co-operating with us untenable. It is therefore of vital importance, if we are to regain our ascendancy in the Bay, to have every possible long-range and Leigh Light night aircraft that we can possibly get into action.[32]

However, Brian Baker, the new commander of 19 Group, believed that Coastal Command's rigid patrol tactics and centralized control were part of the problem. In a bold letter to Slessor in late September, he declared that

> although the enemy has changed his tactics, we have not and it is submitted that by sticking to an old groove which did produce results under a certain set of circumstances, but which are not producing them now, we are making a desperate mistake. In fact, the flexibility of air power has been forgotten.

The answer, argued Baker, was

simple and straightforward. Let us shake ourselves out of the groove into which we have fallen, use the flexibility of air power to the maximum and try to find new areas of operation where the enemy will not be expecting us. With Liberators we can get to 24 degrees West. And finally allow the Groups who should be conducting the operations some measure of initiative. Time was when the Groups were allowed full control and I would suggest that they have staffs sufficiently experienced to do it again.

He concluded, 'Let us shake ourselves free from the stereotyped system of patrols with which the enemy must now be fully acquainted.'[33]

Yet the situation was not nearly as bleak as it seemed. For the Reich's ascendancy in the Bay was of little use if it did not change the course of the Battle of Atlantic. Improved protection of the U-boats off the French and Spanish coasts could not be an end in itself, but only a means to regaining the ability to cut the Allied supply lines. But by the autumn of 1943, the convoy system was so secure that the Germans were unable to inflict much damage when they resumed their operations. If the trunk was still alive, the branches had now withered. Not only was the Atlantic gap firmly closed, but air support in the middle of the ocean had been dramatically reinforced by an agreement secured by the persuasive diplomacy of Foreign Secretary Sir Anthony Eden with the Portuguese government to allow Allied planes to operate from the Azores. This meant a further extension to Coastal Command's global empire. The commander of the new base on the island of Terceira was the cool-headed Geoffrey Bromet, former head of 19 Group, with the first planes, a pair of Flying Fortresses, arriving in October. Further reinforcements followed, among them Leigh Light Wellingtons of 172 and 179 squadrons and Hudsons of 269 Squadron. The *Daily Telegraph* reported:

With the Azores at our disposal, we shall in future be able to exercise virtual control over the entire Atlantic crossing, winter and summer alike. Instead of having to fly the 1,800 miles to Newfoundland or 900 miles to the mid-Atlantic and back from either Newfoundland or Northern Ireland, our coastal aircraft will now have a valuable and central base in the south.[34]

The Allies' strength was quickly demonstrated when the Germans tried to renew the attacks on the convoys from mid-September 1943. An initial success by the Kriegsmarine in sinking six merchantmen in the westbound convoys of ONS18/ON2, in return for three U-boat losses, proved misleading. Not only had 90 per cent of the Allied ships reached their destination, but the next three convoys suffered no damage at all, thanks to heavy air cover which prevented the wolf packs going on the attack.

Coastal Command's force was not just more numerous but also better equipped than ever. The advanced Liberator VI, the first production version fitted with a nose turret, was coming into service, eventually making up five Coastal Command squadrons. There was also a growing establishment of Liberators fitted with 10-cm radar, rocket projectiles and Leigh Lights. An illustration of their potential for devastation came in mid-October, when a wolf pack targeted the westbound convoy ON126, only to lose six U-boats, four of them to Liberators. By the end of the month twenty-eight German submarines had been sunk, twenty-two of them by aircraft.

A further addition to Coastal Command's anti-U-boat armoury in October came with the arrival of a small number of De Havilland Mark XVIII Mosquitoes, fitted with a 6-pounder, 57-mm anti-tank gun. Incongruously, the gun was built by the Molins company of Peterborough, which before the war had specialized in the production of machines for packaging cigarettes. The Mosquito was the ideal aircraft for this weapon, not only because of its speed and manoeuvrability but also because its wooden structure could easily absorb the tremendous recoil from the Molins gun. Once other modifications had been made to the Mosquito, such as extra ammunition tanks, the removal of outer machine guns and further armour in the nose and cockpit to deal with enemy anti-aircraft fire, tests proved the practicality of the plane, which was a fearsome sight when the gun fired, with flames 30 feet long spouting from its barrel with each round. Symbolic of Coastal Command's sharpening lethality, these Mosquitoes, sometimes called Tsetses, were sent to Predannack as a specialist detachment of 618 Squadron to fight alongside the Beaufighters of 248. Having scored their first hit on a U-boat on 7 November, when a Mosquito flown by Canadian officer A. J. L.

Bonnett unleashed eight rounds at U-123's conning tower and hull, rendering the vessel unable to dive and in urgent need of repairs. Further successes led to the creation of a second Molins-armed anti-submarine squadron, though the Mosquito really came into its own as an anti-shipping aircraft.

By the end of October it was clear that the attempted revival of U-boats in the Atlantic had been foiled. Out of 2,468 merchantmen which had crossed the Atlantic in the last two months in sixty-four convoys, only nine had been sunk. The Naval Staff's Anti-U-boat Division wrote to Slessor that 'U-boats have fared worse in their present campaign against the North Atlantic convoys than they did in April and May 1943, when they were withdrawn from this area on account of the unfavourable situation. It is assumed that early disengagement from the present campaign is expected.'[35] As ascendancy appeared to become a reality, Coastal Command's own in-house journal concluded in December, 'The year 1943 has many claims on history. High among them will be that it saw the defeat of the U-boat menace in the Atlantic, which at the beginning of the year bade fair to strangle our strategy in Europe.'[36] But it was far too early to write-off a military machine as tenacious as the Reich's.

12

Wing

O N 18 MAY 1943 Slessor wrote to Portal in bullish terms about Coastal Command's recent anti-shipping operations, led by the recently established strike force based at North Coates in Lincolnshire.

> The torpedo boys are putting up a great show – 489 got a couple of ships on the Norwegian coast last week and 455 got a 10,000-ton tanker full of naval fuel oil yesterday, and today the North Coates wing got into another convoy on the Dutch coast, hit two merchant vessels with torpedoes and one with a bomb, and left three escort vessel well blazing.[1]

But that optimistic assessment was in contrast to the narrative of struggle that had characterized Coastal Command's previous anti-shipping work. As recently as January 1943, just before Slessor had taken over, Coastal Command had flown 461 anti-shipping missions but sank only two ships. Nor had there been much early glory for the North Coates Strike Wing, which was hampered by poor co-ordination and lack of training.

The concept of a strike wing had evolved after long discussions within Coastal Command. A key influence in its adoption had been the experience of the war in the Mediterranean, where some success had been achieved against Axis shipping by torpedo bombers flying at low level in tight formations, making astern attacks and co-ordinating with other aircraft that used cannons and machine guns to quell the enemy flak or create diversions. With its speed, ruggedness and heavy armament, the Beaufighter was the ideal plane for the strike wing, especially when Coastal Command found that it could be converted to carry torpedoes, creating a new type known as the Torbeau. But the potent versatility of the Beaufighter was also a problem since it was in high demand by Fighter Command, as well as in the Middle East and India. Indeed, Pound wrote to Portal in May 1942 to warn that the drain of Beaufighters had left 'Coastal Command in a most unsatisfactory state', with the result 'that a long dated programme of expansion for torpedo bomber aircraft is much overdue'.[2] There had been, however, sufficient Beaufighters and Torbeaus to form a strike wing, part of No. 16 Group, with additional training and trials of equipment undertaken at Leuchars in Scotland.

By November, Coastal Command HQ had deemed the new unit ready for its first anti-convoy operation, which was to have three main elements: an advance section to hit the ships' defences, followed by the torpedo bomber section, with both guarded by an escort of Spitfire fighters. On the eve of the maiden assignment, the RAF's Torpedo Development Unit stressed the need for simplicity: 'The only form of attack likely to succeed is the simplest in every case. As soon as any complicated manoeuvring is introduced, things will start to go wrong.'[3]

In fact, the very first mission of the North Coates Strike Wing, on 20 November 1942, had gone badly awry before it had even left England. Comprising twenty-four Beaufighters of 236 and 254 squadrons, it had been led by veteran pilot Mark Bateman and targeted an Axis convoy of sixteen ships off the Hague. In poor weather, it had failed to meet its fighter escort over Kent, while four Beaufighters had become lost and returned to base. Further mishaps followed as the reduced, unprotected formation came under heavy Luftwaffe fighter attack, torpedoes failed to explode and flak defences proved deadly. The trip had proved an expensive disappointment. In return for one tug definitely sunk plus inconclusive reports of two hits on merchant ships, three RAF aircraft had been shot down and six badly damaged. Joubert had been forced to order the suspension of any further operations by the wing so that further training could be undertaken.

The botched trip to the Hague epitomized the continuing struggles of the RAF's anti-shipping arm after three years of war. Altogether in 1942, Coastal Command had sunk just twenty-six vessels for 55,424 tons, compared to twenty-eight vessels for 51,965 tons in 1941. In another telling statistic, twelve of the fifteen Axis ships that acted as blockade runners during that year along the western European coast were intercepted by aircraft, yet not one was sunk. Further attempts to damage the German ships *Prinz Eugen* and *Scharnhorst* proved equally fruitless. There were occasional successes, however, particularly on the Norwegian coast where there was a greater volume of German shipping, much of it handling vital iron ore imports from Sweden. Even the Hampden, deemed obsolete by Bomber Command, came into own in this theatre, sinking 45,000 tons of shipping between September 1942 and mid-1943. One noteworthy Hampden torpedo attack was led by Flying Officer Tony Mottram, who was to become a tennis star after the war, reaching the quarter-finals of Wimbledon in 1948. On 17 September he was in a formation of three Hampdens despatched to attack a convoy of two large merchant ships, with five escorts, off the south-west coast of Norway. Having sighted the vessels, as he recorded in his debriefing report,

We went in together and released our torpedoes almost simultaneously. I flew past the convoy and, as I turned to come back, I saw a big mushroom of water go up into the air just across the beam of the larger ships. As the water fell away, another spout shot up, showing that a second torpedo had scored a hit. Shortly afterwards a dense pall of chocolate-coloured smoke arose from the ship and, in a short while, almost completely enveloped it. All this time they were throwing up a lot of flak at us. At first it was inaccurate but then they seemed to get our range, and shells began bursting uncomfortably close. A pom-pom shell hit the cowling of one of my engines and blew a bit off, but it kept going and got us home safely.[4]

The temporary suspension at North Coates did not lead to the abandonment of the strike wing experiment. On the contrary, plans were formulated early in 1943 for the creation of two further wings within No. 18 Group in Scotland. There were also intense discussions within Coastal Command about the development of better tactics, communications, weaponry, training and use of intelligence. Typical was a paper by the Directorate of Torpedo Operations of 11 February, which suggested that in a torpedo attack 'the primary role of the accompanying diversionary aircraft is to keep down the flak of the escorts and of the target ships themselves. In order to do this the escort vessels must be attacked by an adequate number of aircraft armed with rocket projectiles or cannon or preferably both.' The paper added that

> the ration of diversionary aircraft to aircraft taking part in the main strike should certainly be 2 to 1 and probably 3 to 1, and if this is accepted the present planning of 10 Beaufighter squadrons for Coastal Command equally divided between torpedoes and diversionary aircraft is cutting things too fine on the diversionary side.[5]

Aircraft numbers also cropped up during a major conference at the Command's headquarters on 22 February, called to improve co-operation with Fighter Command. Among other measures, the planners decided that 'a minimum of two single-seater fighter squadrons (24 aircraft) should be employed to escort the strike wing, one as close escort, and one as cover'.[6]

By 18 April, after months of intensive practice overseen by Wing Commander Neil Wheeler, the North Coates strike squadrons were ready to go into action again. The target this time was a heavily escorted convoy that had been sighted by RAF reconnaissance off the Hook of Holland. Assigned to the attack were nine Torbeaus of 254 Squadron under the command of the redoubtable New Zealander Squadron Leader Bill Sise; they were supported by twelve anti-flak Beaufighters of 143 and 236 squadrons, each of them armed with four 20-mm cannon and two 250-pound bombs, one slung under each wing. The tension in the build-up at North Coates was captured by David Ellis, a pilot in 236 Squadron:

> After briefing, activity on the station increased. Ground crews put the finishing touches to the aircraft, caterers provided rations and in due course our WAAF [Women's Auxiliary Air Force] driver delivered us with all our equipment to our aircraft. Watches had been synchronised at briefing and, at the appointed time, 42 Hercules engines roared into life. After warm-up and checks, 21 Beaufighters began to taxi to their take-off positions. Then section by section they followed the Wing Commander into the air.

Soon they were over RAF Coltishall, where they successfully picked up their escort of twenty-two Spitfire Mark Vs and six American Mustangs, the exceptional American fighter with unrivalled range and speed. Ellis's account continued, 'Crossing the Norfolk coast, the wing commander took the formation down to wave top height, our normal height to avoid radar detection. It was even more exhilarating when flying as part of a large formation skimming the sea.' After forty minutes, the strike wing approached the Dutch coast. 'I peered ahead but the visibility was deteriorating. I locked my gunsight into position and turned off the safety catch on my safety button.'

Following Wheeler's lead, the formation climbed to 1,500, the Beaufighter crews knowing from the whine in their headphones that they had been picked up by German radar. Then the convoy came into view, made up of two lines of four merchant ships each, escorted by six flak ships and two minesweepers. As he prepared to attack one of the flak ships and puffs of smoke from anti-aircraft fire appeared around his plane, Ellis felt 'a mixture of excitement, fear and pumping adrenalin' run through him.

> The formation turned to starboard, the Torbeaus remaining low over the sea and preparing to drop their torpedoes. The rest of us dived towards the flak ships and as I settled into the dive I brought my gunsight to bear on the target and saw cannon shell splashes in the sea move towards the ship. At the same time, tracer shells were rising to meet me. This was the crux of the attack when pilot and ship's gunner faced each other like duellists.[7]

Fortunately for Ellis, the tracer missed his plane and he released his two bombs as he skimmed over the target before weaving his way from the convoy, where the heaviest ship, the 5,000-ton Norwegian-registered collier *Höegh*, was now belching smoke, having been hit by two torpedoes. One of them was dropped by a Torbeau of 254 Squadron, whose navigator was Raymond Price. He later recalled:

> We were most conscious of what sitting ducks we and the other torpedo-carrying aircraft were. We were lucky, however, and were not hit by flak. As soon as the torpedo had been released we weaved up

and down and approached the convoy which was only a few hundred yards ahead of us. We were firing our four cannons all the time at the target and as we were about to fly over the convoy at mast height, I managed to take a photograph of the ship's bows.[8]

The returning crews felt elation and relief when they landed back at North Coates, where they were given an ecstatic welcome. Roy Conyers Nesbit wrote:

All the ground crews, with WAAFs, motor mechanics, sick-bay attendants, operations room staff, and indeed the majority of the 1,000 personnel on the station, were lined up outside the crew rooms in front of the hangars. Each time a Beaufighter landed, they waved and cheered thunderously, counting in the aircraft. It was as though the fliers had won the Cup Final at Wembley.[9]

The whole attack had lasted just four minutes; it achieved such complete surprise that the Germans did not have time to scramble their fighters from their coastal aerodromes. Not a single aircraft had been lost, while the collier had been sunk and four escorts badly damaged. What delighted Slessor almost as much was the impact of the strike wing's cannon fire, as he wrote in his post-war despatch: 'Gun crews of the escort vessels were seen leaping overboard, and there could be no doubt that heavy casualties were inflicted on personnel.'[10]

Before the month was over, the North Coates wing had undertaken another destructive mission under Wheeler's command against a convoy off the Dutch coast, with Bill Sise again leading twelve Torbeaus of 254 Squadron, supported by fifteen other Beaufighters. On this occasion two merchant ships and a flak ship were sunk, though one aircraft from 143 Squadron was lost. Referring to these opening operations by the wing, Slessor wrote, 'Each of these so-called strikes was a carefully planned, highly organized and hard-fought action involving thirty or more aircraft, each of which had its own particular role in the attack.' Slessor also had high praise for the fighter escorts: 'So excellent was their co-operation that the Strike Wing crews were imbued with a feeling of security from interruption by enemy fighters that was a stimulating influence on their morale.'[11] Far less successful, however, was an attempt two days later by the wing to hunt down the German cruiser *Nürnberg* off the Norwegian coast, which was out of range of the available RAF fighters. The squadrons paid a heavy price for their absence, as the exposed Beaufighters were set upon by Messerschmitt 109s and Focke-Wulf 190s, with five of them shot down. For the next attack, on 17 May, a stronger fighter escort was provided, enabling the Beaufighters to evade the German defences and sink three vessels without any losses.

Provided the right tactics were followed, Coastal Command at last seemed to have found a means of presenting a real threat to Axis shipping. Its potency looked as if it would be further enhanced by the introduction of rocket projectiles in April 1943, the racks for which began to be fitted to the Command's aircraft from April. The first rocket-armed Beaufighters arrived at North Coates in May and went into action on 22 June, when the entire wing was instructed to intercept a convoy of Swedish merchantmen, escorted by seven German flak ships and five minesweepers, off the Hague in the Netherlands. The strike force comprised five fighter squadrons, twelve Torbeaus, each armed with cannon and an 18-inch torpedo, plus twenty-two cannon-armed Beaufighters, which all carried 60-pound rocket projectiles with explosive heads. But lacking combat experience with the new weapon, the crews only hit two ships from a barrage of 176 rockets. Even worse, two Beaufighters were shot down and four were damaged, while none of the torpedoes hit home. Another massed rocket attack five days later produced only slightly better results; two flak ships were claimed but neither kill was confirmed by the Admiralty. It was obvious that more training and tactical modifications were needed, such as firing from a closer range and using several aircraft to unleash their rockets simultaneously at one target. But it was also found that there were problems with the accuracy of the rocket projectile that carried a 60-pound high-explosive warhead, which tended to curve when it was fired because of the wind resistance it generated. As an alternative, the projectile with a 25-pound solid metal head turned out to be more reliable and lethal in action, as a later internal report confirmed:

The 25-pound rocket projectile because of its underwater trajectory is most effective as a sinking weapon against either merchant or flak vessels. In addition, it can also be harmonized effectively with cannon, thus allowing the cannon to be fired during the initial approach. This not only inflicts damage but acts as a deterrent to enemy gunners. The 60-pound head has none of these advantages but experience has proved that it is capable of doing considerable damage to merchant vessels and is especially effective against destroyers.[12]

One of the first pilots outside the North Coates wing to use rocket projectiles on anti-shipping operations was Wing Commander Hugh McConnell of 235 Squadron on a mission to attack a merchant vessel that had become stranded in a Norwegian fjord near Trondheim. The plan was for three of his squadron to shoot up the ship with rocket projectiles, while three other Beaufighters were to act as a fighter escort. In poor weather, McConnell led the formation at low level up the Norwegian coast, their task made all the more difficult by the steep hills surrounding the fjord and the flak from shore batteries. As he recounted in his combat report,

> we had to be quick on the trigger or we would have passed over the enemy ship. In fact, I did not have sufficient time to fire at first, nor did my No. 2 Beaufighter, but No. 3 spotted the ship a little sooner and opened fire with his RP [rocket projectile]. I turned round up the fjord and made a second attack, this time scoring hits on the ship; No. 2 following me scored several more. Meanwhile the Beaufighters of the other squadron were circling as protection against enemy fighters. I saw the ship catch fire at the stern and she was burning brightly when two Messerschmitt 109s appeared and attacked No. 2 Beaufighter. At the time the Beau's observer was busy holding a camera over the side, taking photographs, and the first he knew that enemy fighters were about was when a bullet hit his camera. We flew out to sea and managed to shake off the fighters.[13]

Norway remained of strategic importance to Coastal Command throughout 1943 because of its vital roles as a supply route, a centre of Nazi occupation and a base for the Kriegsmarine. In addition to regular reconnaissance and anti-shipping missions, the Command carried out covert mining operations there and clandestine support for the Norwegian resistance behind German lines, such as transporting agents whose intelligence was invaluable for the Allies. This latter dangerous work was carried out by a unit called Flight 1477 under the label 'reconnaissance', using Catalinas, but in April these were supplemented by much faster, better-armed Mosquitoes. A month later the unit was renamed No. 333 (Norwegian) Squadron. At the same time, in mainstream operations in the Norwegian theatre, the obsolescent Hampdens were phased out in favour of Beaufighters. One of the Hampdens' last successful actions there occurred on 4 April, when torpedo bombers of 435 and 489 squadrons, exploiting cloud cover to evade the flak escort, sank the 6,800-ton Dutch merchant vessel *Altair*, which had been commandeered by Germany. It was estimated that there were 190 men on board at the time of the attack. Even in the faster Beaufighters, German fighter defences remained a serious danger, as Squadron Leader Aubrey Hilliard of 235 Squadron, found when he ended up in a dogfight with a Fw 190 over the North Sea:

> During the combat when the fighter was attacking from behind, I carried out corkscrew evasive action by diving to port, then climbing again and turning to starboard on top of the climb, then diving again, repeating the action as necessary. The action was carried out from 0 to 700 feet, and as you can imagine, executing steep turns and skipping the waves was hair-raising in itself, let alone being attacked by any enemy fighter at the same time.

The one advantage Hilliard had was that 'I could fly lower than him due to the excellent cockpit view from the Beaufighter'. Despite the severe damage to his plane, he made it to the Fleet Air Arm station at Arbroath, where he found that cannon shells had pierced the fuselage, starboard engine, wing and navigator's seat.[14]

By the summer of 1943 the Allies were gaining the ascendancy against the Axis. In Burma, Bill Slim was masterminding the fightback against Japan, whose empire was falling back in the Pacific war against the USA. On the eastern front, the Reich was in retreat after the Soviet Union's epic victory at Stalingrad. Germany had also been cleared out of Africa, enabling the Allies to land on mainland Italy. Vast preparations were under way for the Allied invasion of France, helped by the failure of Dönitz's U-boat campaign in the Atlantic. Speaking to the *Daily Express* in early August, Sir Max Horton, the head of Western Approaches, said that 'particular credit is due to Coastal Command' for 'the vigour of the offensive against the U-boats on passage and the determination and gallantry shown by captains of aircraft and their crews against the powerful armament of the U-boat'.[15]

Having played its central part in that victory, Coastal Command continued to grow in capability and confidence. On 4 August the *Daily Telegraph* reported that the Command 'had its most active month of the year in July, all records for sorties being broken'.[16] A fortnight later, a meeting of the War Cabinet chaired by Deputy Prime Minister Clem Attlee agreed to send a message of congratulations to Slessor for 'the achievements of Coastal Command in the last month'.[17] Tony Spooner, who had been serving in Malta, was struck by the transformation in mood when he returned to England in 1943 to serve on Liberators in 53 Squadron. 'It was completely unrecognizable. We put the fear of God into the enemy.'[18]

As well as rocket projectiles, other new equipment was becoming available, like the highly sophisticated Mark 24 ASW, developed by American scientists and nicknamed Fido, which was actually a torpedo propelled by a battery-operated electric motor. When dropped from an aircraft, it used four hydrophones placed around its mid-section to pick up acoustic signals from an enemy vessel before steering itself towards the target. Under conditions of great secrecy whereby crews had to sign an oath on the Bible that they would never divulge any information about this weapon, Fido was first deployed in action by Coastal Command on 11 May 1943, when a Liberator of 86 Squadron successfully dropped it on U-456 in the Atlantic. Although it did not sink instantly, the U-boat was severely damaged and was finished off the next day by a Royal Navy destroyer summoned to the scene by the Liberator. During the remainder of the war, the Mark 24 was used mainly by the USAAF and US Navy, but sixty-two attacks with the device were made by RAF aircraft. Altogether, it is estimated that thirty-seven Axis submarines were sunk by this mine.

The Command made less progress with the new ASV Mark VI

radar, which used the 3-cm wavelength. More powerful than the 10-cm Mark III, and undetectable by German receivers, this device seemed to represent a key breakthrough in the fight against the Kriegsmarine. Part of the impetus behind the project were fears that the Germans were developing their own new radar detector to replace the flawed Metox apparatus. In fact, just such a device had been created, called Naxos, though the high hopes invested in it by the Germans turned out to be misplaced. Because of its short range, Naxos was of limited use on U-boats, providing only a minute's warning of an approaching aircraft, while its antenna was not waterproof so it had to be stowed before submerging. But, as had happened before, the British development of countermeasures had been hampered by another inflammatory clash in the long-running Battle of the Air.

On this occasion, the flames of acrimony over the new radar were first ignited by Slessor's anger at the low priority given to Coastal Command after the TRE had built a working 3-cm set, which had then gone into production with an initial order of 200. The Mark VI had a much longer range than previous types, and also had a facility whereby the operator, once locked on to a contact, could reduce the radar's output so that its pulses did not get any stronger as the plane homed in on the target, thus deceiving the enemy about the imminence of an attack. Given these qualities, Slessor urgently wanted the Mark VI for Coastal Command and, annoyed at delays, called on Bernard Lovell at the TRE to find out what was happening with his share of the planned production. In a post-war interview, Lovell recounted the tale.

> I said to him, 'Yes, we've got 3 cm ready for operations but I'm afraid the responsible people have not provided the right fittings to get it in your aircraft.' He was absolutely furious, took off his blue jacket and said, 'Could you get me a piece of paper?' He then wrote a most extraordinary letter to the Air Ministry, using phrases such as 'Nobody but a congenital idiot would expect this equipment to be of any use without the means for it to be fitted into aircraft.' The letter led to another confrontation with Bomber Command.[19]

Soon afterwards, Lovell was summoned to a meeting in the Cabinet War Rooms, where he found Slessor and his Coastal Command team on one side of the table, opposite Robert Saundby, the deputy head of Bomber Command, and his colleagues. Lovell and Slessor made the case for Coastal Command to be given some of the Mark VI's production run, which was eventually agreed. But as soon as the meeting was over, Saundby phoned Harris to tell him this decision. At once, Harris contacted Churchill and got the agreement reversed, with the result that all the ASV Mark VI sets went to Bomber Command. 'This was the sort of antagonism and infighting that went on,' recalled Lovell.[20]

Another, less fraught, development was the 35-pound retro bomb, used in conjunction with a magnetic anomaly detector (MAD), which could pick up the presence of a large metal object in the water by identifying tiny variations in the earth's magnetic field. The problem with MAD was that it could only make a detection when it was directly over a vessel, so a conventional depth charge or bomb, carried forward by the motion of a plane, would be useless. American engineers came up with an imaginative solution: the backward-firing retro bomb. Fitted with a solid fuel rocket which cancelled out the plane's forward velocity, this fell vertically when released and exploded on impact with a U-boat, generating enough force to crack a hull. These 35-pounders were installed on launching rails in Catalinas, twelve under each wing, and were fired in three salvos of eight. From 1943 Coastal Command deployed another sensor, the sonobuoy, in limited numbers. Code-named High Tea and mainly used by Sunderlands of 210 Squadron, this was the aerial equivalent of ASDIC in its ability to detect submerged U-boats.

Aircraft themselves were becoming more advanced. The Mosquito, the most versatile British plane of the war, was now serving in a variety of roles from photo reconnaissance to anti-shipping work, where twenty-seven of the deadly new Mark XVIII 'Tsetses', with their devastating front guns, were now in action. In the same vein, 236 Squadron was re-equipped in July with the high-performance TF Mark X Beaufighter, the first variant specifically designed for anti-shipping strikes as reflected in its lethal armoury that featured four cannons in the nose, six Browning machine guns in the wings, eight rocket projectiles and either two 250-pound bombs or one torpedo. The TFX went into action on 2 August as part of a well-organized strike by the North Coates Strike Wing against a convoy off the Dutch island of Texel that sank one ore carrier and damaged four flak ships.

But just as crews were gaining experience so Slessor began to turn against the idea of the unit, primarily as a result of his remorseless focus on severing the trunk of the U-boat campaign in the Bay. In his determination to acquire more planes for that offensive, he came to see it as an expensive, uneconomical luxury which consumed too much in proportion to its effectiveness. In a critical letter to the Air Ministry of 8 August, he pointed out that the North Coates Strike Wing tied down sixty front-line aircraft and their crews, as well as ground staff totalling seventy-two officers and 1,309 other personnel. These numbers, he wrote, had been based on his conjecture that the wing would make five attacks a month but in reality so far they had only been making two, partly because Fighter Command could not always provide cover. The unit's resources, he argued, could be better deployed in the Bay.

Statistics appeared to back his claim, for in the year to May 1943 just twenty-one enemy ships had been sunk by aircraft, compared to seventy-nine by mines. Everything, he wrote later, 'seemed to point to the break-up of the North Coates Wing'.[21] But his views fell on stony ground. A major conference was called on 20 August to debate the strike wing's future, at which there was widespread hostility to Slessor's proposal. Sir John Tovey, the commander-in-chief of the Nore (a long-standing naval command that covered the Thames estuary, named after a sandbank at the mouth of the River Medway), who in a previous post as commander of the Home Fleet had urged the Admiralty Commissioners to threaten resignation to pressurize the government into providing more air support in the Atlantic, argued that the threat of North Coates's attacks was forcing many German convoys to sail at night, which made them more vulnerable to his motor torpedo boats from the East Anglian coast. A compelling case was also made by the Ministry of Economic Warfare. Pointing out that sinkings were not the only criterion, the ministry highlighted the remarkable decline in recent German trade through Rotterdam, especially in Swedish iron ore. Because of the pressure of air assaults, much of the trade had been rerouted through the German port of Emden, whose facilities and transport links were much limited, putting a brake on the Reich's industrial production. Far from down-grading the strike wing, the ministry believed that it should be provided with greater operational support.

That was the unanimous view of the conference. The wing concept was endorsed, North Coates was saved, and the planning for additional units proceeded rapidly. In November a second wing was formally established at Wick in Scotland, comprising Torbeaus of 144 and Beaufighters of 404 squadrons, armed with solid head rocket projectiles, which proved an excellent weapon in the narrow fjords. The official first mission by the Wick wing was undertaken on 22 November against a German convoy off Stadlandet, when the 404 Beaufighters sunk a Norwegian freighter and damaged two others. This was followed at the start of 1944 by the creation of the Leuchars Wing, made up of 455 and 489 squadrons.

At the same time that winter Coastal Command was stepping up its harassment of Axis blockade runners sailing from the Far East to western Europe. Notable actions included the sinking of the Italian cargo ship *Pietro Orselo*, which sailed from Singapore bound for Germany only to be hit by torpedoes from the Beaufighters of 254 Squadron on 18 December. Another blockade runner, the *Alsterufer* was sunk little more than a week later on its way to Brest, an action in which Leslie Baveystock, a Sunderland pilot of 201 Squadron, took part along with several other Coastal Command attackers. As he recalled in his memoir,

> By the time we had spotted the ship we were down to 200 feet with our quarry dead ahead in what should have been an ideal position. If I released our bombs we just couldn't miss, but their forward speed, being the same as that of our aircraft, would have resulted in explo-sions directly under us, with the consequent dire damage to ourselves. This I could not risk.

Instead, the Sunderland flew over the *Alsterufer*, spraying it with a continuous stream of tracer before climbing to 1,000 feet and dropping its bombs and depth charges using radar as the means of aiming. Predictably, given the height, the damage to the ship appeared to be slight and having 'cursed the stupid Armaments Office for not giving us delay fuses on our bombs, as he should have done', Baveystock embarked on the long journey back to his squadron's base at Castle Archdale in Northern Ireland. But almost out of fuel, they had to come down near St Mary's in the Scilly Isles, where he made a perfect landing on the water.[22] Meanwhile other aircraft, alerted by Baveystock, had gone into action against the *Alsterufer*, among them a Liberator of 311 flown at low level by a Czech crew which managed in the face of intense flak to fire eight rockets at the ship, five of which scored direct hits. The damage was compounded by two well-aimed bombs that hit the stern and set the vessel ablaze. As she began to go under, another Liberator and four Halifaxes arrived with more explosives to ensure her demise.

Throughout the year, Coastal Command had grown in effectiveness, sinking 84,759 tons of enemy shipping compared to 55,424 in 1942. Even more impressively, its squadrons were responsible for eighty-eight U-boat kills, four of which were shared with the Royal Navy, compared to twenty-eight in 1942. British naval ships themselves, in contrast, accounted for the destruction of only forty-eight U-boats.[23] With deepening experience, the co-ordination of attacks could now be brutally efficient, not just between the two British services but also with other Allies, as was highlighted by an incident on 10 November when U-boat U-966 under the command of Eckehard Wolf was engaged in a nine-hour running battle in the Bay of Biscay with an assortment of planes flown by British, Americans and Czechs. The attack was opened at 4 a.m. by the crew of a Coastal Command Wellington of 612 Squadron in moonlit conditions so bright that the Leigh Light was unnecessary. Having spotted the submarine on the surface 4 miles away, the plane, piloted by Warrant Officer I. D. Gunn from Renfrewshire, dived and released its stick of depth charges on the target, at the same time raking the hull with machine-gun fire. The U-boat crew responded with their deck guns before taking evasive action, as Gunn recalled in a contemporary account. 'I should say that the U-boat dived about three minutes after the attack. We flew over the area for nearly two and a half hours and searched a radius of 5 or 6 miles but saw nothing more.' But a US Liberator, piloted by Leonard Harmon from Rhode Island, sighted Wolf's vessel and ran in on his port quarter to attack from 60 feet, only for the U-boat to put up a barrage of fire. 'The sky around us seemed full of 20-mm shells. We attacked with all the guns we could bring to bear,' said Harmon. Unfortunately for the crew, the depth charges failed to release, as they did again when Harmon came in for a second attack. With the aircraft's interior full of smoke and its hydraulic system out of action, he climbed to 2,000 feet and started to circle the target.

> We then found we had one hit in the port wing and two in the bomb
> bay; the bow turret gunner worked for half an hour, slithering about
> in the oil, trying to free the bombs but without success. We circled for
> two hours, waiting for another aircraft to arrive. Every time we went
> close enough, the U-boat opened fire at us. Altogether we made three
> strafing attacks on the submarine, and as we turned for home we saw
> it surfaced, making away as fast as it could.

The Allies were still in pursuit. Another US Navy Liberator, flown by Kenneth Wright, sighted U-966 and hit it with depth charges, followed by a third Liberator that came out of the sun after seeing the U-boat 3 miles away, opened fire with machine guns and dropped its charges on the stern of the submarine. With an astonishing survival instinct, the U-boat limped on, unable to travel at more than two knots, making it an easy target for a Czech Liberator that machine-gunned its conning tower as it ran aground on the coast of Galicia. The forty-two members of the fifty-strong crew who survived then scuttled the submarine, took to the dinghies and were soon appre-hended by the Spanish authorities.[24]

Yet for all this success, Slessor was not a contented leader at the end of 1943. Like his two wartime predecessors, he felt that his command was not given the priority it required for the maritime war. Slessor's innate gift of leadership meant that he was in demand to take command in other theatres as the Allies advanced. But the process of his departure and his exact destination were complicated by the competing claims of other senior officers, particularly those of Sir

Sholto Douglas, the former head of Fighter Command who was now in charge of the RAF in the Middle East. With Churchill's backing, Sinclair had offered Douglas the prestigious job of Allied commander in south-east Asia, but his candidacy was vetoed by the Americans, led by Eisenhower and Roosevelt. They had lost faith in him after the disastrous adventure of Operation Accolade, a failed attempt to capture Rhodes and the Dodecanese Islands in the Aegean. For the US military establishment, there were two other serious problems with Douglas. One was his alleged prejudice: 'When he has had a drink or two he speaks contemptuously of the Americans,' Churchill was told by Sir John Dill, the head of the British Joint Staff Mission in Washington.[25] The other was his politics, for, rare in an Allied military commander, Douglas was a committed socialist. It was an outlook that incurred the suspicion of the Americans, with their fear of communism, though Churchill, as an admirer of Douglas's forcefulness, was determined to elevate him.

Having fruitlessly pressed Douglas's case with Roosevelt, the prime minister then tried to have him appointed vice chief of the Air Staff in place of Evill, but Sinclair adamantly refused these entreaties. There was then an attempt to make him the deputy Allied air commander in the Mediterranean under the US lieutenant general Ira Eaker, but Douglas bristled at the idea, both because he felt American hostility towards him would make the job impossible and because he had much more experience and a higher rank than Eaker. Indeed, Douglas considered resigning before he accepted the unwanted appointment with bad grace after a lecture from Portal who told him that it was not 'for you to say where you will be employed'.[26]

But then he was saved from his fate by an act of extraordinary selflessness from Slessor. Keen for a move himself and drained by the rows over the Bay campaign, Slessor, who was trusted by the Americans, volunteered to become Eaker's deputy, thereby enabling Douglas to take over Coastal Command. There was relief all round at this solution made possible by Slessor's generosity in accepting what was technically a demotion, despite the wide scope of his position. Douglas himself was delighted at having a real command, later writing in his memoirs, 'I now look back upon what was the happiest period of my service during the Second World War.'[27] Churchill, who was also relieved, wrote to Roosevelt to correct any misapprehensions about Douglas's views:

> As I am moving Sholto Douglas from the Mediterranean to British Coastal Command to replace Slessor, I hope you will not mind my putting on record the fact that, after having made the most careful and searching enquiries in every direction, I am completely convinced that there is no foundation for the suggestions which have been made that this most capable officer has shown a lack of goodwill or loyalty towards the United States and its officers.[28]

Like all three of his wartime predecessors, Douglas had served with distinction in the Great War, first as a second lieutenant in the Royal Field Artillery, then as an officer in the Royal Flying Corps, ending up a captain in the RAF and winning the DFC. Born in 1893, he was the son of a former Anglican priest who had been secretary of the Church of England Temperance Society but later became a Roman Catholic, a citizen of the United States, an expert on Italian art, a multiple divorcee, and the father of eighteen children, ten of them illegitimate. Bright and inquisitive, Sholto Douglas had won a scholarship from Tonbridge School to Oxford, where he joined the officer training corps and the Fabian Society, the intellectual powerhouse of the fledgling Labour Party. At the end of the war he left the RAF to become a commercial pilot, but in 1922 was persuaded by none other by Trenchard to enrol at the new Air Staff college in Andover, where among his fellow students were Charles Portal and Keith Park, later one of the heroes of the Battle of Britain. After stints as a commander in the Middle East and an instructor at the Imperial Defence College, he joined the senior ranks of the Air Ministry in 1936, becoming deputy chief of the Air Staff in 1940 before succeeding Sir Hugh Dowding at Fighter Command. Yet for all his intellect, drive and presence, he never attained the stature within the RAF that he felt he merited. As the historian Vincent Orange wrote, 'Douglas's military career, though distinguished, left him unsatisfied. He arrived in Fighter Command after the Battle of Britain, in Egypt after Rommel's departure, in Coastal Command after victory over the U-boats.'[29] Politics, American antipathy and the Aegean campaign record played their part, but just as important was his personality, which some found overbearing and arrogant. 'A stuffed shirt' was one description relayed by Dill to Churchill.[30] Edward Shackleton, the St Eval intelligence officer who later became a government minister, had this memory of him.

> An interesting man, a socialist and classicist. I thought he was very competent, able and intelligent, but most hated his guts. He was not very popular. I remember my Group Captain sitting with his head in his hands, saying, 'Oh my God, not that man.' He had rather raffish friends and was terribly keen on women.[31]

Indeed, when it came to relationships, Douglas took after his priapic father. Thrice married, his numerous infidelities and voracious sexual appetite aroused strong disapproval at the top of the Air Staff. When a vacancy arose for the vital position of Air Member for Personnel, Portal wrote to Sinclair,

> Douglas is ruled out in my opinion because of a reputation for serious indiscretions in his private life and because he is personally somewhat undisciplined and therefore most unlikely to be able to maintain discipline in the service. This is a pity because he is a strong character and has a fine record in command.[32]

Sir Wilfrid Freeman went even further at the end of the war, describing Douglas as 'socially and morally beneath contempt . . . I don't suppose any decent parent would allow his son to join the RAF (still less his daughter to join the WAAF) if he was Chief of the Defence Staff.'[33]

Regardless of his character, Douglas had a big task ahead of him when he took over on 20 January 1944. Coastal Command was soon to have a starring role in the biggest maritime operation in history.

13

Rescue

IN EARLY 1944 the screenwriter and film director Charles Bennett, on a visit to England from Hollywood, stayed with his old friend Sholto Douglas. At one stage the commander-in-chief invited him to see Coastal Command's headquarters at Eastbury Park, Northwood, an experience that left a deep impression on Bennett, as he recorded.

> The most exciting point was when Sholto took me down in Coastal Command's vast underground operations room. To say that I was overwhelmed by the efficiency of this undertaking, not to speak of the spectacle, would be an understatement. On one side of this vast chamber were box-like cubicles in which sat important air officers and their assistants. Facing them was a perhaps 150-feet wide wall map of the Command's extent. It was a huge section of the world displaying, like a mural, not only the shores of the British Isles, but almost the entire North Atlantic, stretching south to the Caribbean and north to the shores of Newfoundland. Swarming over the great map on ladders were young members of the Women's Auxiliary Air Force, planting flags or markers to indicate the last known positions of the Atlantic convoys, Nazi wolf packs and the like for Coastal Command to strategize. As Sholto and I emerged from the deeply descending elevator and came into this vast room, he stopped beside a box where an air commodore appeared to be in charge of the evening's observations. Sholto asked, 'Everything in order?' The answer was crisp, 'Moving along, sir, no complaints.'
>
> Sholto glanced across to where three WAAFs were planting markers on the southern tip of Greenland. He asked entirely casually, 'Cape Farewell?'
>
> 'No change since my last report. There are two down below but air frigates have 'em marked and are working on it. They won't get away.'
>
> 'Keep me informed,' said Sholto.

'This was a fleeting glimpse of real war on a grand scale,' concluded Bennett.[1]

The capacious operations room was symbolic of Coastal Command's expansion and modernization. By 1944 Cinderella had truly come to the ball. The early days of scarecrows, shortages and Stranraers belonged to the past. At the start of that year, the Command had fifty-five squadrons and 910 aircraft, compared to eighteen squadrons and 265 aircraft at the outbreak of war, the majority of which were steady but lumbering Ansons. Now its establishment included 180 Beaufighters, 105 Liberators (added to which were 36 US Navy and Army Liberators under its control), 84 Sunderlands, 32 Fortresses, 30 Halifaxes and 18 Mosquitoes. Its workforce was now 82,000 strong, 13,700 of which were WAAFS. Its network of bases ran in Britain from Thorney Island in West Sussex to the Outer Hebrides in Scotland, while in the western hemisphere its reach encompassed the West Indies and West Africa.

There was even an informal operation in north-west Eire, over which so many RAF planes flew from their bases in Ulster for duty in the North Atlantic. In secret defiance of Irish neutrality, a unit with an armed trawler and eleven British personnel had been established in June 1941 at the port of Killybegs to provide a rescue and refuelling service. The impetus behind the unit's creation was an incident in April that year when Pilot Officer Dennis Briggs, returning from an anti-submarine patrol, was forced to ditch his Saro Lerwick off the Donegal coast after running out of fuel. He was towed by a local fishing boat into the seaside town of Bundoran where he was taken prisoner by the Irish Army, whose commander disappeared to make a phone call. Briggs expected to be interned for the remainder of the war, but to his surprise an RAF truck turned up from across the border with 80 gallons of aviation fuel and he was allowed to fly back to Lough Erne. According to the historian Joe McGowan, co-operation between the British and Irish authorities was 'commonplace'.[2]

Life on the Coastal Command bases in Britain did not have the glamour or excitement that typified Fighter Command stations in the summer of 1940. Like the patrols themselves, the work was of a more pounding, relentless nature, 'a wearisome' routine punctuated 'by moments of high tension', in the words of Graham Harrison, a Wellington crewman, who was based at Chivenor in Devon for much of the war. He recalled how the recruits entertained themselves, when not on duty, with a music club, films, visits to the pub and dance evenings. He admitted, however, that some of his time was also occupied with erotic fantasies:

> Though the generality of WAAFs inspired few lustful thoughts in me – perhaps it was the flat shoes, lisle stockings and brass-buttoned tunic or shapeless battledress – it was generally agreed that the ops room girls were a cut above the average and I confess to having on occasions stumbled into the outer darkness after a briefing with the fading image of a well-filled tunic and thighs taut in the placing of a symbol on the chart.

Occasionally, the desires went beyond fantasies. One evening, Harrison came across a couple in action on a pneumatic bed they had installed in the airframe of an abandoned Wellington on the base. 'Clearly this had been a repeat assignation, understandable in view of the frustrating lack of privacy on the station . . . Barnes Wallis's geodetic fuselage could become a tunnel of loving dreams.'[3]

Some disciplinarians among the higher ranks were confounded in their suspicions about amorous liaisons as Edward Shackleton recalled of life at St Eval:

> I was in charge of the Photographic Section and the senior WAAF officer was a great stickler; she did not like her girls being alone with airmen. She asked that only men should do night duties but I overruled her. One evening she burst into the darkroom, hoping to catch a couple in flagrante delicto. All she succeeded in doing was damaging the photos that had been taken of Brest, though that had no bearing on the escape of the *Scharnhorst* and *Gneisenau*.[4]

Edward Nichols, who served a spell in 518 Squadron based on the remote Scottish island of Tiree, used other comforts to cope with the isolation. 'Living quarters: the usual Nissen hut. The one I shared with three other officers was several hundred yards from the mess.'

The station had a 'fairly large contingent of WAAFs, a very bright bunch of young ladies who could recognise by their morse rhythm who was sending the coded messages from way out in the Atlantic'.

> But there was nowhere to go for entertainment, no pubs, nothing. We had our mess bars, which we put to good use and we had our fun and games, some a bit crazy. The odd cinema show and the even odder, very occasional, thank God, ENSA show . . . When not on duty, it was not unusual for me to have a whisky chaser followed by six or seven pints of wartime brew beer . . . Quieter times would be for writing letters home or playing Ludo at a bob a corner, even the odd doze in comfortable armchairs.[5]

The rigours of wartime life in Coastal Command were also described by Dorothy Williams, a wireless operator who was billeted in a private hotel when she served at Oban from 1942 to 1944. 'There were seven us in the room. You had a bed, a chair and that was it . . . When we first went to Oban they were very strict about cleanliness and kit, with regular inspections of feet and head.' Her station ran a four-watch system round the clock, which meant each operator did a shift of six hours. In theory there was plenty of time for sleep, but in practice the quarters were too noisy. 'That was the biggest drawback. There were no carpets to absorb the sound, just a bit of oilcloth. Everything had been stripped. One never had any quiet. You spent your time having short catnaps.' Of her work, she said,

> even when weather conditions were good and you got very little crackling and atmospherics, it became very apparent when crews weren't receiving you. They kept asking for repetitions. We sometimes got a little impatient with them and tended to transmit quicker. It should have been the other way round.

To gain an appreciation of what the air crews faced, she and her comrades were taken on occasional familiarization patrols.

> It really was a most fascinating experience. It made you realize what the aircrew were up against. One minute you were receiving signals at

full strength, the next you heard nothing at all, then you were back to full strength. That taught us a lot. After that my attitude to work changed completely.

One feature of station life that Williams disliked was the influx of conscripted recruits.

I never felt they did their work conscientiously. Their attitude was different, constantly grumbling. It was amazing how infectious that could be; always banging on about something or other, nothing was ever right. It did affect the whole atmosphere. People who were normally cheerful were mentally dragged down by these conscripts, who went on and on and on. I was always of the opinion that we would have been better off without them.[6]

Another WAAF, Gwen Webster, worked as a cook at St Eval. Not only was the station large, with 'many thousands of personnel' but so was her equipment. 'By the sides of the huge coal ranges were two 40-gallon boilers, one for hot water, the other for cooking cabbages and puddings. The frying pans were so large we were able to cook 20 eggs at a time.' There were three shifts, the last from 9 p.m. to 8 a.m. 'The work was hard and being a member of the shift was no joke, especially as you were on for a month at a time. Our social lives were limited, as we were too tired to do much after a shift.' Although the WAAFs were clothed and housed, their pay was poor, which 'could be embarrassing when we mixed socially with civilians who were generally paid more. However, there was a wonderful rapport in the forces and we were all very proud to be serving our country.'[7]

Like the WAAF Dorothy Williams, electrical officer Bryant Wolstenhome worked at Oban and found aspects of his job frustrating.

As on any flying boat station much of the available working time is lost in getting to and from the aircraft no matter how efficient the Marine Craft Section may be. Add to this the time lost in travelling to and from the island workshop and an estimate of 40 per cent available man hours would probably be low.

But, as he wrote in his wartime diary, Wolstenholme felt the greatest handicap was that 'all sections are under strength. For six whole weeks my own electrical station was left to carry on with three tradesmen, including a sergeant, out of an establishment of ten.' He later moved in 1943 to Castle Archdale, Northern Ireland, and, again like Dorothy Williams, he gained an insight into the experience of operational crews by taking part in one of their patrols in February 1944:

> Up at 0300 when most civilized people are still sleeping. I don my borrowed flying boots and Irwin jacket, complete with helmet and Mae West. I grope my way down to the Ops Room to meet the rest of the crew. A good breakfast of bacon and egg, then briefing where we learn that we are going south and west to look for a U-boat reported approximately 500 miles north west of the Azores. We go out by dinghy to the Sunderland. In the black night she presents an eerie sight as we glide alongside – it beats me how those dinghy owners find the right one out of 36 identical kites! Once aboard, each member of the crew carries out his preliminary checks – navigator's maps and charters, oil, guns, ammunition, bomb trolleys – all are checked while somebody gets the primus stove going in the galley for an early morning brew.

As dawn began to break, the skipper received approval from Flying Control to taxi out: 'After the usual engine checks, the captain makes his run up the flare path and we become airborne.' Thus began

> one of the usually monotonous and typical sorties we are carrying out every day by Sunderlands, Catalinas and Liberators . . . We see nothing – nothing but water and the occasional friendly ship – oh and porpoises! – for fourteen hours. A flying boat captain's dream is a lovely U-boat gliding along the surface but that is all a matter of chance. Some crews get through a full operational tour of 800 hours without an enemy sighting.

On the journey back, as it began to become dark, Wolstenholme was surprised to see the four engines glowing red hot. 'Quite normal,' said the skipper, 'they don't show up in the daylight.' Soon afterwards the

plane reached Castle Archdale, where the flare path guided the plane
in to land.

A dinghy takes us to our buoy and another sortie is successfully
completed. All switches off, hatches and portholes closed and we are
whisked away for debriefing, a good hot meal and with the engines
still whirring in my ears, bed, wonderful bed. Amazing to reflect we
have travelled over 2,000 miles since getting up.[8]

What Polish navigator Bernard Połoniecki remembered of his time
at a base in the Outer Hebrides was the bitter weather. 'The wind was
always a problem and could sometimes get up to 100 knots, which
made landings difficult. Life there was harsh. The climate was the
enemy rather than the Germans.'[9] Many pilots found the conditions
in Iceland even tougher. The harsh weather made flying difficult, but
sometimes dramatic, as Liberator pilot Jack Colman recounted of
carrying out sweeps in December 1942. 'It was dark most of the time,
apart from a couple of hours of twilight in the middle of the day.' One
typical sortie was 'murky and miserable' with the sea 'alarmingly
rough, the wind ripping spray in great, long grey tails off the top of
breaking rollers'. On another mission, he had a disturbing experience
of the natural phenomenon of St Elmo's fire:

I began to get bloody scared as the rings round the prop tips got
brighter and brighter until the whole of each prop looked like a great
big luminous disc of changing colours and bits seemed to be flying off.
What a queer place the Atlantic was – one minute filthy rough
weather, bouncing up and down and maybe picking up ice, then
queer balls of fire floating around like weightless genies, then beautiful
clear blue skies.[10]

The freezing conditions also inspired some imaginative technical
innovations, according to the memoir of pilot Ted Rayner. In his
squadron, in order to prevent icing on the wings, they were equipped
'along the leading edge with adjacent strips of pneumatic "boots",
the lengths of which, when switched on, inflated to a prescribed
order, producing a corrugated effect sufficient to crack any thin layer

of ice which might form before it had the strength to become thick enough to affect the lift supplied by the wing. The carburettors could be heated as necessary, and it was possible to cover the props with a fine spray of oil from the constant speed hub cover. Add to this formidable protection some Kilfrost de-icing paste on important parts of the aircraft and we would be ready for anything.'[11] Some crews in Iceland found the attitude of many islanders as frosty as the weather, as Arthur Beech spelt out in a post-war interview. 'It was rotten. Nice country but the people did not like us. They made that quite clear. They had not joined in the war and they had been taken over by us.'[12]

Like the rest of Coastal Command, training had undergone a major expansion as the war progressed. The number of Operational Training Units reached eleven in 1943 and at its peak in August that year, No. 17 Group, now with over 1,000 aircraft at its disposal, ensured that 238 crews completed their training. Altogether in 1943, no fewer than 11,482 men were trained on fourteen different types of aircraft for a total of 255,800 hours, 'about half the flying achieved by the whole Command', as the historian Chris Ashworth has pointed out.[13] Improvements in training also brought a steady decline in the accident rate, down from 3.3 per 1,000 recruits to 2.5 by 1944. The ascendancy of the Allies in 1944 meant the gradual closure and merger of some of the OTUs, but the advance in technology also led to greater specialism; the number of different syllabuses taught increased from twenty-six in 1943 to thirty-eight in 1944, while courses also became longer. The quality of the specialist training impressed Roy Conyers Nesbit, who undertook an observer's course that he found 'extremely efficient. It lasted 12 weeks with a mixture of work on the ground and in the air. There was a very high standard of instruction. The hours were long and the pace was fast but this was welcomed by almost all the trainees.'[14]

Apart from training, Coastal Command had other important non-combat arms which again mirrored its expansion from the dark days of 1939. One was its meteorological service, a vital requirement given the importance of the weather for RAF operations. At the outbreak of war the Air Force had just one meteorological flight, made up of Gloster Gladiator and Gauntlet biplanes, supplemented by reports from reconnaissance aircraft. But by March 1941, under pressure from the front-line operations for better information, the Air Ministry had created four more flights, which were placed under the control of Coastal Command and provided with Blenheims and Hurricanes. Two further units, equipped with Hudsons, were established in the autumn. From 1942 Spitfires and Mosquitoes, capable of flying at high altitudes, began to enter the units, supplemented by the fast, twin-engined Lockheed Ventura, though this American plane, despite its speed, was never popular with RAF crews because of its unreliability. The growth continued in 1943, with the creation of three new squadrons from the absorption of several flights, as well as the introduction of long-range Halifaxes, modified by the installation of dedicated observers' stations in the nose. Further meteorological units were set up in Iceland, Gibraltar and the Azores, again under Coastal Command's oversight. It has been estimated that in the crucial six months in the run up to D-Day in June 1944, the Command was responsible for 91 per cent of all Allied meteorological flights in the western theatre.

Just as crucial to operations was the intelligence provided by photo reconnaissance. Dissatisfaction within the RAF during the first year of war over the quality of material produced by Fighter Command's 212 Squadron, the specialist detachment responsible for this task, had led to the establishment of the Photographic Reconnaissance Unit in June 1940 under the control of Coastal Command. Bomber Command had wanted to take charge of the PRU but the Air Ministry decided that Coastal was a better choice, partly because of the Admiralty's involvement and partly because the Command already had visual reconnaissance as its top priority. In the wake of that decision, four operational flights were created at the PRU, each with three medium- and one long-range Spitfire, as well as one Hudson and a Tiger Moth biplane. At the time of the threatened German invasion, the PRU's intelligence about the build-up of barges in the ports of occupied western Europe was an essential ingredient of Britain's defence. Once Hitler's planned Operation Sea Lion had been postponed, in September 1940, the PRU continued to carry out important missions, like keeping watch on the Biscay ports and Norwegian fjords. Meanwhile, the unit maintained its expansion with the arrival of the US Martin Maryland light bomber, new duties in the Mediterranean and the introduction of low-level operations for close-up photography of key targets. These highly dangerous missions, undertaken by Spitfires, were known as dicers because their pilots were dicing with death.[15] By September 1941 the PRU had thirty-seven Spitfires, two Marylands and two Mosquitoes, the rapid growth continuing into 1942 to reach eight flights, more than 1,000 personnel and seventy aircraft flying from six different bases as far apart as Wick in Scotland and St Eval in Cornwall.

Despite some changes to the organization, which, at the behest of Portal, became No. 106 PR Wing in June 1943, Coastal Command retained administrative control for the rest of the war, just as the Spitfire remained the prime weapon of the wing, not least because improved variants were constantly evolving, such as the highly successful PR Mark XI. The photographs taken by the pilots played their part in many of the key episodes in the defeat of the Reich, like the Dambusters raid, the destruction of the German V1 and V2 rocket sites, the resumption of the Russian convoys and the assault on the *Tirpitz*. At the end of 1943, a year in which 106 Wing had flown 3,000 sorties, producing a total of 750,000 negatives, Slessor paid this tribute:

> The enormous extent to which we rely on this wing for our knowledge of every aspect of the enemy's activity, is perhaps not generally realized; the science, not only of air photography, but of interpretation, has made enormous strides in the last four years and the intelligence staffs would be blind without the courage and skill of the pilots and ground personnel of No. 106 wing.[16]

In terms of life and death for RAF crews, there was no more valuable service in Coastal Command's realm than its air-sea rescue organization, given how much time the Allies' planes spent over hazardous stretches of water. It is another reflection of how ill-prepared Britain was in 1939 that at the outbreak of war there were no such unit for crews who were shot down or had to ditch in the sea. Instead, the RAF relied on a makeshift array of RNLI lifeboats, salvage tugs, private vessels and naval high-speed launches, though there were only eighteen of these in 1939. Coastal Command's job

was limited to acting as a spotter and co-ordinator of rescue oper-
ations. But all that changed with the fall of France and the Battle of
Britain. As casualties mounted dramatically in home waters, the first
ASR service was formed by Fighter Command and the Admiralty at
Dover, which evolved into the Directorate of Sea Rescue in January
1941, using Westland Lysanders for scouting and Supermarine
Walruses for dropping supplies. The directorate soon proved itself,
with the recovery rate for downed aircrews rising to 35 per cent by
June 1941, and it was further beefed up in the autumn under the leadership of Sir John Salmond, the former chief of the Air Staff. Under
his auspices, Coastal Command's rescue service was significantly
strengthened by the addition of two new Hudson squadrons and the
supply of sets of Lindholme Gear. Each Lindholme set, joined together
by a floating rope, had five cylinder-shaped containers, one of which
held a nine-man inflatable dinghy; in the others were emergency
rations, flares and clothing.

Chances of survival were further improved by two additional
developments: the installation of dinghies, complete with automatic
inflation, in larger aircraft; and the creation of an airborne lifeboat
that could be dropped by a plane. As experiments with this lifeboat
continued, the directorate chose as its carrier the Vickers Warwick, a
close relative of the Wellington. The Warwick had been meant for
Bomber Command, but it had proved a disappointment because of its
under-powered engines. In total, fifty-seven had been built by January
1943 and the Air Ministry decided that, for all its drawbacks, it would
be useful for rescue work, particularly when an improved Mark II
version became available. In November 1943, No. 281, based in
Thornaby, north Yorkshire, became the first squadron to be equipped
with the Warwick lifeboat carriers. That year, Coastal Command had
rescued 1,684 men out of 5,466 who were reported to have ditched
in the sea, a highly impressive ratio give the number of aircrew who
would have been killed on impact with the water. Indeed, the
Command's heroic ASR work prompted American commander Ira
Eaker to write to Slessor,

Your superlative Air Sea Rescue Service has been one of the prime
factors in the high morale of our own combat crews. This

organization of yours picked up from the sea nearly 600 of our combat crewmen since we began operations in this theatre. This is a remarkable achievement made possible only by the highest efficiency and the greatest courage and fortitude. It has our unbounded admiration.[17]

The first drop of a lifeboat by a Warwick took place on 7 January 1944, when a Mosquito crew was successfully rescued off Land's End. At the same time more RAF surface rescue craft became available, reaching a total of 182 in early 1944, just as the Allies were preparing to invade western Europe. During the month of D-Day, 355 aircrew were saved by these vessels, part of the magnificent rescue effort by the RAF. According to Chris Ashworth, a total of 10,663 people were rescued in ASR operations during the war, made up of 5,721 Allied aircrew, 4,665 non-aircrew and 277 enemy aircrew.

The experience of ditching in the sea was one of the toughest that airmen faced, giving rise to some extraordinary tales of valour in the face of suffering. None was more moving than the final flight of David 'Bud' Hornell of 162 Squadron in the Royal Canadian Air Force, based at Wick. On 24 June 1944 he was on a routine patrol north of Scotland in his Consolidate Canso amphibian, a Canadian-made version of the Catalina. After an uneventful ten hours in the air, he spotted a U-boat, U-1225, 5 miles ahead to his port side. As he turned the aircraft to go on the attack, his men took up action stations. The U-boat was ready for them. Remaining on the surface, its crew put up a heavy barrage of anti-aircraft fire. Shells ripped through the Canso's wings, aerials, fuselage and starboard engine, which was quickly engulfed in flames. 'The whole side of the ship popped full of shrapnel holes till it looked like the top of a salt shaker,' recalled gunner Sydney Cole.[18] Despite extensive damage and violent shaking in the aircraft, Hornell carried on towards the target and at 1,200 yards the Canso's machine guns opened fire, striking the submarine's conning tower. Moments later, the blazing engine broke free from its mounting and fell to the sea, leaving burning petrol to spread the conflagration across the plane. Still Hornell did not give up, as his co-pilot Bernard Denomy described:

Bud fought with the controls which were damaged, either from the anti-aircraft shells or the fire, we did not know. With one engine gone and the aircraft afire, we had a tough time trying to keep the aircraft trimmed and at the same time press home the attack. This, however, he did and we coasted in to within 30 or 40 feet above the enemy sub and loosed our depth charges.[19]

Hornell flew over the U-boat, whose flak had now ceased, dropping his depth charges in a perfect straddle. At once the sea was convulsed by explosions, throwing the submarine into the air before it fell back down into the foaming waves and began its descent beneath the water. But once Hornell tried to climb from the scene on one engine, he quickly realized that his stricken, burning plane was finished. The only hope for him and his seven-man crew was to ditch the aircraft and take to the two inflatable dinghies stowed on board. The first task was accomplished expertly, and all eight were able to make it out of the plane after Hornell had landed with one bounce on the choppy water. According to Denomy, 'We set her down surprisingly easily but we got out in a hurry because we were afraid she would blow up, she had been on fire for so long. The cabin was full of smoke so we could not stay in it long anyway.'[20]

But their ordeal was about to become worse. Due to an equipment malfunction, one of the dinghies proved unusable. Only five of them could cram into the tiny remaining craft, so the crew had to take it in turns for three of them to hang from the sides up to their necks in the icy Atlantic. To compound their torment, the weather deteriorated as darkness fell, with strong winds whipping across the water and making the overladen dinghy bob up and down violently. During the night, chilled to the bone, they abandoned the routine of alternate shifts and all of them squeezed into the dinghy, having jettisoned everything they could, even emergency rations. Then, to their relief, a flare that one of them had fired into the black sky was spotted by a passing Catalina, whose pilot radioed for ASR and dropped flame floats and sea markers around the dinghy. As the pilot waited for the rescue service to arrive, he circled for fourteen hours. During his vigil a Vickers Warwick arrived and dropped a lifeboat, but the strong winds and waves carried it away from the survivors.

Time was beginning to run out. On several occasions the Canso crew's dinghy almost capsized and was only righted with great difficulty. As the long wait continued, two of the crewmen died from exposure, their bodies consigned to the sea by the survivors. 'There was no ceremony, but it was just as reverent and heartfelt as any funeral held on dry land,' said Cole.[21] Hornell himself, who had been badly burned in the attack and was almost blind, was beginning to succumb to exhaustion despite his efforts to keep up morale. Close to death, the six men were finally rescued when an HSL, guided by a Sunderland, arrived twenty-one hours after Hornell had crash-landed. It was too late for the skipper. He had fallen into a coma and, despite frantic efforts of the HSL team to revive him once he was hauled on board, he never regained consciousness. Posthumously, he was awarded the VC, a medal that Cole felt could not have been more fitting, saying,

> The way he drove that one-engined, flaming half-a-plane straight into flak almost too terrific for the imagination, levelled her off right over the U-boat as coolly as if he was on a practice run, and dropped his depth charges for the perfect kill, brings a lump to my throat whenever I think about it.[22]

Cole himself was awarded the DFM.

In September 1943 Jack Foss of 233 Squadron was flying as the co-pilot in a Liberator on anti-submarine patrol near Gibraltar when he came under deadly attack from four Ju 88s. The hail of cannon shells raked the fuselage from nose to rear, killing the pilot and the rear gunner and forcing Foss to take over the controls as the plane lost height. Having ditched in the sea, an experience he likened to 'hitting a brick wall at 100 mph',[23] the crew managed to reach the Liberator's dinghy. Incredibly, they were at sea for the next seven days, enduring a nightmare of freezing cold, gangrenous wounds, delirium, thirst and hunger, as well as danger from U-boats and ocean swells. Eventually they were picked up by a naval rescue ship, guided to their location by a Catalina. 'All our feelings had gone out of our bodies', recalled Foss, who was one of just three survivors out of a crew of nine.[24] That same month six members of a Halifax crew of 58 Squadron managed to survive eleven days in a dinghy after they were shot down off south-west Eire by anti-aircraft flak in an attack on a

U-boat. With remarkable fortitude, they kept themselves going on hope, stoicism, tiny rations and innovation, as the diary of one of them, Roger Mead, revealed. About their seventh day at sea he wrote:

> Frightened by a couple of whales basking and bellowing 400 yards away. All wounds healing well. Had a discussion on what action to take. Now obvious searching aircraft are unlikely to find us. Time we did something. Decided to reach patrol area of the Bay. Still trying hard to catch fish. Made fishing net from half a mast and a seat of an old pair of pants. No fish but about 6 p.m. caught an unlimited number of jelly fish, all sizes and what looked like baby octopi. Tried to make a drink out of them. Foul. Seem to be mainly water. Dubious stuff altogether. Kept it in case we got thirsty. Night warm and dry. Sea calm.

His last entry for the eleventh day was much shorter: 'Weather cleared midday. Divided one tin of water among us – two ounces each. A little chocolate.'[25] Soon after that, Mead and his five comrades were spotted by a Royal Navy destroyer and rescued.

At the opposite extreme Kenneth Harper, a Hudson wireless operator and gunner, had a far briefer time at sea when his crew had to ditch west of Gibraltar in late 1941 after their plane was hit by anti-aircraft fire from a Portuguese ship which then rescued them. In a post-war interview, Harper recalled,

> The first touch on the water was a horrible lurch as the plane hit the top of a wave, then there was an almighty crash as the nose went in. The Perspex at the front broke off and the plane was immediately flooded. It stood up on its tail before it settled on an even keel. We had previously jettisoned the cockpit canopy and the escape hatch on the rear of the cabin. The pilot and I climbed out onto the port wing to find that the other two crew members were in the water alongside the dinghy, which had released itself automatically from the door of the aircraft. One of the snags was that we should have been able to cut the dinghy free with the pair of clippers that were attached to the dinghy but some idiot had tied them up with insulation tape, so we could not get them undone fast enough. The second pilot went back into the aircraft, then released the door to which the dinghy was fastened. We

took that with us in the dinghy. We were in the dinghy for about a quarter of an hour. The ship had stopped and put a boat out and picked us up. We were taken on board the ship. We were given dry clothes, a bath and a meal. The ship was heading for Portuguese West Africa and we remained on board for three days. On third day we sighted two destroyers, steaming north. The captain of the steamer sent them a message and one of them stopped to pick us up. We reached Gibraltar.[26]

Jim Hunter of 217 Squadron was less fortunate in the nature of his rescue when his Beaufort was shot down during an attack on the *Scharnhorst* in July 1941. Heavy anti-aircraft fire from the ship set the plane on fire, wrecked the controls, shot away much of the nose and killed the wireless operator, though the captain of the *Scharnhorst* was deeply impressed by the courage of Hunter's crew in trying to press home their strike. 'The aircraft did not allow itself to be deflected by fire,' he recorded. Forced to ditch in the sea, the three surviving crew were picked up by a craft from the battleship, taken aboard, given dry clothes and hot drinks before being incarcerated for the remainder of the war.[27]

Even when crews made it back to their bases, landing in wartime could be difficult, especially in the dark or with a damaged aircraft. The complexity of guiding a Sunderland down off Gibraltar was described by Leslie Baveystock of 201 Squadron, who recalled that the 'technique was utterly different to that used on an airfield. There was no glide path indicator to bring us in at the right angle of descent; neither was there a long runway with its double row of lights.' Instead the way was indicated by lights, powered by car batteries and mounted on masts held by a series of dinghies, which were spaced at 800-yard intervals. 'As it was necessary for the lights to be visible from all directions, reflectors could not be used to increase their intensity. They were so dim that they were only just visible from a circuit height of 1,000 feet.' The layout of the dinghies was organized by a flying control officer in a pinnace, which doubled up as an emergency crash boat.[28] Emergencies occurred regularly on land, as Bernard Połoniecki witnessed before a mission in 1944, when a Wellington was in obvious trouble as it made its descent.

The crew must have failed to perform the cockpit drill prior to land-ing; they had not changed the pitch (of the propellers) to fine so that the engine could develop full power on demand. They left it on coarse. This, with the undercarriage and flaps down, meant that the pilot could not get the engine to deliver enough power. As we sat in our aircraft, waiting for our take-off clearance, we could hear the engines labouring. Both my skipper and I as second pilot had our radio/telephones switched on and our microphones ready to transmit. Yet we watched the aircraft losing height until it crashed, engines labouring to the last. We guessed what was wrong but neither of us had the presence of mind to shout over the radio/telephones, 'Pitch! Pitch! Fine!' I can see and hear the scene now. There was a flash as the ammo started going off, sounding like machine-gun fire. Then, after a brief silence, one enormous bang as the whole plane exploded. No one had a chance.[29]

At St Eval in 1943, Harry Platt witnessed an incendiary collision between a Whitley that was landing after an aborted take-off and an American Liberator which was waiting to go on a sortie:

I dived on the concrete of the perimeter trench as the first explosion blew everything about 20 or 30 feet in the air. After standing up, I noticed the familiar pinkish sparks arising and threw myself down again as a second explosion occurred. From about three hundred yards away, the blast of hot air from each explosion could be felt. It was thought that the petrol tanks and the American anti-U-boat bombs exploded the first time and our depth charges the second. I have never before witnessed such carnage and didn't eat anything else that day, especially as we were all detailed to help clear the runway that morning.[30]

14

Invasion

THE DAPPER AIR Secretary Sir Archibald Sinclair rose to his feet, ready to address the House of Commons. It was the end of February 1944, and now in the fifth year of war, he was able to give MPs a positive tale on Coastal Command as he opened the debate about the Air Estimates. 'The combination of air and naval power is the fruit, not of radical changes of organization or of direction from above, but of the steady efforts of Commanders and Staff Officers of the two Services engaged in the pursuit of a common enemy,' he declared, then added: 'The many units of Coastal Command, in which American squadrons are now serving alongside our own, stretching from Iceland to Gibraltar and the Azores, sweeping the whole of the Atlantic, have a long task of vigilance and of danger too.' But even in the face of 'formidable opposition', the Coastal crews had pressed home their attacks as 'they fly in low to drop their depth charges'. Against German shipping too, 'the Command has had a year of extended activity and considerable success', sinking 'quite a proportion of the traffic' between the Rhine ports and Norway. Sir Archie's optimism was infectious. The MP for Cumberland North, Wilfrid Roberts, expressed his belief

> that the part which the aircraft of Coastal Command play in the Battle of the Atlantic is recognized more today than it was in the early days of the war. I would like to add my word of tribute to the part which has been played in that long and at one time rather desperate battle by the pilots and personnel of Coastal Command.[1]

The mood in Parliament reflected the growing confidence in the Command's operations. On the anti-shipping offensive, three dedicated strike wings were now operational from North Coates, Leuchars and Wick, the first overseen by No. 16 Group, the latter pair by No. 18. In addition to more lethal weaponry like the solid head rocket projectile and the pulverizing Molins gun, Coastal Command was adopting new, more sophisticated tactics such as 'Gilbey' operations off the Dutch coast. The Gilbey attack, made at night, began once an enemy convoy had been sighted by reconnaissance, often assisted by decrypts from Bletchley Park about German naval traffic. Then, acting on this intelligence, the group sent a Wellington, equipped with ASV, to illuminate the way to target with flares, ready for the Torbeaus that followed. The method was described in a private memoir by Wing Commander E. P. W. Hutton, who served with 248 Squadron:

> On locating a convoy the Wellington would lay a rendezvous of ten marine markers, some ten miles from the seaward side of the convoy. This position would be broadcast to the Beaufighters who would then fly to this position. When 60 per cent of the Beaufighters located the rendezvous, the Wellington would drop flares to enable an attack to be made. There were two forms of Gilbey, one in which the Beaufighters were airborne, patrolling a line not far from that covered by the Wellington, and another in which the Beaufighters were kept at scramble readiness on the ground.[2]

First used successfully on the night of 5/6 March 1944 when a formation of strike aircraft sank a merchantman and three minesweepers, the Gilbey method was helped by progress in the use of sea markers resulting from work by the RAF's pyrotechnic research experts at Drem in Scotland. The specialists at Drem had already devised a lighting system to help aircraft land at night and had also radically improved the target indicators used by Bomber Command's Pathfinders, which lit the way for the main force in nocturnal raids. Now the maritime Drem flares were proving useful for Coastal Command and were also deployed on 'Ashfield' operations, a version of the Gilbey raids adopted for the Norwegian fjords.

By early 1944 the pressure of the anti-shipping offensive had forced the Germans all but to abandon Rotterdam, rerouting traffic to the more heavily defended ports of Emden and Bremen. But Germany was not safe territory either. The support of Mustang fighters enabled the North Coates Strike Wing to mount a heavy attack on the Ems–Elbe route at the end of March with six Torbeaus and ten Beaufighters armed with rockets and ten anti-flak cannon carriers. Two merchant ships were sunk and several flak escorts damaged. The burgeoning spirit of aggression was recalled by Squadron Leader Peter Hughes, of 489 Squadron, which formed part of the ANZAC Strike Wing at Leuchars, made up of crews from the Royal Australian and Royal New Zealand Air Forces.

> We were operational with our new craft and tactics in January 1944. No longer did we depend on cloud cover for an attack, nor were we passively vulnerable to the flak as we made our torpedo runs. We went over in force. The leading Beaufighters attacked the flak ships with their four cannons to discourage the anti-aircraft gunners, so allowing the following torpedo-carrying aircraft a relatively clear run in. We now rarely arrived on the Norwegian coast without seeing a target. We assumed this was because of intelligence received from the Norwegian resistance, which may well have contributed in this way, but we now know that the cracking of the Enigma code was mainly responsible.[3]

A further insight into Coastal Command's new capacity can be found in some of the combat reports of the North Coates wing in early 1944, like this from 1 March about an attack on a convoy, headed by a 6,000-ton merchant ship, south of Den Helder, by an anti-shipping patrol escorted by Spitfires.

> Four aircraft attacked the merchant vessel with cannon and three with rocket projectiles, eight of which scored direct hits. Seven aircraft attacked the leading tug with cannon, scoring numerous hits and setting it on fire. The second tug was also hit by cannon fire from one aircraft. The remaining aircraft attacked the escort vessels with cannon fire, one being seriously damaged and possibly on fire, two more being damaged. Very little flak encountered and aircraft suffered no damage.[4]

In March alone, planes from No. 16 and No. 18 groups sank seven vessels totalling 13,634 tons, while in the period from January to April Coastal Command was responsible for the loss of 38,000 tons of enemy shipping. The Ministry of Economic Warfare calculated that in May 1944 the export of Swedish iron ore had fallen to 420,000 tons compared to 1,307,000 in May 1943.

The anti-U-boat offensive was also in the ascendancy. With 430 anti-submarine aircraft at his disposal, including ten squadrons of Liberators, five Wellington squadrons fitted with Leigh Lights and seven squadrons of Sunderlands, Douglas commanded a force whose strength severely restricted the Germans' scope for any recovery by the wolf packs. As Sholto Douglas wrote in his post-war despatch, the year 1943 had

> witnessed the repulse and defeat of the enemy's main U-boat effort . . . Our shipping losses, which had averaged 215,000 tons per month during 1943, as compared to 520,000-a-month in 1942, had fallen in the last months of the year to a figure which gave just cause for satisfaction. December, with losses of 87,000, was the third consecutive month in which tonnage sinkings were under 100,000.[5]

The success rate continued at the opening of 1944. Determined to launch a counter-attack after remaining on the defensive for so long, Dönitz mustered twenty-two U-boats west of Ireland to target a series of convoys in late January. But through the decrypts from Enigma, which had been permanently cracked by Bletchley Park, British intelligence uncovered his plan, and provided strong air cover, including fifteen Cansos ordered to Iceland and a squadron of Beaufighters sent to Northern Ireland to tackle any Luftwaffe support for the U-boats. On 28 January, two submarines were sunk, the precursor to weeks of destruction. By 19 February, half of the formation assembled west of Ireland had been lost, part of a wider pattern of obliteration that saw sixty U-boats destroyed in the Atlantic during the first three months of the year.

Yet the Germans, with the heavy armament on their U-boats and supported by the Luftwaffe near the coast of occupied Europe, still put up a tenacious fight, as Polish pilot J. F. Jaworzyn found when he took part in a night patrol in his Wellington of 304 Squadron in early 1944. After hours in the air off France, the crew spotted a U-boat up ahead. It seemed to be under attack from another RAF aircraft. As Jaworzyn's Wellington headed to the scene, the other RAF pilot radioed to report that he was returning to base because of serious damage to his plane. Beginning to descend when the U-boat was just 2 miles ahead, Jaworzyn then told his crew to stand by for attack. At a height of 800 feet, he ordered the Leigh Light to be lowered. A mile from the target, the bomb doors were opened and the light switched on. According to his own vivid record of the incident,

> everything was happening at once. A flash of powerful light dazzled me. Fifty feet, bomb doors open. I saw nothing, blinded by a flare from the U-boat. Fighters attacking. 'Evasive action.' I counted to ten, ignoring the voices, then dropped the bombs and pulled the bomb door lever up. 'Leigh Light up.' I tried to turn the aircraft slowly, gently pushing the throttles forward. A single hasty move now and we should be in the water in two and a half seconds. Outside in the darkness I could see the tracers moving in our direction. Our rear gunner was firing in long bursts at one aircraft, now the other, trying to keep them away while we were in this vulnerable position. Finally I was able to open the throttles fully and start to turn. 'Attacking again, turn, turn.' Tracers again, a furious exchange of fire. 'The U-boat's still there,' said the radio operator. The attacks continued while we flew at top speed in a westerly direction, twisting and turning. Single engine fighters were not supposed to be keen to follow, yet the tracers seemed to be as vicious as ever.

The Wellington was hit several times before the fighters broke off the chase and Jaworzyn made it back to England. The flight had lasted ten hours.[6]

Dönitz had long recognized the great disadvantage of the standard U-boat was that it had to remain on the surface for sustained periods to recharge its batteries and replenish its air supply. Moreover, when underwater, it could only travel at an average speed of just 4 knots. A brilliant German engineer, Professor Hellmuth Walter, had come up with an advanced new type of craft which seemed to overcome these drawbacks. Powered by a closed-circuit propulsion system that ran on Perhydrol, a stabilized form of hydrogen peroxide, Walter claimed that his invention would have an endurance of 2,500 miles and could travel at 30 knots underwater, compared to 17 knots on the surface for the Type VII, the standard vessel of the Kriegsmarine's fleet. But in practice, the Walter submarine turned out to be a doomed project because of both difficulties in construction and problems with Perhydrol, which was highly flammable and therefore dangerous in combat. Only three were ever commissioned and none saw wartime action.

But there was another, more practical invention, which held out the promise of a transformation in the U-boat's capabilities. This was the *Schnorchel*, which had been pioneered by the Dutch navy before it fell into German hands with the blitzkrieg conquest of western Europe in 1940. Essentially it was a pair of tubes, fastened together, that allowed the submarine to expel foul air and take in fresh air from above the surface so its diesel engines could continue to operate while submerged. After successful trials in the Baltic during the summer of 1943, from early 1944 the device began to be fitted to operational U-boats. In all its simplicity, this breathing device apparently offered the chance to restore the U-boat's original assets of concealment and surprise that had been lost in the face of the Allies' countermeasures. Yet, although it allowed the U-boats to operate below the gaze of the RAF, the *Schnorchel* was not ideal. It made the U-boat permanently slow, because any speed above 6 knots would break the mast holding the tube. Nor was detection made impossible, for experienced aircrews could pick up the trail from the mast or the exhausts from the diesel engines. Furthermore, in the absence of regular surfacing, garbage and waste had to be stored on board. Even worse, the ballcock valves tended to slam shut in rough weather, with the result that the diesel engines sucked air from the interior of the boat, causing a severe loss in pressure and pain to the crews, some of whom experienced perforated eardrums. The engines would then have to be shut off as the U-boat was forced to surface, thereby abnegating the benefit of the *Schnorchel*. Nevertheless, after the recent disastrous setbacks, it offered hope for the U-boat fleet to retake the initiative.

By June 1944, half of the submarines based in the Biscay ports were fitted with *Schnorchel* tubes, which meant they could operate under the surface in the shallow waters of the English Channel, just as the Allies were planning to launch the greatest amphibious invasion the world had ever seen. The threat of the U-boat was a prime concern of the Allied planners, and the vital task of nullifying this potentially deadly menace fell to Douglas's force. It was a daunting responsibility but Douglas was certain his command was up to the job, having been impressed with its spirit since he took charge. As he later wrote, 'At Coastal Command I was called up to exercise a more single-minded concentration than I had known previously in any of my work', but was ably assisted by two crucial figures at his side in the headquarters: Peyton-Ward, who 'never allowed' his 'obvious pain to interfere with his work'; and Aubrey Ellwood, the senior Air Staff officer who had been a distinguished naval pilot in the First World War and was later to be chief of Bomber Command. A calmness prevailed across the organization, he discovered. 'Coastal Command was constantly on the go more than any other command in the RAF but the whole atmosphere and tempo – which above all else was one of great endurance – were more relaxed and less hectic than in other commands,' he wrote.[7]

But the planning for the invasion, code-named Overlord, also looked at one moment as if it might cause a severe reduction in Coastal Command's resources. In February 1944 the Air Staff issued an appreciation of the needs of the Allied Expeditionary Air Force, which were estimated to be 650 aircraft and 27,000 men. This vast requirement could not be met from increased production and recruitment, so the Air Staff, under Portal's influence, suggested that in addition to transfer from the Mediterranean, Africa and India squadrons, around half the men and planes could come from the shift of seventeen squadrons from Coastal Command to the Expeditionary Air Force. In a paper of 17 March, Portal maintained that 'the enemy menace at sea was so much reduced that Great Britain was greatly over-insured against it'.[8] This paper was discussed at a meeting of the Air Ministry on 22 March, at which Douglas mounted a powerful case against Portal's proposal, stressing the negative impact of the break-up of experienced units. Portal adopted a different approach, where he called for a study into the efficiency of Coastal Command before assessing how the air requirements of Overlord could be met. The investigation revealed how much the Command had tightened its management since the introduction of the Planned Maintenance Flying regime two years earlier, on the advice of Professor Blackett's Operational Research Section. Portal's scheme for major cuts was abandoned and Coastal Command remained intact in the run-up to D-Day. In fact, its unique role was highlighted by the fact that it was the only part of the vast Allied invasion armada that was not placed under the control of the supreme commander Dwight Eisenhower.

But as the hour of destiny approached, Douglas was troubled by the new anxiety that he had not been given explicit enough instructions by Allied headquarters as to what was expected of Coastal Command. So he went to see Sir Andrew Cunningham, the widely admired naval commander who had become First Sea Lord on the death of Pound in 1943. Decisive and dynamic, Cunningham gave Douglas short shrift: 'You know perfectly well what you've got to do, Sholto. Get on with it.'[9] Even so, at Douglas's insistence, Cunningham produced a directive which, in six vague clauses, emphasized that Coastal Command's priority was to keep the U-boats out of the invasion zone through extensive air cover and patrols.

That was exactly what Douglas had been planning. At the heart of his scheme was the idea of putting 'the cork in the bottle' by which the skies over the western entrance to the English Channel would be saturated with air patrols to block the movement of U-boats. In practical terms, 20,000 square miles of sea were to be divided into twelve rectangular sections, each of their peripheries covered by frequent 'cork patrols' mounted by aircraft from a total deployment of twenty-one anti-submarine squadrons, eight of Liberators, five of Wellingtons, two of Halifaxes and six of Sunderlands. Theoretically, this meant that any submarine on the surface that ventured into these waters would be seen at least once every thirty minutes. In addition to five further anti-submarine patrols at the eastern end of the Channel and the southern part of the North Sea, the strike wings would be deployed day and night against enemy surface vessels. There would also be four Fleet Air Arm squadrons to provide anti-U-boat cover and escorts to the invasion convoys.

Douglas set out his plan to his group commanders in a directive of 18 April which opened in appropriately stirring words:

We are now approaching the time for the supreme trial of strength between the United Nations and their German enemies which is to take the form of the invasion of occupied Europe and has been designated by the code name Overlord. Coastal Command has already played – and is still playing – a leading role in ensuring the safe transit across the Atlantic of the troops and war material which has alone made it possible to launch this great offensive. It has now, in addition, to bend its energies to securing the safety of the Allied convoys of invading forces in their passage to the continent. The Germans still dispose a very formidable U-boat fleet and may be expected to have some 200 available at any one time. They will undoubtedly use an all-out effort to disrupt our invasion convoys.

His directive went on to warn that the Germans had ninety E-boats and thirty-five heavily armed destroyers, while they might 'attempt a breakout' with a force of heavy ships in the North Sea. But he emphasized that the vast bulk of Coastal Command's forces would be concentrated on the south-western approaches to the St George's, Bristol and English Channels, flooding 'the areas to kill or keep the submarines submerged'. Fighter cover would be vital, particularly against Ju 88s, while 16 and 19 Groups would have to counter a likely offensive by surface vessels. He concluded:

the task set for all squadrons is much in excess of that now being flown . . . All ranks must realize that they will be required to work much longer hours than they do at present. Leave has already been cancelled and rest periods will have to be curtailed. At any given moment, to be notified by this Headquarters, all squadron training will be discontinued and all efforts directed to the conduct of operations. Lower standards of living and domestic comfort must be accepted; congestion on airfields will in some cases necessitate recourse to tented accommodation . . . Inconvenience and hardship must be cheerfully accepted and I look to all officers, airmen and airwomen to give their best and their all to the accomplishment of this great task.[10]

A stream of more detailed instructions followed. On the 'Cork' oper-ations, commanders were told that each section was to be designated 'a closed circuit' and would be covered by aircraft all flying at the same speed. The planes would be

> fed into the Section from the datum point at pre-determined intervals so that although they make several circuits of the Section, they are always evenly spaced. By this means, the entire section comes under observation at regular intervals. In almost every case three waves of aircraft will be required in each section to cover it continuously both by day and night.[11]

Guidance for No. 16, headquartered in Chatham, explained that

> when it is established that U-boats in large numbers are attempting to penetrate to the Eastern flanks of the Battle Zone through the North Sea, Air Officer Commanding 16 Group is to employ the four 19 Group Anti-U-boat squadrons that will have been transferred to him in providing continuous cover.

Turning to the anti-shipping operations, this paper further warned that the enemy, 'with his forces of destroyers and light surface craft, will make a sustained effort to interrupt our coastwise convoys sailing between Land's End–Portsmouth and North Foreland–Portsmouth and to attack the flanks of our supply routes across the Channel'. Interestingly, the instructions stated that 'owing to the shallow draught of destroyers and the small targets presented by E-boats, the torpedo will not be used during Overlord. Reliance will therefore be placed on rocket projectiles and bombs against destroyers, with cannon as the anti-flak weapon.'[12] For the anti-U-boat squadrons, 'all aircraft equipped to carry the 250-pound Mark XI depth charge only are to carry the maximum number possible' while aircraft 'equipped to carry the 600-pound depth charge are to carry one on every daylight sortie'.[13]

Inevitably, further concerns arose as D-Day drew near. A note by Ellwood of 13 May warned of the inadequacy of the proposed levels of daytime reconnaissance on the enemy coast by patrols of single-seater fighters at two-hourly intervals, given the scale of potential activity by E-boats from French, Dutch and Belgian ports. 'It would be appreciated if consideration could be given to the provision of more frequent reconnaissance of the coast between Dieppe and Texel,' he wrote to Fighter Command.[14] The Admiralty also worried about the correct identity recognition procedures between aircraft and surface vessels at night, while Sir John Tovey, the commander of the Nore, felt there were insufficient Coastal Command aircraft to maintain patrols between Ostend and Orford Ness. 'I do not regard daylight attacks in this area as very probable but I consider that the U-boat threat cannot be entirely disregarded,' he told Douglas.[15]

These minor issues were soon resolved as the gargantuan scheme for Overlord took its final shape. Nothing like it had ever been previously contemplated. 'We are on the fringe of something so tremendous that one hardly dares measure what may happen,' wrote the Coastal Command publicity officer Hector Bolitho in his diary.[16] On 4 June, as in other arms of the Allied Air Force, all Coastal Command planes were painted with black and white invasion stripes on their wings and fuselages so they could be recognized from the ground. Wellington gunner Graham Harrison remembered how, on the eve of the invasion, the commander of 19 Group, Air Commodore Brian Baker, tried to inspire air crews gathered at Mount Wise, Plymouth. 'I want every man of you', he was barking into the fresh southerly, 'to keen yourselves up all round.'

> Take risks, go over to the attack whenever the enemy exposes himself . . . Patrols will be flown with clockwork precision. They've been worked out to cover every inch of the Bay and the Channel by day and night, 24 hours. A five-minute error might mean a U-boat slipping through the net, so any slackness will not, repeat not, be tolerated. Well, that's it. Go to it and keep at it until Winston's got Hitler's remaining ball as a watch fob [laughter].

After the briefing, Harrison found that

> the excitement was heightened when we were each issued with a revolver, holster and gun belt, seemingly of Great War vintage. I don't

recall anyone explaining how we were to deploy these side arms over the Bay, the inference being that if things didn't go well we might be flung into the land battle.[17]

The sense of apprehension at Douglas's headquarters on the momentous morning was conveyed by Squadron Leader Michael Wilson and Flight Lieutenant A. S. L. Robinson, who were both present in the Northwood operations room.

In the south-west was concentrated the heaviest number of anti-U-boat squadrons in the history of aviation. In the Operations Room, the patrols into the Bay were plotted. On an additional large-scale map of the Channel, the special invasion anti-U-boat sweeps zigzagged across the entrance to the Channel, the bright red tapes of the aircraft routes standing out startlingly clear against the background of green sea and yellow sand. Everyone in the room was tense and keyed up. The final effort of the War, to which we had worked for these past three years, had begun.[18]

All the planning paid off once the invasion was launched. From the early hours of D-Day, Coastal Command undertook its 'cork patrols' but the expected U-boat resistance never materialized. Predictions that Dönitz would deploy more than 100 U-boats in the western approaches to the Channel proved wildly exaggerated, just as the fears that the Germans might attack from the east turned out to be unfounded. At the start of the invasion Dönitz had issued a bold proclamation to his U-boat crews: 'On you, now more than any other time, the future of the German people depends. I therefore require of you the most unstinting action and no consideration for otherwise valid precautionary measures.'[19] Yet that rhetoric never translated into action. It was an indicator of German disarray that twenty-one U-boats in Norway, assigned to anti-invasion duties, actually remained in harbour. The submarine units that ventured out from Biscay ports had a torrid experience. During the first four days of the invasion, thirty-six U-boats were sighted by Coastal Command aircraft off Brest and in the mouth of the Channel; twenty-six were attacked, with six destroyed and three seriously damaged. According to Sholto Douglas, captured German prisoners of war said that, because of the intense air cover, 'it was a nightmare trying to penetrate the Channel'.[20] Only the *Schnorchel* appeared to offer a degree of protection. That was reflected in the order issued on 12 June by Theodor Krancke, the German admiral commanding naval forces in the west: 'All submarines operating without the *Schnorchel* in the Bay of Biscay have been ordered to return to their bases, as the enemy air attacks are causing too many losses and too much damage.'[21] There could be no more powerful vindication of the work of Coastal Command than those words.

The morning of D-Day was recalled by Leslie Baveystock of 201 Squadron.

I awoke on the 6th to find the whole station alive with the news that the invasion had commenced. At the flight office I found I was scheduled that night to fly on a special trip down off Gijon in Spain, to find a known U-boat which had been harried for two days without success.

Shortly before midnight, as they flew in their Sunderland, Baveystock's crew picked up a blip on their radar at a range of 9 miles. Baveystock was certain this was his quarry, but soon afterwards the Sunderland lost contact. A flame float was dropped where the target had last been detected and Baveystock kept circling the location, sure that the U-boat would have to surface given that its batteries must have been low after so many hours of harassment. His tactic was rewarded. The Sunderland's radar screen picked up the blip again. Descending to 250 feet, Baveystock homed in on the submarine, which began to fire its anti-aircraft guns at a half-a-mile range.

We must have been silhouetted against the faint light of the clouds. We immediately started dropping flares and our U-boat was fully lit up a little to port and turning sharply to his starboard. As he came broadside on, his four 20-mm cannon opened up with tracer streams all around us as the front-gunner fired with his twin Brownings; the whole area was a criss-cross of tracer bullets and shells but when 200 yards away, all return fire stopped for we had smothered the guns with continuous fire from six Brownings.

Baveystock then released six depth charges, straddling the U-boat at an angle of 15 degrees abaft the vessel's port beam. The subsequent explosions sent the submarine, U-955, to the bottom of the ocean, with all fifty crewmen lost.[22]

The atmosphere at the end of the first day was captured by Hector Bolitho, based at St Eval. Having just been told by the intelligence officer that 31,000 Allied airmen had been over enemy territory in the last twenty-four hours, he walked into the night air to reflect on the historic moment:

> Outside were four aircraft due to take off during the night. I waited beside them in the closing darkness. One imagines that aircraft become physical and alive when they have flown many times, as ships that have sailed the seas. There were drops of oil on the lips of a gun. The Leigh Lights were ready to be switched on to their power and the fish-like bellies of the Liberators seemed stained by salt air.[23]

Based on the testimony of crews, Bolitho was impressed with the execution of Douglas's 'Cork' plan. 'The entire system of patrols is so punctual that the pilots call it "the bus service" and even when an aircraft attacks a U-boat it is expected to resume its place in the continuity when the attack is ended.'[24]

But amid the routine of scanning the sea, there were moments of high drama, like on the night of 7/8 June when Kayo Moore, the Canadian skipper of a Liberator from 224 Squadron, was on patrol between the Scillies and Ushant. His navigator Alec Gibb recalled that it was 'a wizard night: a calm sea and a full moon that just laid a white path down the water'. At about 2.15 in the morning they picked up a contact with a U-boat and soon saw its conning tower. 'We flew in and attacked, opening up with the nose gun. They returned the fire, but we silenced them,' said Moore, who continued,

> We passed dead over the conning tower and dropped six depth charges in a perfect straddle, three either side. The rear gunner saw the plumes and he squealed with delight, 'Oh God, we've blown her clean out of the water.' We ran in and passed over the spot once more and saw the heaving water and distinct patches of black oil on the dark green sea.

Just after the wireless operator had sent a message back to base with the news of a 'definite kill', another blip was picked up, so Moore dropped his height and headed towards the second U-boat. According to Gibb,

> it was an exact duplicate of the first attack. The U-boat was dead up moon, slightly to port, so we did a slight turn and opened fire on him at about one mile. His return fire was heavy and there was a perfect fan of tracer from the conning tower. As we passed over, the depth charges straddled a line ten feet behind the conning tower. Four fell on one side, and two on the other.

Initially the U-boat looked as if it had survived, but then its bow went high in the air and the vessel slowly sank under the water. Moore was immediately awarded the DSO.

Because of German defensiveness and disorganization, Coastal Command's anti-shipping forces saw little hard action on D-Day or in its immediate aftermath. So limited was the Kriegsmarine's surface activity around the invasion zone that normal patrols along the Norwegian and northern European coasts resumed within barely a week. It was a sign of the Command's dominance that when on D-Day itself a convoy of three heavy destroyers was spotted sailing down the Gironde estuary towards the Bay of Biscay, the North Coates Strike Wing, led by David Lumsden, was scrambled to devastating effect. In what the Coastal Command Review called 'a model attack',[25] the first two ships were peppered by several solid warhead rocket projectiles fired by the Beaufighters, though the third vessel at the rear escaped damage. That night, the flotilla limped into Brest where emergency repairs were carried out, then set sail again, this time escorted by a torpedo boat, only to be spotted near Ushant by a Liberator of 547 Squadron. A report was radioed to the Royal Navy, which rushed to intercept. One of the ships was sunk, another beached and was destroyed by twelve aircraft from 404 Squadron. Relieved to escape the combination of air and sea firepower, the other two hurried back to port without any hope of reaching the Channel.

That firepower was again illustrated on 15 June when a German convoy comprising two large armed ships protected by seven minesweepers was sighted off Rotterdam. In response, the largest strike force yet assembled by Coastal Command went into action. Led by Tony Gadd, an outstanding pilot who had dropped over a thousand torpedoes in trials, this was made up of forty-two Beaufighters, including Torbeaus and rocket firers, plus ten Mustangs as escorts. Although the Germans tried to fight back with their anti-aircraft guns, they were overwhelmed by the sheer scale of the Allies' attack. The two biggest vessels were sunk, as were two of the mine-sweepers, while the rest of the convoy was badly damaged. Coastal Command suffered no losses at all.

But air superiority did not diminish the dangers inherent in many sorties. On the night of 11 June Peter Cremer, the captain of U-333, came under attack from a Sunderland of 228 Squadron. As the big flying boat came in, Cremer opened fire with his deck gun, setting one of the starboard engines ablaze. The Sunderland carried on with its bombing run but was now doomed. In Cremer's account, it 'lost height and nearly hit the conning tower; it was not more than three feet above. The aircraft crashed into the sea amidst exploding depth charges. The sea was burning all around us. It was an incredibly brave and death-defying attack.'[26]

The fighting spirit highlighted in that tribute from Cremer was also embodied in the incredible bravery of John Cruickshank, the fourth man from Coastal Command to win the VC. Cruickshank was apprenticed in an Edinburgh bank when he volunteered for the Royal Artillery at the outbreak of war before transferring to the RAF in 1941; he won his wings the following year and joined 210 Squadron based at Sullom Voe in the Shetlands. Six weeks after D-Day, on 17 July, he was flying on a nocturnal patrol off the Norwegian coast west of Narvik when his navigator John Appleton picked up a blip on the Catalina's radar. Cruickshank began to home in on the target, whose status as an enemy U-boat was confirmed by fire from its 37-mm gun. In Appleton's memoir of the incident,

The skipper manoeuvred into a perfect attacking position astern of the submarine, just keeping out of range of the enemy gunfire. He gave a blast on the Klaxon and started the attack run-in from about two miles. At this, I got up on my lookout position again and looked over

Cruickshank's right shoulder at a textbook attack. The flak was coming up fast and bursting around us at the rate of about two a second. As we got closer, the two pairs of 20-mm cannon on the U-boat's bandstand opened up.[27]

Even confronted by this increasing barrage, Cruickshank flew on and appeared to release the depth charges to perfection over the conning tower.

But the bombs had hung up. 'The disappointment of all this happening after an attack was indescribable,' wrote Appleton. Miraculously, all the German fire seemed to have caused little damage to the Catalina, so Cruickshank then took the plane to 250 metres, out of range of the U-boat's defences, while his crew rearmed their own guns and checked the bomb release mechanism. 'Everyone ready! Here we go again,' said Cruickshank over the intercom. Of the second attack, Appleton recounted, 'This time all the flak was burst-ing much closer to us and I was surprised at how thick it could be. We seemed to be flying into a wall of black explosions. The skipper went straight in without hesitation and again the aircraft passed precisely over the conning tower.'[28] Seconds later, the plane was caught by more bursts of enemy fire. Flames and smoke began to fill the aircraft; the radar was wrecked, the nose canopy was shattered, one crewman was dead and four others were badly wounded, includ-ing Cruickshank, who had been hit in his chest and legs and was bleeding heavily.

But all was not lost. With the use of extinguishers, some of the uninjured crewmen put out the fire. As the co-pilot took over the controls, Cruickshank was carried aft to lie down. The tremendous pain he was suffering was obvious, yet he refused any morphine from the emergency safety kit because he wanted to keep his faculties in order to help bring the Catalina home to Sullom Voe. With almost superhuman fortitude he insisted on being carried to the co-pilot's seat for the final descent on to the water at 4 a.m., just as dawn was breaking. On landing, water began to pour through all the holes in the Catalina's hull, but with a final burst of power from the engines the plane was run up the beach before it sank. When Cruickshank was taken to Lerwick hospital, a total of seventy-two pieces of shrapnel were removed from his chest and legs. He had also lost a dangerous amount of blood. Yet he survived and, after recuperation, took up a staff job at Coastal Command headquarters, having been awarded the nation's highest military decoration on 1 September. His citation read,

> By pressing home the second attack in his gravely wounded condition and continuing his exertions on the return journey with his strength failing all the time, he seriously prejudiced his chances of survival even if the aircraft safely reached its base. Throughout, he set an example of determination, fortitude and devotion to duty in keeping with the highest traditions of the service.[29]

The only Coastal Command VC holder not to have been awarded the medal posthumously, Cruickshank returned to his career in banking at the end of the war. In 2020 he became the first VC recipient to reach the age of 100.

Coastal Command, too, had distinguished itself heroically in Operation Overlord. Rightly attacked over the Channel Dash in 1942, the Command was showered with praise two years later for its successful guardianship of the Channel. Its in-house journal boasted that 'U-boats putting to sea met such a blast from Coastal Command aircraft that the enemy's ambitions were defeated from the beginning'.[30] Admiral Sir Bertram Ramsay, the commander of the Allied naval expeditionary force, sent a message to Douglas to 'record my appreciation of the important part that Coastal Command has played throughout this period', which had ensured

> the failure of the U-boat to achieve anything but the most meagre results within the Channel. Anti-shipping operations have been equally successful and must have added a further unwelcome burden to the enemy's already overloaded transport system, while your aircraft so harried the enemy's coastal forces that they did not inflict the damage to our convoys which might otherwise have been expected.[31]

Even more fulsome was Winston Churchill, who telegrammed Douglas:

I send you and to all your officers and men my congratulations on the splendid work of Coastal Command during the last three months. In spite of all the hazards of weather and in the face of bitter opposition from the armament of enemy U-boats and escort vessels, your squadrons have played a vital part in making possible the great operations now going forward in France. Working in close concord with the Allied navies, they have protected so effectively the host of landing craft and merchant vessels that the enemy campaign against them has been a complete and costly failure.[32]

In private, Portal, who had been an advocate of slashing Coastal Command only months earlier, now gave Churchill a glowing, detailed endorsement of its work.

The U-boat threat to our sea communications with France appears to have been dealt with so effectively between D-Day and D + 4 that during the first three weeks of Overlord not one U-boat is believed to have reached our shipping lanes to Normandy. In all during June, Coastal Command aircraft made 109 sightings and 64 attacks in the course of over 40,000 flying hours, an effort some 11,500 hours greater than in any previous month. The results were 15 U-boats sunk or probably sunk and 15 damaged. Thus from 15 May to the end of June Coastal Command aircraft sank or probably sank no fewer than 21 U-boats and damaged 18. These results entailed considerable casualties to aircraft. During June, 26 aircraft were lost on anti-U-boat operations, i.e. two aircraft for every five U-boats attacked.

Portal then turned to the other plank of the Command's operations, telling Churchill:

The anti-shipping activities of Coastal Command reached their peak in July. In June they were confined principally to the attack of E-boats and destroyers in the Channel and its Approaches, involving approximately 2,000 sorties and 190 attacks. Since over 60 per cent of the attacks occurred at night, information about the results has necessarily been meagre. The failure of the enemy to interfere seriously with the invasion shipping nevertheless testifies to the efficiency of the attacks as a harassing measure. As a result it was possible toward the end of June to reduce the air effort against E-boats and to put more into the attack of coastal convoys. In July, a total of 1,900 sorties produced the record figures of 227 attacks, involving 550 aircraft.[33]

On this memorandum Churchill penned in his own handwriting the word 'excellent'.[34]

Arthur Harris had told Churchill that Coastal Command was an obstacle to victory in 1942. Now the air chief had informed the prime minister that Coastal Command had helped to make victory possible.

15

Victory

T HE SUCCESS OF the D–Day landings and the Allies' subsequent
advance through northern France transformed the balance of
the maritime war in western Europe. It was no longer feasible for the
Kriegsmarine or the Luftwaffe to operate from bases on the Biscay
coast. From August 1944, Dönitz ordered his naval forces to Germany
and occupied Norway, a task that was accomplished with surprisingly
few losses thanks to their *Schnorchel*. Some Germans were relieved to
escape the relentless threat of attack from Allied ships and aircraft in
the west, as Hans Goebeler recorded:

> Overhead, a virtually constant flow of RAF bombers shuttled back
> and forth between England and Gibraltar, creating a corridor of death
> between our sailing ports and the Atlantic which we called Suicide
> Stretch. If a boat was spotted and escaped destruction from the air,
> groups of destroyers were despatched to the spot.[1]

The drastic reduction in U-boat activity in the Bay enabled Coastal
Command to transfer several squadrons from 19 Group in the south-
west to 18 Group in Scotland, concentrating on Norway, and 15
Group, covering the Western Approaches and the northern transit
area for any renewed breakout into the Atlantic. Despite this ascendancy, Douglas was not remotely complacent. He believed that the
Schnorchel could open a deadly new period in submarine warfare. On
30 August he wrote to George Johnson, the head of the Royal
Canadian Air Force's Atlantic Command, setting out his anxieties:

> In my opinion it is definitely not the time when we can afford any
> relaxation of efforts and in fact the reverse. As I told you, we have put

scientists on the problem and they are trying to find a quick means of improving the capacity of various types of ASV to pick up and home in on the Schnorkels. Furthermore, I am starting an intensive training campaign designed to improve the efficiency of our radar operators to pick up and home in on the Schnorkels by day and by night.

Nonetheless, Douglas feared that however effective the training and equipment, 'we shall never be able to pick up the Schnorkel at the range at which we used to pick up a fully surfaced U-boat'. The only answer, he thought, was to flood the area of enemy operations. He concluded, 'On the assumption that the European war will last for another six months we shall require more and better aircraft in order to achieve success against this new U-boat threat.'[2]

The *Schnorchel* problem also featured heavily at a Coastal Command conference on 7 September where Douglas warned that 'the enemy use of this equipment was affecting the number of sightings of U-boats by Coastal Command and it might be that some changes in tactics would be necessary', though he admitted that 'there was not sufficient information available yet' to make such decisions.[3] Among the countermeasures discussed were: the possibility of laying long wires across the surface of the sea in targeted areas in order to catch the masts of the *Schnorchel* submarines; an increase in the setting for depth charges; and the use of infrared equipment for detection. None of these ideas, however, was implemented that autumn or winter, mainly because of their impracticality. 'The possibilities of infra-red at this stage could only be highly speculative',[4] one meeting was told, while another learnt that subsequent trials of infrared were 'very discouraging'.[5]

Douglas's concerns had some justification, especially because *Schnorchel* allowed the U-boats to penetrate British waters. 'The enemy has found it possible to operate inshore in a manner that would have been certain death if it had still been necessary to surface periodically for a few hours in order to charge,' warned an Admiralty paper in September.[6] For the first time since Bowhill's spell in command, the U-boat menace was close to home, as the German military historian Dr Jürgen Rohwer explained:

The Schnorkel U-boats which the Commander U-boats sent into the Channel and into the Coastal waters of Great Britain from August 1944 onwards reported being able to stay in these areas for weeks without being detected by aircraft or surface anti-submarine groups. Even when they attacked single ships or convoys and escort vessels tried to hunt them to death, they could often evade pursuit by using high-density layers in coastal waters which reflected the sonar beams. And now HF/DF [Huff-Duff] was only of limited use, because the U-boats received their orders before departure or by radio signals in special cipher settings for individual boats which could not be broken by analytical means. The U-boats were, however, almost stationary and could not intercept the traffic. They mainly had to wait for the targets to come their way, because air coverage was so dense and the surface anti-submarine groups so efficient.[7]

The reality of the threat was highlighted by U-482, a Type VIIC, which sailed from its new base in Norway to the west of Ireland in late August and in just nine days sank five Allied merchant vessels totalling more than 33,000 tons. Emboldened by this success, Dönitz reorganized his U-boat forces to concentrate them in the North, St George's and Bristol channels. In October nine Allied ships were sunk by U-boats, followed by another nine in November, with the total more than doubling to twenty-two ships of 72,000 tons in December. But the impact should not be exaggerated. Even in the worst months of late 1944, these were nothing like the losses that had been sustained at the height of the Battle of the Atlantic in 1942 and 1943. Moreover, despite *Schnorchel*, the combined superiority of the Allied air and naval forces was overwhelming. In August forty U-boats were lost, followed by twenty-one in September, thirteen in October, seven in November and fifteen in December. What made the German position all the more difficult was that U-boat production was not keeping pace with these crippling losses due to the Allied bombing offensive, which was now devastatingly effective after gaining mastery of the skies over the Reich's homeland. It was not so much that the German yards themselves building the U-boats were being wrecked in 1944, for the submarines were constructed in huge, reinforced concrete pens that were almost impenetrable to conventional bomb attacks, but that the workforce, transportation networks and supply factories were being disrupted by constant air raids.

Coastal Command's own superiority in north-western Europe was reinforced later in 1944 by the transfer of 202 Squadron, now equipped with Catalinas, from Gibraltar to Castle Archdale in Northern Ireland, and the move of two Leigh Light Wellington squadrons from the Mediterranean theatre to No. 19 Group in the south-west to enhance convoy patrols. Equipment was becoming more sophisticated, epitomized by the sonobuoy receivers, code-named High Tea, that were now installed in an increasing number of Liberators. Coastal Command also staked a claim for the powerful new Mark VII radar developed by the Telecommunications Research Establishment. Following a lull after D-Day, the Mark VII programme was given a fresh impetus by the advent of the *Schnorchel* and an Air Ministry meeting in November agreed to proceed with further research and trials. The end of the war came, however, before the new ASV radar could go into service with Coastal Command.

There was a brighter story with the ASV Mark X and Mark XI, which operated on even shorter wavelengths, initially the X-band at 3 cm and later the K-band at 1.25 cm. The Mark X was installed on select Liberators from the summer of 1944 and proved able to pick up the periscope of a *Schnorchel* if the sea were reasonably calm. The Mark XI was mainly used by Fairey Swordfish of the Fleet Air Arm, though its bulk meant that there was no room for a torpedo, so any Mark XI Swordfish had to be accompanied on a bombing mission by another aircraft, equipped with a bomb but without radar. A further advance was made in the Mark XII, which was specifically developed for use in anti-shipping operations, becoming part of the Beaufighter's bristling potency late in the war.

Coastal Command was now in by far its strongest position of the conflict, exerting a dominance over the U-boat fleet. The value of radar was captured in an account left by Flight Lieutenant Gilbert Potier of 53 Squadron of a nocturnal attack on a submarine in his Liberator in the eastern Atlantic in mid-August, having made a contact: 'Everything depended on the radio operator. If he failed, we might easily be shot into the sea. We were flying at 200 feet but we could not see the water.' Then Potier heard the radar operator's voice.

' "Steady, skipper, steady!" And, "Oh, she's a wonderful blip, steady as a rock, skipper. Oh, she's a beaut."' The Leigh Light went on. 'For a fraction of a second I could see nothing at all, then all hell broke loose. Our front guns were blazing away for all they were worth and I saw little red balls of fire coming up towards us and racing away beneath our starboard wing.' The bombs were released on the target as the plane straddled the U-boat just aft of the conning tower. 'The Leigh Light went out and the blackness was intense.' At seven o'clock the next morning the Navy found the U-boat limping along under the surface so badly damaged that it was moving at only a mile an hour. 'They finished off what we began and one more of the bastards went to the bottom.'[8] By the end of 1944, 158 U-boats had been sunk by the Allies, fifty-one of them by Coastal Command alone, plus an additional nine kills shared with the Royal Navy.

The scales had also tilted dramatically in favour of Coastal Command's anti-shipping force, which was now able to flex its considerable muscles. An insight into how high morale now was can be found in the report of a strike by the North Coates wing on 21 July against a large convoy heading towards Heligoland. Doug Young, a Beaufighter navigator of 489 RNZAF Squadron, was amazed at the sight of a flotilla as he flew towards it as part of the large Coastal Command formation. 'Over several square miles of sea, indeed as far as the eye could see, an ordered array of ships was proceeding like a great Armada.' The Germans opened up with their anti-aircraft guns, but the wing could not be deterred, said Young. 'Down we went and our four cannons burst into life with a shattering roar above the noise of the engines.' His Beaufighter hit one vessel, which seemed

> almost to leap out of the water as we pulled out of our dive only feet above the now smoking decks. In the space of perhaps three or four minutes absolute havoc had been inflicted from the skies on that convoy. Almost every ship was belching think clouds of oil smoke.[9]

By the end of August German naval activity in the west had almost ceased and strikes on the Norwegian coast acquired increasing significance, as a Coastal Command paper stressed:

The attack on shipping on passage between North German and Norwegian ports has assumed great importance. In particular it is vital to the enemy that he should be able to maintain his sea transport in the Kattegat and Skagerrak both for the movement of troops and supplies and for the maintenance of his U-boats in the Norwegian ports.[10]

To strengthen the fight on the Norwegian coast, a new strike wing was established by transferring 235 and 248 squadrons from Portreath in Cornwall to Banff in Aberdeenshire, with a satellite airfield at nearby Dallachy. Further south in Lincolnshire, another wing was set up at Strubby as a lodger unit at a Bomber Command station, having been previously based at Davidstow Moor in Cornwall. Initially the Strubby wing concentrated on the German and Dutch coasts, but, as *Coastal Command Review* explained, 'the enemy was wary of exposing his shipping to the risk of air attacks and targets for daylight strikes had to be sought further afield', so patrols were mounted into Heligoland Bight and southern Norway.[11]

Altogether the wings now had four squadrons of Mosquitoes, the ideal aircraft for anti-shipping operations because of its unique capacity to carry a range of weaponry, its tremendous manoeuvrability and its ability to outpace most German fighter escorts. According to Roy Conyers Nesbit, the Mosquito 'handled more like a fighter' and was better in combat than a Beaufighter, but the Bristol plane was 'more robust flying into flak', its radial engines could absorb 'phenomenal' punishment, and it was a safer aircraft to ditch in because 'its stressed skin acted like a skin on the water' whereas the 'wooden ply of the Mosquito, with little tensile strength, could easily rip off on contact'.[12] In one typical spell in mid-autumn, eighteen Beaufighters and eight Mosquitoes rendezvoused on the night of 9 October over a pattern of markers laid by a Coastal Command Warwick on reconnaissance, then attacked their targeted convoy off Egersund, sinking a freighter of 2,000 tons and an escort vessel. On 15 October twenty-one rocket-carrying Beaufighters and seventeen Mosquitoes sank a tanker and a flak ship off Kristiansund South without any loss. Six days later, eleven Mosquitoes and six Beaufighters attacked a convoy in Haugesund harbour and sank two merchant vessels.[13]

In these missions across the North Sea, Coastal Command made extensive use of Norwegian expertise, as the historian Christina Goulter noted:

> One of the Mosquito squadrons, based in the north of Scotland, was manned by Norwegians and during the year this unit developed one chief function: advanced reconnaissance guide to other anti-shipping squadrons operating over Norway. Known as outriders, these aircraft squadrons flew ahead of the main force, seeking out enemy shipping which could be reported to the following strike aircraft. With their intimate knowledge of their homeland, the Norwegians proved invaluable.[14]

Halifax pilot James Sanders gave a description of a bombing mission at night to the Norwegian coast in September 1944. Approaching the shoreline, the radar operator picked up a contact from a ship 8 miles ahead.

> I rely on the advice of my radio altimeter and feel my way along the surface of the waves at 200 feet ... Now begins a very close and meticulous liaison ... The radar operator must guide us on to the target. The bomb aimer must, by stop-watch precision, know the distance to run and the pilot must be the faithful, non-swerving servant of his two team-mates. It is time for me to climb to a safe bombing height. I power the Halifax to 1,200 feet and begin our bombing run. We are very tense.

Sanders followed the aimer's instructions as the target came into view and the bombs were released.

> There is a pregnant pause. And then, above the steady rumble of our Rolls Royce engines comes a roll of explosions, and six yellow welts of light break the darkness below. The aircraft bucks and wallows in the blast as the bombs, with air-burst pistols, explode on the surface of the sea. We do not know if we have destroyed the target ship; that information will have to reach our intelligence officers later. But there is no point in lingering over the scene.[15]

The pressure on German shipping continued to the end of the year, even in poor weather. December saw seven wing strikes by Mosquitoes and two by Beaufighters, which also carried out armed reconnaissance patrols of the coast. During the month Coastal Command sunk ten merchant vessels and an escort vessel as well as badly damaging fourteen other ships.

Time was now running out for the Germans. On every front the Reich was staring at defeat. But Dönitz, ever resourceful, made one last bid to seize the initiative, putting his desperate but defiant hope in new types of U-boat to replace the dangerously vulnerable VIIs and IXs that had made up the majority of his fleet. One was the small, highly manoeuvrable XXIII, which was designed to operate in shallow waters and could remain submerged for long periods due not only to its *Schnorchel* but also to its large battery capacity. After successful trials, the first six XXIIIs went on patrol around the British Isles in January 1945. Even smaller was the XXVII midget submarine, carrying a pair of torpedoes and a crew of two. Having gone into service in December 1944, the XXVII represented a dangerous problem for the Allies because its small size meant it could not be picked up by ASDIC while its slow speed left it almost immune to detection by sonobuoys. Even more promising was the large XXI. Along with its capacity to stay long underwater as a result of its many battery cells, triple the number in the traditional Type VII, this large submarine, over 250 feet long, had a higher speed and better handling characteristics than preceding types because of an improved hull design. It also had a long range and packed a heavy punch, capable of carrying up to twenty-three torpedoes. Dönitz himself crowed about the potential transformation in the Kriegsmarine's fortunes:

> The advent of these new types put an end to the supremacy which the enemy's defences had enjoyed over the U-boat since 1943 and which had been due to the introduction of ultra short-wave radar. The U-boat would remain undetectable by radar under water, it could now operate at a depth at which it was safe and deliver its attack from the same depth. New possibilities had opened up for the boats, new successes were within our grasp.[16]

British apprehension about a renewed threat was explicitly set out in a paper of 7 December 1944 by Lieutenant Commander Dick Raikes, a Coastal Command staff officer who had previously served with distinction in the Royal Navy. In gloomy tones, Raikes warned that 'the moment is psychologically for the Germans to launch their greatest U-boat campaign of the war. There is a feeling of acute disappointment in Great Britain at the prospect of another year of war after the unprecedented advances across France and Belgium.' Citing the devastation caused by the V1 and V2 rockets in 1944, Raikes continued that 'the new types of U-boats are in fact something quite revolutionary in performance', yet the Allies had shown little urgency in countering them. 'We are basically muddling along with what we've got in the vague belief that the enemy is again too late.'[17]

Raikes's point seemed vindicated in January 1945 when twenty ships of 89,500 tons were sunk by U-boats, almost all of them in the waters off the British Isles. Particularly grievous was the loss of the aircraft carrier HMS *Thane*, which was hit off the Clyde by a torpedo from U-1172. In the middle of the month Douglas proposed to go on the offensive through 'co-operation on an unprecedented scale between air and surface forces', by switching the focus of the air patrols from inshore waters to the northern transit zone, targeting three areas: between the Shetlands and the Norwegian coast, between the Shetlands and the Faroe Islands, and north of the Shetlands. In conclusion, he wrote to Portal that

> the enemy has for the present put us at a serious disadvantage. He is in fact compelling us to play into his hands by dispersing our air and surface effort in areas unsuited to either air or ASDIC search . . . It seems therefore that we should strike out with a bold offensive with air and surface craft in close co-operation. U-boats must no longer be allowed to arrive unhurried in their inshore billets. They must be hunted remorselessly while in transit. For this the maximum number of aircraft and surface ships will be needed and must be provided at the expense of close escort to convoys.[18]

The Admiralty, however, were not supportive of the plan to focus on the northern transit area, believing that effort should for the time being be concentrated on the Irish Sea in an endeavour to drive the U-boats out of that area. They further considered that the implementation of such a plan should be postponed for a month or two until better weather conditions and longer hours of daylight can be expected.[19]

As it turned out, the Admiralty's hesitancy was justified. There was no need for alarmism. By the first months of 1945 Germany was so battered that Dönitz was unable to mount any sort of powerful new offensive. Only two Type XXIs actually entered wartime service and neither sank any ships. The hope that there would be a big expansion in numbers was dashed when RAF Lancasters, using the colossal 22,000-pound Grand Slam bomb, destroyed the huge concrete bunker under construction at Farge, near Bremen, where the XXI would be built. Similarly, only six of the manoeuvrable Type XXIIIs went into operational service. Far more of the Type XXVII, known as the Seehund, saw action, 285 of them having been constructed. They sank a total of nine merchant vessels, but thirty-five were lost, most of them to poor weather. Sir Charles Little, the naval commander-in-chief of Portsmouth, expressed the relief of many when he said, 'Fortunately these damn things arrived too late in the war to do any damage.'[20]

Despite the reduction in the threat, there were changes to the RAF's deployment to strengthen anti-U-boat operations, with the result that 17, 27 and 489 squadrons were moved from the Mediterranean to Coastal Command while US Admiral Ernest King, more co-operative than in the past, approved the transfer of two Liberator squadrons equipped with Mark X ASV, a Catalina squadron and a Ventura squadron. The numbers of Fairey Swordfish with Mark XI ASV were also increased and proved useful in hunting midget U-boats off the southern English coast. The Admiralty refused, however, to shift two Sunderland squadrons from West Africa, explaining that these planes were 'almost the sole protection in that area' since 'practically all surface escorts' had gone.[21] Contrary to the dark predictions in January, it was the German maritime forces that were endlessly harassed. By the spring of 1945 Coastal Command had reached the peak of its wartime strength with 1,115 aircraft, including no fewer than 225 Liberators, of which eighty-four belonged to the

US Navy and US Army Air Forces but were under Douglas's control. The commander-in-chief himself admitted, 'I had formidable air power under my control.'[22]

That power made itself felt in the final weeks of the war as the Reich crumbled. Anti-submarine sweeps across the Baltic and the North Sea brought a savage harvest in German losses. During a mission on 3 March, for example, four Liberators of 206 (Czech) Squadron sank two U-boats, an enemy coaster and a destroyer. Such was the Command's supremacy that the anti-shipping forces regularly joined the attacks on U-boats. On 9 April the Banff Strike Wing, made up of thirty Mosquitoes armed with cannon and rockets, accompanied by Mustangs, sank three U-boats in quick succession off the Norwegian coast. Even more decisive was the action of the Beaufighters of the North Coates Strike Wing on 4 May when they flew to liberated Holland, spotted four U-boats off the coast and sank every one of them. The *Coastal Command Review* exulted in the strike force's predominance:

A continuing and increasing pressure has been directed on the enemy's anchorages throughout the winter of 1944/5, with the Germans constantly changing their hiding places and our aircraft just as consistently finding new ones. The enemy has tried hard to meet this situation by selecting remote fjords, by anchoring still further up them and finally by tying right up under steep cliffs, but the Mosquitoes and Beaufighters of the Banff and Dallachy Wings have succeeded for the greater part to overcome these obstacles.

The journal noted that these two wings alone had sunk over 75,000 tons of shipping and seriously damaged another 28,000 tons.[23]

Yet even at this late hour the anti-shipping arm could still suffer disastrous losses due to the continuing resilience of the anti-aircraft and fighter defences. Indeed, in Norway, the Luftwaffe's presence was the strongest it had been since 1940. In the Trondheim area alone there were eighty-five single-engined and forty-five twin-engined fighters plus a squadron of night fighters. Furthermore, just as with the U-boats, improved types of aircraft were now available, such as the Focke-Wulf 190 D series, which was 40 mph faster than the

Messerschmitt 109. Casualties in Coastal Command's anti-shipping operations actually increased in the last seventeen weeks of the war, not least because of limited fighter cover as a result of the need from the advancing Allied armies for tactical air support.

No ordeal illustrated more gruesomely the dangers faced by the strike wings than 'Black Friday' on 9 February, when thirty-two Beaufighters, armed with cannon, machine guns and rocket projectiles, set out from Dallachy on course for Førdefjord, east of Vevring, where a Narvik–class destroyer had been seen by reconnaissance. The crossing was uneventful but that changed once they reached the target, as Spike Holly of 144 Squadron, on the last trip of his operational tour, recalled.

> Due to the terrain, we were flying much higher than usual and so were in the dive much longer during the attack. It seemed an age before the cannons opened up and filled the fuselage with their thundering racket, shuddering vibration and fumes. As we started our dive, there was another Beau 100 feet on our port side. Suddenly without warning, it exploded into a ball of orange flames. One of the tailplanes broke off and fell away like an autumn leaf.

Holly's plane completed its attack, then climbed away, only to come under attack from an Fw 190. As the shells tore into the aircraft, one engine and the intercom were put out of action while Holly himself was badly wounded in his stomach and legs. He was drifting in and out of consciousness when the broken plane came down in the water. Having just managed to get out through the escape hatch before the Beaufighter sank, he was then rescued by two local men in a fishing boat. After six weeks in hospital, he spent the remainder of the conflict in a POW camp.[24]

Stan Butler was another airman whose plane was attacked by a Fw 190. Even before then, Butler had endured a barrage of flak as he dived at the German ship.

> Being the last into the attack, and probably their only remaining target, we were getting plenty of unwelcome attention. It was a frightening moment . . . Just before we cleared the destroyer there was a loud bang

and a spurt of liquid gushed up from the front of my cockpit. My jink-
ing caused it to splash over the windscreen and over me, seriously
impairing my vision.

But Butler managed to weave his way out of the fjord and away from
the fighter, 'pumping the control column backwards and forwards
quite violently at random intervals'. Despite the damage, he managed
to nurse the Beaufighter back to Dallachy where he had to make a
belly landing, a shell having pierced the fuselage on the port side,
puncturing the hydraulic system.[25] Butler's crew was among the luck-
ier ones on Black Friday. In the carnage nine Beaufighters were shot
down, seven by flak, two by Fw 190s. They were the heaviest losses
that the strike wings experienced in a single operation during the
war.

To provide greater protection for the wings, Douglas specifically
asked Portal for a squadron of Mustangs.

At present we have a call on two squadrons only which is hardly sufficient in view of the scale of the opposition. I realize, of course, that
my demands conflict with those of Bomber Command, but I feel that
in view of the weakness of the defences in Germany, the withdrawal
of one Mustang squadron from bomber escort work would make all
the difference to my anti-shipping strikes.[26]

It was a sign of how important the Command had become that on 11
April more Mustangs were transferred. Nor did Black Friday inhibit
the anti-shipping operations in the final period of the war. In early
March the Banff Strike Wing was equipped with long-range
100-gallon drop tanks, enabling it to penetrate deep into Norway.
The results were compelling; indeed, 1945 was to be the most successful year for these squadrons, accounting for eighty-one ships, seventy-
three of them off Norway or in the Kattegat, though Coastal
Command lost 103 aircraft in the process. In April, the Command
had sunk twenty-four vessels totalling 48,500 tons, prompting the
Coastal Command Review to claim that 'the past seven months have
been outstanding in the war against enemy shipping. In the Norwegian
area a considerable strategic success has been achieved, while in the

southern North Sea a heavy and continuing attack on our shipping has been neutralized.'[27] The last major sortie was conducted on 4 May when a formation of forty-eight Mosquitoes, escorted by eighteen Mustangs, attacked a seven-strong convoy in the Kattegat, sinking a 3,750-ton merchantman and damaging two other vessels. Further operations planned for 5 May were cancelled as it became clear Germany was about to surrender.

The end of the war was also close for the anti-submarine arm. The last U-boat to be sunk by a Coastal Command aircraft was U-320, a Type VII, which was hit on the morning of 7 May by a Catalina flown by Flight Lieutenant K. H. Murray of 210. Although the Catalina's depth charges did not immediately sink the vessel, so great was the damage that the German skipper just managed to limp to Norway, where he scuttled the boat the following day, just as the Allies accepted the unconditional surrender of Germany from none other than Admiral Dönitz, whom Hitler had chosen as his successor before his suicide in his Berlin bunker. In a reflection of Dönitz's ruthless stubbornness, his U-boat fleet had fought on to the bitter end. Even after the capitulation of the land forces, the Allies were concerned that the Kriegsmarine would not abandon the struggle. In the concluding volume of his epic history of the Second World War, Churchill wrote, 'The final phase of our onslaught lay in German coastal waters. Allied air attacks destroyed many U-boats at their berths. Nevertheless, when Dönitz ordered the U-boats to surrender, 49 were still at sea. Such was the persistence of the German effort and the fortitude of the U-boat service.'[28] Recognition of the U-boat crews' determination also shone through Douglas's poignant last wartime signal to his squadrons and ground staff, on 6 May:

We may expect the continuance of intense U-boat operations from Norwegian bases. All ranks must realize that for Coastal Command the war goes on as before. We started first. We finish last. I call upon all squadrons for a great final effort against the old enemy. It falls to Coastal Command to strike the final blow against the enemy's one remaining weapon.[29]

Even after Dönitz had signed the instrument of surrender, Coastal Command took no chances and kept up its patrols, in the search for any recalcitrant German submarines. Finally, on 4 June 1945 the last mission was undertaken by Wing Commander J. Barrett of 201 Squadron, flying his Sunderland back to its base at Castle Archdale on Lough Erne. The event was reported by the local Ulster paper, the *Northern Whig*: 'A Sunderland flying boat alighted on the placid waters of Lough Erne yesterday morning. The four big propellers slowed down and stopped, and Coastal Command's last patrol of the war had ended.' The paper then noted that 'Coastal Command has had throughout the war at least one machine in the air every day somewhere in its territory, stretching from Iceland to Norway, the Baltic, the Azores and Gibraltar.'[30]

That tribute was fully justified. Coastal Command had fought the war from the beginning and had been instrumental in the defeat of Nazi tyranny. In the words of the wartime Under-Secretary of State for Air Harold Balfour, speaking in Margate about the men of the Command as the tide turned in the Battle of the Atlantic in 1943,

Day in, day out, whatever the weather, they fly the oceans on their allotted duties. Theirs is not the sharp glory of the fighter combat, nor the satisfaction of the concentrated destruction of Germany's war machine by the bomber offensive. Theirs is the physically arduous and equally hazardous job of flying far out to the west in the front line.

Their 'constant attacks' and wide sweeps of the seas 'for scores, sometimes hundreds of miles' at the 'extreme limit of aircraft range' had thwarted the enemy. He concluded by telling his audience, 'Give praise to Coastal Command for their unsung glories and feats.'[31]

Epilogue: Exodus

THE MOTTO OF Coastal Command was 'Constant Endeavour', words that were triumphantly fulfilled by its part in the war. From a troubled start, the service had emerged as a decisive factor in the Allied victory, helping to defeat the U-boats, protect Britain's shipping routes and degrade the enemy's naval capacity. Its journey from a limited force, restricted mainly to reconnaissance duties in home waters, to a global arm of the RAF with bases throughout the western theatre, was symbolized by its wartime beginnings with Wildebeest biplanes and its wartime end with radar-equipped, rocket-carrying Liberators.

The story of that odyssey is also told in statistics. In the first three years of the war Coastal Command sank just three U-boats, with one additional kill shared with the Navy. In 1944 the Command sank forty-eight German submarines and shared in ten further kills. Its own wartime research showed that altogether its planes were probably responsible for the destruction of 209 U-boats during the war, including twenty-one shared with naval forces. Another 290 U-boats were damaged by its aircraft, quite an achievement for an organization once dubbed the Cinderella Service. From 1939 to 1945 the service escorted over 1,250 convoys, flew 123,372 anti-U-boat sorties totalling 905,000 hours in the air, made 1,664 attacks and dropped 4,236 tons of depth charges. The impact of Coastal Command on the German submarine fleet was brought home to the Allies immediately after the end of hostilities when a group of senior RAF officers visited the headquarters of the U-boat staff at Flensburg, where, according to an internal report, they

> learned of the high opinion of Coastal Command aircraft held by the average U-boat captain. The U-boat staff stated that of the air

269

opposition they had encountered, Coastal Command was by far the most effective. When questioned about the aspect which impressed them most, the Germans agreed that the efficiency of our air/sea co-operation was uncanny. It would seem that it was almost an everyday occurrence for a U-boat to dive on sighting a Coastal Command aircraft, and then some hours later for surface craft to arrive and start hunting.[1]

Like the anti-U-boat offensive, the attack on enemy surface craft grew more deadly as the war progressed. From March 1941, when the campaign against shipping started in earnest, until May 1945 Coastal Command sank 166 merchant vessels of 470,000 tons and damaged another 351 of 1.1 million tons. In addition, the Command sank 107 German naval vessels and damaged another 401. During the war Coastal Command anti-shipping planes flew 85,382 sorties, amounting to 244,295 hours in the air, and fired 10,214 rocket projectiles and 749 torpedoes.

But this was not just a question of direct losses inflicted on the enemy's shipping. The threat of air attack meant the Reich had to pour resources into defending Axis shipping, from armaments to Sperrbrechers, a process that denuded the capacity to fight in other theatres. Around 204,000 Germans were engaged on minesweeping and merchant escort duties. As Christina Goulter has pointed out, 'half the material allocated to the 64 merchant vessels in the Emergency Shipbuilding Programme for 1944–45 could have been used in U-boat manufacture'.[2] The effectiveness of the anti-shipping offensive was highlighted after the war by the British Bombing Survey, which concluded that for 3,000 man hours spent on the strike wings the cost to Germany was 8,000 man hours, a factor of almost three to one in the wings' favour, whereas, according to this analysis, the bombing of Germany cost Britain more in man hours than the value of German manpower expended on the damage it caused. 'The only conclusion that can be drawn from these findings is that it would have been far more advantageous for the Allied war effort if resources had been diverted from Bomber Command to Coastal Command,' wrote Roy Conyers Nesbit.[3]

The Command's own statistical research outlined the extent of the overall effort. In total 238,313 sorties were flown by its crews, who spent 1.3 million hours in the air. 'At a conservative estimate this represents over 200 million miles or 800 circuits of the globe,' declared its in-house journal.[4] Every part of the service fought tirelessly. Over 3 million images were taken by its Photographic Reconnaissance Unit. Its meteorological flights undertook around 12,000 missions. More than 10,500 people were saved by its air-sea rescue operations. Its planes shot down nearly 300 Luftwaffe aircraft and laid 1,200 mines. In the process of all this diligence, its crews had won four VCs, seventeen George Medals and eighty-two DSOs. But the Command paid a high price for such heroism: 8,180 aircrew and 694 ground crew lost their lives during the conflict. Another 141 were missing in action, 516 were taken prisoner and 2,601 were wounded.[5]

Coastal Command's eventual triumph was not achieved without a tremendous struggle within the government and the top ranks of the armed forces, driven in part by the RAF's continuing faith in the primacy of the bomber offensive. It was a fight epitomized by restrictions in the supply of Liberators, which had a decisive influence on the Battle of the Atlantic once they became available in sufficient numbers. Professor Blackett believed that the case for Coastal Command was irrefutable, as he set out in a telling post-war essay for the 1953 edition of *Brassey's Annual*, where he wrote:

a long-range Liberator operating from Iceland and escorting the convoys in the middle of the Atlantic saved at least half a dozen merchant ships in the service lifetime of some 30 flying sorties. If used for bombing Berlin, the same aircraft in its service life would drop less than 100 tons of bombs and kill not more than a couple of dozen enemy men, women and children and destroy a number of houses. No one would dispute that the saving of six merchant ships and their crews and cargoes was of incomparably more value to the Allied war effort than the killing of two dozen enemy civilians, the destruction of a number of houses and a certain very small effect on production.[6]

In his own autobiography, Slessor wrote that 'the whole story of Very Long Range aircraft for convoy cover is one of misunderstanding, argument, procrastination and delay'.[7] Much of the responsibility can be put on Churchill, Portal, the Air Staff and Harris, whose collective attachment to urban bombing undoubtedly distorted the RAF's strategic priorities. Stephen Roskill even described the prime minister's failure to support Coastal Command sufficiently as 'his most tragic and far-reaching error', given that the shipping limitations 'delayed every offensive by the United Nations in every theatre'.[8] In his magisterial, three-volume account of the war at sea, Roskill wrote that

> in the early spring of 1943, we had a very narrow escape from defeat in the Battle of the Atlantic. Had we suffered such a defeat, history would have judged that the main cause had been the lack of two more squadrons of very long range aircraft for convoy protection duties.[9]

Another distinguished historian, Correlli Barnett, believed that the RAF's approach was too heavily influenced by Harris's dynamic personality. 'None of the men at the top of Coastal Command, Bowhill, Joubert or Slessor – who had great political skills – had quite the relentless, egotistical shove of Harris.'[10] The wartime officer Michael Lyne, later head of Air Force training, once said, 'I never thought that the Royal Air Force had a proper gut understanding of what was at stake in the Atlantic.'[11] In the view of Sir Edward Chilton, who was station commander at the vital Coastal Command base of RAF Chivenor in Devon during the war, the combination of Harris and Churchill had a negative impact: 'It was Churchill really; he was siding all the time with Harris, wanting him to bomb Germany.' On one specific point about long-range aircraft, Sir Edward held that Bomber Command should have been more generous about the use of Lancasters in the maritime war, particularly the Mark IIs with their Bristol Hercules radial engines, which Harris felt were inferior to the predominant Merlin-engined Lancasters.

> Harris should have released the Lancasters that had radial engines. They were not really popular in Bomber Command but properly handled and modified to take more fuel, they could have done almost as well as the Liberator. A few more squadrons of these would have made all the difference.[12]

After the war the Admiralty's former political chief, A. V. Alexander, complained bitterly that 'whatever good Coastal Command did, the credit was primarily due to Sir Dudley Pound and the other Admirals who fought the Air Ministry and the Air Marshals tooth and nail'.[13] The Navy had to fight the prime minister as well. But Slessor, who was a pragmatist, also felt some of the blame could be pinned on the Admiralty. In a revealing letter of 1947 to the Labour Secretary of State for Air Philip Noel-Baker, Slessor wrote that 'the implied suggestion that the Air Ministry and the Air Marshals were wicked and subversive in not yielding to each and every demand made upon them is nonsense'. With some justification, he went on to tell Noel-Baker that the Admiralty could be criticized for its failure to support the maritime air wing. 'One of our main troubles in the early stages of the late war was the complete lack of a coherent strategic policy', as demonstrated in the Navy's 'undue reliance' on ASDIC,

> the rejection of the idea that air power could be a serious menace to shipping [and] the emphasis on fleet action as the be all and end all of Naval Warfare. It is therefore hardly surprising that the Air Staff were not as impressed as they ought to have been with the menace of the U-boat or the need to build up the anti-submarine air force . . . Actually old Dudley Pound was far more broad-minded and far seeing than many of his staff. But with far too many admirals, the trouble was that they just did not believe that Air Power could have and was in fact having the decisive effect we now know.[14]

In the crucible of war, the practical needs of the Allies eventually triumphed over dogmatic theory, turning Coastal Command into a lethally effective arm of the RAF. By the time of victory over Germany, in May 1945, it was a formidable organization with 1,115 aircraft, including 225 Liberators, 88 Mosquitoes and 78 Sunderlands. Inevitably, the arrival of peace brought a rapid contraction. Within just a month twenty-two squadrons had been disbanded, all the remaining Liberator units had been transferred to Transport Command and the strike wings had been drastically cut. 'Very substantial reductions have already been made. In consequence, approximately 4,000 aircrew and 30,000 ground crews will become available for disposal,'

Douglas Evill, vice chief of the Air Staff, told Churchill just a month after VE Day.[15] The wheel now went full circle as Coastal Command became the Cinderella Service once more, with low priority for new equipment and its scope of operations limited. It saw action again briefly in late 1948 in Palestine and in the Berlin Airlift, where its increasingly elderly flying boats were invaluable in transporting bulk salt, but the rundown continued with final disbandment of the strike wings and the transfer of the Photographic Reconnaissance Unit to Bomber Command.

The one bright development for Coastal Command at this time was the introduction of the Avro Shackleton, its first post-war reconnaissance landplane. Derived from the enormously successful Lancaster, the Shackleton had its first flight on 9 March 1949 and, with its reliability and range, soon became the mainstay of Coastal Command in the 1950s, serving as a vital part of NATO's aerial defences in the Cold War against the Soviet Union by keeping watch on the Atlantic and European waters. There was a certain irony in the Shackleton's dominance, given that Sir Arthur Harris had so fiercely opposed any moves during the war to transfer any Lancasters to Coastal Command, but it proved a formidable operator, remaining in RAF service until 1991. Indeed, it far outlived Coastal Command itself, which continued to shrink throughout the 1950s despite its Cold War role. In 1953 the Command comprised just eight Shackleton squadrons of sixty-four aircraft, covering Gibraltar, the North-Western Approaches and the Atlantic, plus four Sunderland squadrons and four squadrons of Lockheed Neptunes, one of the first operational aircraft to be fitted with both jets and piston engines. There were also sixteen Bristol Sycamores, a highly versatile helicopter that could be adapted for several different functions: air rescue, training, anti-submarine warfare, and freight transport.

Coastal Command was again in action during the Suez Crisis in 1956, flying out Bomber Command ground crews to Malta and Cyprus, but within two years the service had been reduced to just sixty-seven aircraft, the vast majority of them Shackletons, though the Westland Whirlwind helicopter had come into service from 1954. Defence rationalization and the withdrawal from empire ensured that the contractions continued in the early sixties, though there was a brief revival of operational urgency when the Cuban Missile Crisis exploded in October 1962. In perhaps the most serious confrontation of the Cold War, Coastal Command squadrons were put on six hours' readiness and surveillance patrols were significantly increased before an uneasy settlement was reached. There were other flare-ups in the awkward peace of that decade, like Operation Chacewater in 1963 when Shackletons carried out long hours of reconnaissance to deter Soviet intelligence gathering by disguised fishing trawlers in British waters.

But, despite further overseas deployments such as the Aden Emergency in 1967, the end was near for Coastal Command. In late 1969 the RAF took delivery of the Nimrod, a derivative of the Comet jetliner that was designed to replace the Shackleton, and the start of a new era was the occasion to signal the passing of the old one, as the government took the decision that Coastal Command should be absorbed into RAF Strike Command, which had been formed in 1968 by the merger of Bomber and Fighter commands.

The formal disbandment came on 27 November 1969 at St Mawgan airfield in Cornwall, when the last commander-in-chief, Sir John Lapsley, who had flown Gloster Gladiator biplanes from a base on Malta during the war, took the salute from nine Shackletons, two Whirlwinds and a Nimrod. Coastal Command's existence, lasting thirty-three years, was over, but those who had served in the force had left behind the richest of legacies. The defeat of tyranny might well have been impossible without their valour and endurance.

Acknowledgements

This is my thirteenth book and I hope it is up to the standards of the previous ones. But I have to confess that it has been the most difficult one to write, not because of the subject matter but because I had to labour under two serious handicaps. The first came early in the research when the Covid pandemic suddenly limited access to libraries and archives.

This was compounded by the onset of Parkinson's disease, which placed severe restrictions on my mobility and drained my energy. However, with the aid of a team of diligent researchers, I was eventually able to view, via photographed files, most of the material I needed once the lockdown was lifted. So I am truly grateful to this group for their help, including Carolyn Alderson, Hugh Alexander, John Bruton, Peter Day, Liz Evans, Simon Fowler, Tina Hampson, Graham Hudson, Jennifer Irwin, Alina Nachescu, Russell Shanks and Steven Smith. There were two additional researchers who went far beyond the call of duty with their wise assistance and advice; they are Philip Mills and Dr Kevin Jones, who was magnificent in guiding me to fruitful areas of research.

I am indebted to the staffs of so many research centres for smoothing the flight path of this project. Among them are the National Archives, the Imperial War Museum, Liverpool's Maritime Archives, the RAF Museum, the British Library, the Public Record Office of Northern Ireland, the Churchill Archives at Cambridge University, and Christ Church Library at Oxford University.

I would also like to thank my dear old friend from Cambridge, Ray Harris, for availing me of his military expertise and for reading an early draft of the manuscript so diligently, as did the brilliant Matt Nixson on the *Daily Express*. There are few more warm-hearted or insightful people in British journalism than Matt.

This book would not have been possible without the tremendous backing of the team at John Murray, including Joe Zigmond, Candida MacDonogh, Hilary Hammond, Martin Bryant and Caroline Westmore, who all did a superb job in improving the manuscript, Juliet Brightmore for her excellent work on the pictures, and Xanthe Rendall for looking after the publicity.

As always, I could not have written this book without the wonderful support of my wife Elizabeth, whose fortitude, grace and devotion since my Parkinson's diagnosis have sustained me and enabled me to continue inflicting my words on the British public.

Like the rest of my family, my dear brother Jason has kept me going with his love, and it is to him that this book is dedicated.

Picture Credits

Getty Images: Pages 2 above left, 3 above right and below, 8 centre right. © Imperial War Museum, London: Page 1 above left (CH 14501), centre right (MH 25), below (CH 832). Page 2 above right (CH 9457), below (A 4527). Page 3 above left (CH 11854). Page 4 above (CH 2841), centre (CM 2363), below (CA 122). Page 5 above (MH 5117), centre (HU 91257), below (CM 5312). Page 6 above (CS 354), centre (CM 6221), below (CA 142). Page 7 above (C 4289), centre (CH 14001), below (C 4582). Page 8 above left (ME/RAF/7832), below (CH 15350).

Notes

Introduction: Valour

1. Orange, *Ensor's Endeavour.*
2. Ibid.
3. Ibid.
4. Ibid.
5. Price, *Aircraft versus Submarine.*
6. Bishop, *Wings.*
7. Interview with Peter Beswick, IWM audiotape 34137.
8. Gibbs, *Not Peace But a Sword.*
9. Harrison, *Ops in a Wimpy.*
10. Bolitho, *Command Performance.*
11. Memoir by Peter Burden, IWM document 12781.
12. Bird, *Heroes of Coastal Command.*
13. Klemens Schamong to Ronald Morgan, 11 April 1961, Lloyd Trigg papers, IWM document 09/69/1.
14. *Seek and Sink, Symposium on Battle of the Atlantic, October 1991.* Opened in 1941, Ballykelly was a remote, satellite airfield in the north-western corner of Northern Ireland.
15. Interview with Frank Tudor, IWM audiotape 17773.
16. Bolitho, *Command Performance.*
17. Jaworzyn, *No Place to Land.*
18. Joe Bodien to his sister Malvina, 15 November 1940, Bodien papers, IWM document 17760.
19. Dimbleby, *The Battle of the Atlantic.*
20. Joubert de la Ferté, *Birds and Fishes.*
21. Gartner, *Strategic Assessment in War.*
22. Dönitz, *Memoirs.*
23. Colman, *Liberators Over the Atlantic.*
24. Pitchfork, *Beaufighter Boys.*
25. Churchill to Sinclair, 22 February 1941, National Archives AIR 19/148.

Chapter 1: Reconnaissance

1. Padfield, *Dönitz*.
2. Despatch by Sir Frederick Bowhill, 31 May 1947, National Archives CAB 106/351.
3. Speech by Sir Kingsley Wood, House of Commons, 10 October 1939, Hansard.
4. *Sunday Times*, 29 October 1939.
5. *The Times*, 5 December 1939.
6. Figures from Air Staff Liaison, Air Ministry, 21 November 1945, National Archives ADM 199/690.
7. Joubert de la Ferté, *Birds and Fishes*.
8. Interview with Arthur Beech, IWM audiotape 26581.
9. Paper by Captain Dudley Peyton-Ward on history of Coastal Command, December 1942, National Archives AIR 15/343.
10. Nichols, *We Held the Key*.
11. Interview with Hugh Eccles, IWM audiotape 26581.
12. *Coastal Command Review* (August 1943), National Archives AIR 15/470.
13. Colman, *Liberators Over the Atlantic*.
14. Interview with Harry Prout, IWM audiotape 33808.
15. Dudley-Gordon, *I Seek My Prey in the Waters*.
16. Interview with George Bain, IWM audiotape 26803.
17. Interview with Squadron Leader Tony Spooner, IWM audiotape 13273.
18. Peter Burden, private memoir, IWM document 12781.
19. Terraine, *Business in Great Waters*.
20. Baxter, *The Secret History of RDX*.
21. Despatch by Sir Frederick Bowhill, 31 May 1947, National Archives CAB 106/351.
22. Macintyre, *The Battle of the Atlantic*.
23. Joubert, *Birds and Fishes*.
24. Goulter, *A Forgotten Offensive*.
25. Buckley, 'Coastal Command in the Second World War'.
26. *Daily Mail*, 18 June 1936.
27. *Daily Telegraph*, 18 June 1936.
28. Joubert, *Birds and Fishes*.
29. Debate on the Fleet Air Arm, House of Commons, 30 July 1937, Hansard.

30. Alan Smith, *Oxford Dictionary of National Biography*, s.v. Bowhill, Sir Frederick William.
31. Goulter, *A Forgotten Offensive*.
32. Despatch by Sir Frederick Bowhill, 31 May 1947, National Archives CAB 106/351.
33. Ibid.

Chapter 2: Retreat

1. Monthly summary by Bowhill, 5 February 1940, National Archives AIR 15/758.
2. *Daily Mail*, 31 January 1940.
3. Interview with Hugh Beresford, IWM audiotape 9939.
4. Nesbit, *The Expendable Squadron*.
5. Speech by Hugh Dalton, House of Commons, 7 March 1940, Hansard.
6. Interview with Geoffrey Garside, IWM audiotape 12196.
7. Schuster, 'Aerial Minesweeping'.
8. Report by the Deputy Chief of the Air Staff, 10 February 1940, National Archives CAB 65/5/33. The Messerschmitt Bf 109 was a legendary German fighter and rival of the Spitfire.
9. Monthly summary by Bowhill, 6 April 1940, National Archives AIR 15/578.
10. *Daily Telegraph*, 20 February 1940.
11. Peirse to Brownhill, 4 April 1940, National Archives AIR 15/26.
12. Bolitho, *The Task for Coastal Command*.
13. Ashworth, *RAF Coastal Command 1936–1969*.
14. Account by George Ogwyn's granddaughter Helen, *Guardian*, 12 June 2010.
15. Report by Air Secretary to War Cabinet, 7 May 1940, National Archives CAB 65/7/6.
16. Monthly summary by Bowhill, 11 June 1940, National Archives AIR 15/758.
17. Cole, *Beatrice Webb's Diaries*.
18. The Germans called their rapid-attack craft the Schnellboot, or 'fast boat', but it was designated the E, or 'enemy', boat by the Allies.
19. *London Gazette*, 14 June 1940.
20. Ewan Burnet, *Avro Ansons vs Messerschmitts 109s, Dunkirk 1940*, RAF Museum collections, 7 August 2018, https://www.rafmuseum.org.uk/blog/avro-ansons-vs-messerschmitt-109s-dunkirk-1940/

21. Panton, *Six Weeks of Blenheim Summer.*
22. Speech by Churchill, House of Commons, 4 June 1940, Hansard.
23. Monthly summary by Bowhill, National Archives AIR 15/758.
24. Bowman, *Deep Sea Hunters.*
25. Douglas to Bowhill (draft), June 1940, National Archives AIR 20/2779.
26. Bowhill to Douglas, 17 June 1940, National Archives AIR 20/2779.
27. Douglas to Bowhill, 22 June 1940, National Archives, AIR 20/2779.
28. Douglas to Bowhill, 15 July 1940, National Archives, AIR 15/26.
29. Bowhill to Douglas, 18 July 1940, National Archives AIR 15/26.
30. Bowhill to Portal, 27 July 1940, National Archives AIR 15/26.
31. Despatch by Sir Frederick Bowhill, 27 May 1947, National Archives CAB 106/351.
32. Newall to Bowhill, 16 October 1940, National Archives AIR 15/26.

Chapter 3: Control

1. Bowman, *Deep Sea Hunters.*
2. Monthly summary by Bowhill, 10 August 1940, National Archives 15/758.
3. Despatch by Sir Frederick Bowhill, 31 May 1947, National Archives CAB 106/351.
4. Slessor to Philip Noel-Baker, 20 March 1947, National Archives AIR 75/17.
5. Memorandum by Ivor Lloyd, 22 February 1940, National Archives AIR 15/456.
6. Churchill, *The Second World War*, vol. 2, *Their Finest Hour.*
7. Gilbert, *The Churchill Documents*, vol. 15.
8. Monthly summary by Bowhill, 9 October 1940, National Archives AIR 15/758.
9. Bowhill to Portal, 25 October 1940, Portal papers, Lord Portal Collection, Christ Church, University of Oxford.
10. Despatch by Sir Frederick Bowhill, 31 May 1947, National Archives CAB 106/351.
11. Bird, *Heroes of Coastal Command.*
12. Hendrie, *Short Sunderland.* Bill Gibson was nicknamed Hoot after the Hollywood star Ed 'Hoot' Gibson, who was renowned for playing cowboys.
13. Interview with William Day, IWM audiotape 11221.

14. Bowhill to Portal, 25 October 1940, Portal papers.
15. McKinstry, *Churchill and Attlee*.
16. Denis Richards, *Oxford Dictionary of National Biography*, s.v. Hillary, Richard Hope.
17. Danchev and Todman (eds), *Alanbrooke: War Diaries 1939–1945*.
18. Broadhurst, *Churchill's Anchor.*
19. Note by Portal, 6 December 1940, National Archives AIR 19/554.
20. Paper by A. V. Alexander to War Cabinet, 4 November 1940, National Archives CAB 66/13/14.
21. Terraine, *The Right of the Line.*
22. Faulkner and Bell (eds), *Decision in the Atlantic.*
23. Ibid.
24. Terraine, *The Right of the Line.*
25. Faulkner and Bell (eds), *Decision in the Atlantic.*
26. Slessor to Hilary St George Saunders, 22 June 1949, National Archives AIR 75/17.
27. Simpson, *A Dictionary of Coastal Command.*
28. Sinclair to Churchill, 23 November 1940, National Archives AIR 19/554.
29. Portal to Sinclair, 24 November 1940, Slessor papers, RAF Museum AC 75/9/60.
30. Paper by Sir Frederick Bowhill, 19 November 1940, National Archives AIR 15/288.
31. Paper by A. V. Alexander, 20 November 1940, National Archives CAB 66/13/35.
32. Minutes of Defence Committee, 4 December 1940, National Archives ADM 116/4869.
33. Churchill to Eden, 11 December 1940, National Archives PREM 3/171/2.
34. Slessor to Hilary St George Saunders, 22 June 1949, National Archives AIR 75/17.
35. Note by Portal and Pound to Churchill, 4 December 1940, National Archives AIR 20/2891.

Chapter 4: Research

1. Portal to Bowhill, 6 December 1940, National Archives AIR 15/26.
2. Interview with Hugh Eccles, IWM audiotape 26581.

3. Joe Collins, 'Memoir of a European War', Churchill Archive CLNS, Note 13.
4. Nichols, *We Held the Key*.
5. Memoir by Geoff Walker, website of 95 Squadron, www.95squadron. co.uk
6. Bowman, *Deep Sea Hunters*.
7. Bowhill to Admiralty, 9 June 1941, National Archives AIR 15/288.
8. Interview with Peter Beswick, IWM audiotape 34137.
9. Pitchfork, *Beaufighter Boys*.
10. Bowyer, *Men of Coastal Command*.
11. Memo to Chiefs of Staff Committee, 14 March 1941, National Archives CAB 80/26.
12. Bowhill to Freeman, 14 February 1940, National Archives AIR 15/456.
13. Bowhill to Freeman, 29 December 1940, National Archives, AIR 20/2779.
14. Freeman to Bowhill, 30 December 1940, National Archives AIR 20/2779.
15. Bowhill to Freeman, 25 February 1941, National Archives AIR 20/2889.
16. Cowling, *The Journey*.
17. Interview with William Middlemiss, IWM audiotape 12153.
18. Orange, *Ensor's Endeavour*.
19. Gibbs, *Torpedo Leader*.
20. Interview with Alan Wilson, IWM audiotape 17551.
21. Papers of Group Captain Guy Bolland, IWM documents 12193.
22. Freeman to Bowhill, 7 April 1941, National Archives AIR 15/26.
23. *London Gazette*, 10 March 1942.
24. Budiansky, *Blackett's War*.
25. Ibid.
26. Hankey to Sinclair, 6 January 1941, National Archives AIR 19/148.
27. Air Ministry memo to Sinclair's office, 7 February 1941, National Archives AIR 19/148.
28. Joubert to Pile, 12 February 1941, National Archives AIR 19/148.
29. Beaverbrook to Sinclair, 23 February 1941, National Archives AIR 19/148.
30. Budiansky, *Blackett's War*.
31. Ibid.
32. Sir Bernard Lovell, 'Patrick Blackett, Baron Blackett of Chelsea, 18 November 1897 – 13 July 1974', *Biographical Memoirs of Fellows of the Royal Society* (1975).

33. Interview with Edward Shackleton, IWM audiotape 11454.
34. Roberts, *The Storm of War.*
35. Gilbert, *Winston S. Churchill*, vol. 6, *Finest Hour.*
36. Churchill, *The Second World War*, vol. 3, *Triumph and Tragedy.*
37. Lardas, *The Battle of the Atlantic*, vol. 1.
38. Despatch by Sir Frederick Bowhill, 31 May 1947, National Archives CAB 106/351.
39. Ibid.
40. Hugh Sebag-Montefiore, *Enigma.*
41. Interview with Tony Spooner, IWM audiotape 13273.
42. Minutes of Battle of the Atlantic Committee, 5 April 1941 AIR 205/11.
43. Report by Flight Lieutenant Vaughan, 23 June 1941, National Archives AIR 15/415.
44. Despatch by Sir Frederick Bowhill, 31 May 1947, National Archives CAB 106/351.
45. *Daily Mail*, 29 May 1941.
46. Speech by Churchill on the war situation, House of Commons, 27 May 1941, Hansard.
47. Greenhous et al., *The Crucible of War.*

Chapter 5: Atlantic

1. Churchill to Sinclair, 4 December 1940, Churchill papers CHAR 20/13/9.
2. Churchill to Sinclair, 8 December 1940, Churchill papers CHAR 20/13/9.
3. Orange, *Ensor's Endeavour.*
4. Profile of Joubert by Arthur Longmore for the BBC, 12 December 1966, National Archives DC74/122/36.
5. Joubert de la Ferté, *The Fated Sky.*
6. Freeman to Portal, 14 June 1941, National Archives AIR 20/2779.
7. Joubert to Portal, 14 June 1941, National Archives AIR 15/27.
8. Joubert to Portal, 20 June 1941, National Archives AIR 14/481.
9. Peirse to Joubert, 28 June 1941, National Archives AIR 20/2779.
10. Redford, 'Inter- and Intra-Service Rivalries in the Battle of the Atlantic'.
11. Despatch by Sir Philip Joubert de La Ferté, 1947, National Archives CAB 106/351.

12. Minutes of Battle of the Atlantic Committee, 9 July 1941, National Archives ADM 1205/11.
13. Ibid.
14. Churchill to Portal, 21 July 1941, National Archives PREM 3/97/2.
15. Portal to Churchill, 25 July 1941, National Archives PREM 3/97/2.
16. Ismay to Freeman, 20 August 1941, National Archives AIR 20/3045.
17. Freeman to Ismay, 28 August 1941, National Archives AIR 20/3045.
18. Minutes of AOC's Daily Conference, 29 August 1941, National Archives AIR 15/359.
19. Churchill to Pound and Alexander, 8 October 1941, National Archives PREM 3/97/2.
20. Alexander to Churchill, 14 October 1941, National Archives AIR 20/3045.
21. Minutes of Battle of the Atlantic Committee, 28 October 1941, National Archives AIR 1205/11.
22. Roskill, *The War at Sea*, vol. 1.
23. Joubert to Portal, 1 August 1941, National Archives AIR 15/225.
24. Portal to Joubert, 6 August 1941, National Archives AIR 20/2079.
25. Dudley-Gordon, *I Seek My Prey in the Waters*.
26. Bolitho, *A Penguin in the Eyrie*.
27. Robert Gore-Langton, 'Tail-End Terry', *The Spectator*, 18 March 2017.
28. Dudley-Gordon, *I Seek My Prey in the Waters*.
29. Minutes of Battle of the Atlantic Committee, 11 November 1941, National Archives ADM 205/23.
30. Minutes of Battle of the Atlantic Committee, 28 October 1941, National Archives ADM 205/23.
31. Dimbleby, *The Battle of the Atlantic*.
32. Despatch by Sir Philip Joubert de la Ferté, 1947, National Archives CAB 106/351.
33. Ashworth, *Coastal Command 1936–1969*.
34. Minutes of Battle of the Atlantic Committee, 1 July 1941, National Archives ADM 1205/11.
35. Joubert to Sinclair, 14 September 1941, National Archives AIR 19/183.
36. Despatch by Sir Philip Joubert de la Ferté, 1947, National Archives CAB 106/351.
37. Ibid.
38. Joubert to Freeman, 15 December 1941, National Archives AIR 20/2779.

39. Freeman to Joubert, 17 December 1941, National Archives AIR 20/2779.

40. Despatch by Sir Philip Joubert de la Ferté, 1947, National Archives CAB 106/351.

41. Ibid.

42. Peirse to Joubert, 28 June 1941, National Archives AIR 20/2779.

43. Minutes of AOC's Daily Conference, 15 July 1941, National Archives AIR 15/359.

44. Interview with Alan Wilson, IWM audiotape 17551.

45. Interview with Geoffrey Garside, IWM audiotape 12196.

46. Rayner, *Coastal Command Pilot*.

47. Goulter, 'The Role of Intelligence in Coastal Command's Anti-Shipping Campaign'.

48. Joubert to Pound, 14 November 1941, National Archives AIR 20/2779.

49. Freeman to Joubert, 15 November 1941, National Archives AIR 20/2779.

50. Joubert to Freeman, 16 November 1941, National Archives AIR 20/2779.

Chapter 6: Endurance

1. Bolitho, *Command Performance*.

2. Joubert de la Ferté, *The Fated Sky*.

3. Nichols, *We Held the Key*.

4. HMSO, *Air Ministry Account*.

5. Ibid.

6. Interview with Malcolm Hamilton, IWM audiotape 18264.

7. Leslie Baveystock, *Wavetops at My Wingtips*.

8. Memoir of John Appleton, IWM document 1577.

9. Nichols, *We Held the Key*.

10. Interview with George Bain, IWM audiotape 26803.

11. Baveystock, *Wavetops at My Wingtips*.

12. Sanders, *Of Wind and Water*.

13. Hunter, *From Coastal Command to Captivity*.

14. Baveystock, *Wavetops at My Wingtips*.

15. Memoir of John Appleton, IWM document 1577.

16. Interview with Don Boorman, IWM audiotape 28931.

17. Ibid.

18. Interview with William Middlemiss, IWM audiotape 12153.
19. War diary of John Davis, 1939–46, IWM document 9065.
20. Greenhous et al., *The Crucible of War.*
21. Interview with William Day, IWM audiotape 11221.
22. Interview with Arthur Lane, IWM audiotape 10007.
23. HMSO, *Air Ministry Account.*
24. Coastal Command paper on U-boat tactics, 24 July 1942, National Archives AIR 16/305.
25. Paper by Coastal Command HQ, 17 July 1941, National Archives AIR 15/63.
26. Paper on surfaced U-boats, 19 May 1942, National Archives AIR 15/304.
27. Paper on U-boat warfare,14 November 1942, National Archives AIR 15/343.
28. Paper on surprise in U-boat attacks, 20 March 1942, National Archives AIR 15/304.
29. Coastal Command leaflet, 1942, National Archives Air 15/397.
30. Hans Goebeler, *Steel Boats and Iron Hearts.*
31. Spooner, *Coastal Ace.*
32. Ibid.
33. Coastal Command paper on Terry Bulloch, 29 March 1943, National Archives AIR 15/43.
34. Spooner, *Coastal Ace.*
35. Nesbit, *The Strike Wings.*
36. Interview with Tony Spooner, IWM audiotape 13273.
37. Gibbs, *Torpedo Leader.*
38. Bowyer, *Men of Coastal Command.*
39. *London Gazette*, 24 June 1941.

Chapter 7: Dash

1. Winston Churchill, *The Second World War*, vol. 4, *The Hinge of Fate.*
2. Durston to Freeman, 23 December 1941, National Archives AIR 20/3045.
3. Paper on Admiralty requirements, 14 February 1942, National Archives PREM 3/97/1.
4. Air Staff paper, 14 February 1942, National Archives AIR 20/3045.
5. Terraine, *Business in Great Waters.*

6. Ibid.
7. Roskill, *Churchill and the Admirals.*
8. Mark Simmons, 'The German Channel Dash', *Warfare History Network*, April 2020, https://warfarehistorynetwork.com/article/the-german-channel-dash/
9. Potter, *Fiasco.*
10. Simmons, 'The German Channel Dash'.
11. Byford, 'Executive Fuller'.
12. Interview with Arthur Beech, IWM audiotape 30257.
13. Interview with Edward Shackleton, IWM audiotape 11454.
14. *The Times*, 14 February 1942.
15. Nesbit, *The Expendable Squadron.*
16. Joubert de la Ferté, *The Fated Sky.*
17. Douglas, *Years of Command.*
18. Speech by Lord Winster, House of Lords, 15 April 1942, Hansard
19. Speech by Lord Trenchard, House of Lords, 15 April 1942, Hansard.
20. Byford, 'Executive Fuller'.
21. Greenhous et al., *The Crucible of War.*
22. Joubert to Freeman, 21 February 1942, National Archives AIR 20/2779.
23. Freeman to Joubert, 25 February 1942, National Archives AIR 20/2779.
24. Roskill, *The War at Sea*, vol. 2.
25. Memorandum by Sinclair, 8 March 1942, National Archives PREM 3/97/1.
26. Memorandum by Churchill, 21 March 1942, National Archives PREM 3/97/1.
27. McKinstry, *Lancaster.*
28. Paul Johnson, 'One Man and His Dogma', *The Spectator*, 8 August 2009.
29. Minutes of Chiefs of Staff Committee, 27 March 1942, National Archives PREM 3/97/1.
30. Portal to Churchill, 28 March 1942, National Archives AIR 20/2779.
31. Alexander to Churchill, 13 April 1942, National Archives AIR 20/2779.
32. Note by Portal, 15 April 1942, National Archives AIR 20/3045.
33. Budiansky, *Blackett's War.*
34. van der Vat, *The Atlantic Campaign.*
35. Budiansky, *Blackett's War.*
36. Ibid.
37. Ibid.
38. Roskill, *Churchill and the Admirals.*

39. Pound to Portal, 6 May 1942, National Archives AIR 20/2811.
40. Minutes of Standing Committee on U-boat Attacks, 8 May 1942, National Archives AIR 15/238.

Chapter 8: Light

1. Fraser, *Live to Look Again*.
2. Ibid.
3. Ibid.
4. Ibid. The RAF's nickname for the Wellington, Wimpy, was inspired by the rotund, hamburger-munching character J. Wellington Wimpy in the popular American cartoon series *Popeye*.
5. Greswell, 'Leigh Light Wellingtons in Coastal Command'.
6. Ibid.
7. Joubert de la Ferté, *The Fated Sky*.
8. Air Ministry report, 19 January 1944, National Archives AIR 15/460.
9. Proposal by de Verd Leigh, 23 October 1940, National Archives AIR 15/460.
10. Report by de Verd Leigh on the development of his light, 28 December 1943, National Archives AIR 15/460.
11. Bowhill to Air Ministry, 18 May 1941, National Archives AIR 15/460.
12. Bromet to Bowhill, 17 May 1941, National Archives AIR 15/460.
13. Report by de Verd Leigh on the development of his light, 28 December 1943, National Archives AIR 15/460. Major Jack Savage claimed to have invented the art of sky writing, which in the 1920s became a popular form of advertising.
14. Joubert de la Ferté, *Birds and Fishes*.
15. Fraser, *Live to Look Again*.
16. Report by de Verd Leigh on the development of his light, 28 December 1943, National Archives AIR 15/460.
17. Joubert to Air Ministry, 3 February 1942, National Archives AIR 15/460.
18. Joubert to Cripps, 7 December 1942, National Archives AIR 15/459.
19. Cripps to Joubert, 13 January 1943, National Archives AIR 15/459.
20. Report by de Verd Leigh on the development of his light, 28 December 1943, National Archives AIR 15/460.
21. Terraine, *Business in Great Waters*.
22. Bird, *Heroes of Coastal Command*.

23. Interview with Ken Gatward, printed in RAF Association newsletter, 12 June 2020. The regime of Vichy France collaborated with the Nazi occupation and was headed by First World War hero Marshal Philippe Pétain.

24. Ibid.

25. Quoted in Bird, *Heroes of Coastal Command*.

26. Richards and St George Saunders, *The RAF 1939–45*, vol. 2.

27. Baxter, *The Secret History of RDX*.

28. Ibid.

29. Ibid.

30. Ibid.

31. Ibid.

32. Ibid.

33. *Coastal Command Review* (August 1942), National Archives, AIR 15/470.

34. Dimbleby, *The Battle of the Atlantic*.

35. Paper by Portal, 9 July 1942, National Archives AIR 15/343.

36. Pound to Portal, 13 July 1942, National Archives AIR 20/3400.

37. Joubert to Anderson, 15 July 1942, National Archives AIR 15/368.

38. Minutes of Anti-Submarine Committee, 26 August 1942, National Archives AIR 15/230.

39. Minutes of Anti-Submarine Committee, 23 September 1942, National Archives AIR 15/230.

40. Paper on the development of Coastal Command, December 1942 National Archives AIR 15/343.

41. Dönitz, *Memoirs*.

42. Ibid.

43. Ibid.

44. Dimbleby, *The Battle of the Atlantic*.

45. Portal to Churchill, 4 September 1942, National Archives AIR 20/3045.

46. Cherwell to Churchill, 4 June 1942, National Archives, PREM 3/97/1.

47. Churchill to Portal, 5 June 1942, National Archives PREM 3/97/1.

48. Portal to Churchill, 15 June 1942, National Archives PREM 3/97/1.

49. Churchill to Sinclair and Alexander, 14 July 1942, National Archives AIR 20/2079.

50. Alexander to Churchill, 13 August 1942, National Archives PREM 3/97/1.

51. Churchill to Pound, handwritten note, 24 August 1942, National Archives PREM 3/97/1.

52. Pound to Churchill, 28 August 1942, National Archives PREM 3/97/1.
53. Probert, *Bomber Harris*.
54. Joubert to Portal, 20 September 1942, National Archives AIR 20/2889.
55. Cherwell to Churchill, 15 September 1942, National Archives PREM 3/97/1.
56. Churchill to Sinclair, 16 September 1942, National Archives PREM 3/97/1.
57. Portal to Churchill, 4 September 1942, National Archives AIR 20/3045.
58. Danchev and Todman (eds), *Alanbrooke: War Diaries 1939–1945*.

Chapter 9: Gap

1. *Coastal Command Review* (June 1945), National Archives AIR 15/474.
2. Terraine, *Business in Great Waters*.
3. Tovey to Joubert, 20 September 1942, National Archives AIR 15/284.
4. Report by Joubert, 11 October 1942, National Archives AIR 15/284.
5. Telegraphed instructions to 15, 18 and 19 Groups, 7 October 1942, National Archives AIR 15/284.
6. Joubert to Air Ministry, 25 March 1942, National Archives AIR 15/109.
7. Lovell, *Echoes of War*.
8. Terraine, *Business in Great Waters*.
9. Budiansky, *Blackett's War*.
10. Pound to Portal, 20 September 1942, National Archives AIR 20/3045.
11. Portal to Pound, 1 October 1942, National Archives AIR 20/3045.
12. Minutes of Cripps's meeting, 20 November 1942, National Archives AIR 15/342.
13. Roskill, *Churchill and the Admirals*.
14. Directive on Torch, 22 October 1942, National Archives AIR 16/681.
15. Account in James Louw papers, IWM documents 5/60/1.
16. Intervention by Lord Clark, House of Lords, 29 November 1942, Hansard.
17. Redford, 'The Crisis in the Battle of the Atlantic'.
18. Paper by First Sea Lord, 13 November 1942, National Archives ADM 199/1690.
19. Paper by A. V. Alexander, 8 November 1942, National Archives ADM 205/23.
20. Edwards, *Dönitz and the Wolf Packs*.
21. Speech by Churchill, House of Commons, 15 December 1942, Hansard.

22. Rayner, *Escort: The Battle of the Atlantic.*
23. Alexander to Sinclair, 12 October 1942, National Archives ADM 1/12128.
24. Orange, *Slessor.*
25. Joubert de la Ferté, *Birds and Fishes.*
26. Minutes of 8th meeting of Coastal Command's Anti-Submarine Committee, 16 December 1942, National Archives AIR 15/284.
27. Ibid.

Chapter 10: Convoy

1. Sir Max Hastings, *Oxford Dictionary of National Biography*, s.v. Slessor, Sir John.
2. Macmillan, *War Diaries.*
3. Orange, *Slessor.*
4. Ibid.
5. Ibid.
6. Slessor, *The Central Blue.*
7. Ibid.
8. Minutes of Anti-U-boat Warfare Committee, 15 January 1943, National Archives AIR 15/230.
9. Bolitho, *A Penguin in the Eyrie.*
10. *Seek and Sink, Symposium on Battle of the Atlantic, October 1991.*
11. Memoir of Joe Collins, Churchill Archive Centre, CLNS 2.
12. Dimbleby, *The Battle of the Atlantic.*
13. Buell, *Master of Seapower.*
14. Memoir of Joe Collins, Churchill Archive Centre, CLNS 2.
15. Slessor to Sir Edgar Ludlow-Hewitt, 19 February 1943, National Archives AIR 15/340.
16. Air Ministry to Joubert, 1 November 1942, National Archives AIR 20/2889.
17. Note of meeting at MAP, 15 November 1942, National Archives ADM 205/21.
18. Kimball (ed.), *Churchill and Roosevelt*, vol. 2.
19. Terraine, *Business in Great Waters.*
20. Slessor, *The Central Blue.*
21. Bolitho, *A Penguin in the Eyrie.*
22. Slessor, *The Central Blue.*

23. Orange, *Slessor.*
24. Slessor to group commanders, undated 1943, National Archives AIR 75/18.
25. Joubert to Air Ministry, 15 October 1942, National Archives, AIR 15/284.
26. Dönitz, *Memoirs.*
27. Duncan Redford, 'Inter- and Intra-Service Relations in the Battle of the Atlantic'.
28. Paper by Senior Air Staff Officer, 2 December 1942, National Archives AIR 15/284.
29. Minutes of Anti-U-boat Warfare Committee, 17 March 1943, National Archives AIR 15/284.
30. van der Vat, *The Atlantic Campaign.*
31. Roosevelt to King and Marshall, 18 March 1943, Franklin D. Roosevelt Presidential Library.
32. Padfield, *Dönitz.*
33. Memorandum by Air Ministry and Admiralty, 21 April 1943, National Archives FO 954/32.
34. Bowman, *Deep Sea Hunters.*
35. Goebeler, *Steel Boats and Iron Hearts.*
36. *Coastal Command Review* (July 1943), National Archives AIR 15/470.
37. Ibid.
38. Memoir of H. Platt, IWM private paper 5987.
39. Colman, *Liberators Over the Atlantic.*
40. Bowman, *Deep Sea Hunters.*
41. Cooper, *Sub Hunters.*
42. Ibid.
43. *Daily Telegraph*, 18 May 1943.
44. Speech by Lord Bruntsfield, House of Lords, 2 June 1943, Hansard.
45. Dönitz, *Memoirs.*

Chapter 11: Bay

1. Hendrie, *Short Sunderland* has a thorough account of the episode.
2. Australian War Memorial collection, C157169.
3. Slessor, *The Central Blue.*
4. Slessor to Portal, 15 May 1943, National Archives AIR 75/17.
5. Slessor to Pound, 4 April 1943, National Archives AIR 20/2889.

6. Budiansky, *Blackett's War.*

7. Despatch by Slessor, 1947, National Archives CAB 106/351.

8. Slessor to Trenchard, 6 July 1943, National Archives AIR 75/15.

9. Slessor to Brind, 27 April 1943, National Archives AIR 75/15.

10. Slessor to Blackett, 13 April 1943, National Archives AIR 75/15.

11. Slessor to Trenchard, 6 July 1943, National Archives AIR 75/15.

12. Fraser, *Live to Look Again.*

13. Wilson and Robinson, *Coastal Command Leads the Invasion.*

14. Franks, *Conflict over the Bay.*

15. Teddy Suhren, *Ace of Aces.*

16. Instruction on anti-submarine tactics, 5 May 1943, National Archives AIR 15/32.

17. Minutes of Anti-Submarine Committee, 8 June 1943, National Archives AIR 15/32.

18. Slessor, *The Central Blue.*

19. Nesbit, *The Strike Wings.*

20. Franks, *Conflict over the Bay.*

21. Peter Burden, private memoir, IWM document 12781.

22. Signal by Durston, 12 June 1943, National Archives AIR 15/224.

23. Franks, *Conflict over the Bay.*

24. Ibid.

25. *Melbourne Age*, 15 March 2019.

26. *London Gazette*, 1 October 1943.

27. *Melbourne Age*, 15 March 2019.

28. Slessor to Portal, 15 May 1943, National Archives AIR 75/17.

29. Minutes of Admiralty/Coastal Command Committee, 29 July 1943, National Archives AIR 15/321.

30. Paper by Coastal Command, 31 August 1943, National Archives AIR 15/233.

31. Wing Commander Lionel Cohen to Coastal Command HQ, 8 September 1943, National Archives AIR 15/233.

32. Slessor to Evill, 27 August 1943, National Archives AIR 15/233.

33. Baker to Slessor, 20 September 1943, National Archives AIR 15/233.

34. *Daily Telegraph*, 13 October 1943.

35. Clarence Howard-Johnson, director of the Anti-U-boat Division of the Admiralty, to Slessor, 31 October 1943, National Archives AIR 15/233.

36. *Coastal Command Review* (December 1943), National Archives AIR 15/470.

Chapter 12: Wing

1. Slessor to Portal, 18 May 1943, National Archives AIR 75/17. The two squadrons are 489 Squadron of the Royal New Zealand Air Force, based near Wick in Scotland and flying Hampdens in early 1943 before its conversion to Beaufighters later in the year; and 455 Squadron of the Royal Australian Air Force, based at Leuchars in Scotland and flying Hampdens.
2. Pound to Portal, 8 May 1942, National Archives AIR 20/2891.
3. Memo by the Torpedo Development Unit, 10 November 1942, National Archives AIR 15/633.
4. Goulter, *A Forgotten Offensive*.
5. Paper by Directorate of Torpedo Operations, 11 February 1943 AIR 15/379.
6. Minutes of Conference, 22 February 1943, National Archives AIR 15/379.
7. Pitchfork, *Beaufighter Boys*.
8. Ibid.
9. Nesbit, *The Strike Wings*. The Women's Auxiliary Air Force reached its peak in 1943, with over 180,000 staff.
10. Despatch by Sir John Slessor, 30 January 1948, National Archives CAB 106/351.
11. Ibid.
12. Rocket projectile as a primary weapon, Coastal Command report, 17 July 1944, National Archives AIR 15/167.
13. Bowyer, *Coastal Command at War*.
14. Pitchfork, *Beaufighter Boys*.
15. 'Max Horton: The Man who Beat the U-Boats', *Daily Express*, 2 August 1943.
16. *Daily Telegraph*, 4 August 1943.
17. Minutes of War Cabinet, 16 August 1943, National Archives, CAB 65/35/25.
18. Interview with Tony Spooner, IWM audiotape 13273.
19. Interview with Sir Bernard Lovell, 'Infighting Between Bomber and Coastal Commands', www.webofstories.com/play/bernard.lovell/36
20. Ibid.
21. Despatch by Sir John Slessor, 30 January 1948, National Archives CAB 106/351.

22. Baveystock, *Wavetops at My Wingtips.*
23. Figures from Admiralty Statement to Parliament, March 1946, HMSO Command Paper 6751.
24. Report in the *Daily Telegraph*, 20 December 1943.
25. Katharine Campbell, *Behold the Dark Gray Man.*
26. Ibid.
27. Douglas, *Years of Command.*
28. Churchill to Roosevelt, 4 January 1944, Churchill Archives CHAR 20/154/20.
29. Vincent Orange, *Oxford Dictionary of National Biography*, s.v. Douglas, (William) Sholto.
30. Katharine Campbell, *Behold the Dark Gray Man.*
31. Interview with Edward Shackleton, IWM audiotape 11454.
32. Katharine Campbell, *Behold the Dark Gray Man.*
33. Ibid.

Chapter 13: Rescue

1. Bennett (ed.), *Hitchcock's Partner in Suspense.*
2. McGowan, 'The Donegal Corridor'.
3. Harrison, *Ops in a Wimpy.*
4. Interview with Edward Shackleton, IWM audiotape 11454.
5. Nichols, *We Held the Key.* The Entertainments National Service Association (ENSA) was set up in 1939 to provide entertainment to the British armed forces, and many members went on to become household names, among them Frankie Howerd, Peter Sellers and Vera Lynn.
6. Interview with Dorothy Williams, IWM audiotape 9440.
7. Memories of Gwen Webster, BBC People's War archive, article A4354012.
8. Memoir of Bryant Wolstenholme, IWM documents 726.
9. Bernard Połoniecki, 'Fly for Your Life', website of the Kraków Aviation Museum.
10. Colman, *Liberators Over the Atlantic.*
11. Ted Rayner, *Coastal Command Pilot.*
12. Interview with Arthur Beech, IWM audiotape 30267.
13. Ashworth, *Coastal Command 1936–1969.*
14. Nesbit, *The Expendable Squadron.*
15. Polmar and Bessette, *Spyplanes.*

16. Hendrie, *The Cinderella Service.*
17. Ashworth, *Coastal Command 1936–1969.*
18. *Torontoist,* 14 June 2014.
19. Ibid.
20. Ibid.
21. Ibid.
22. Ibid.
23. Bowyer, *Men of Coastal Command.*
24. Ibid.
25. Ibid.
26. Interview with Kenneth Harper, IWM audiotape 17266.
27. Hunter, *From Coastal Command to Captivity.*
28. Baveystock, *Wavetops at My Wingtips.*
29. Połoniecki, 'Fly for Your Life'.
30. Papers of H. Platt, IWM documents 5987.

Chapter 14: Invasion

1. Speech by Wilfrid Roberts, House of Commons, 29 February 1944, Hansard.
2. Wing Commander E. P. W. Hutton, the North Coates Strike Wing, IWM document 87/39/1.
3. Pitchfork, *Beaufighter Boys.*
4. Ibid.
5. Despatch by Sholto Douglas, 1947, National Archives CAB 106/35.
6. Jaworzyn, *No Place to Land.*
7. Douglas, *Years of Command.*
8. Goulter, *A Forgotten Offensive.*
9. Douglas, *Years of Command.*
10. Sholto Douglas, directive to group commanders, 18 April 1944, National Archives AIR 15/157.
11. Note on South-Western Approaches, 18 April 1944, National Archives AIR 15/157.
12. Paper for 16 Group, 18 April 1944, National Archives AIR 15/157.
13. Note on weapons for Overlord, 18 April 1944, National Archives 15/157.
14. Ellwood to Fighter Command, 13 May 1944, National Archives AIR 15/401.

15. Tovey to Douglas, 8 May 1944, National Archives AIR 15/401.
16. Bolitho, *Command Performance.*
17. Harrison, *Ops in a Wimpy.*
18. Wilson and Robinson, *Coastal Command Leads the Invasion.*
19. Ireland, *The Battle of the Atlantic.*
20. Douglas, *Years of Command.*
21. Terraine, *Business in Great Waters.*
22. Hendrie, *Short Sunderland.*
23. Bolitho, *A Penguin in the Eyrie.*
24. Bolitho, *Command Performance.*
25. *Coastal Command Review* (July 1944), National Archives AIR 15/472.
26. Hendrie, *Short Sunderland.*
27. John Appleton, private memoir, IWM document 1527.
28. Ibid.
29. *London Gazette,* 1 September 1944.
30. *Coastal Command Review* (August 1944), National Archives AIR 15/472.
31. Report in *The Times,* 17 August 1944.
32. Churchill to Douglas, 31 August 1944, National Archives AIR 20/3811.
33. Portal to Churchill, 7 August 1944, National Archives PREM 3/97/2.
34. Churchill, handwritten note, 7 August 1944, National Archives PREM 3/97/2.

Chapter 15: Victory

1. Goebeler, *Steel Boats and Iron Hearts.*
2. Greenhous et al., *The Crucible of War.*
3. Minutes of Anti-U-boat Warfare Committee, 7 September 1944, National Archives AIR 15/434.
4. Minutes of Anti-U-boat Warfare Committee, 11 January 1945, National Archives AIR 15/434.
5. Minutes of Anti-U-boat Warfare Committee, 8 February 1945, National Archives AIR 15/434.
6. Paper by Anti-U-boat Division, Admiralty, 11 September 1944, National Archives AIR 15/296.
7. Rohwer, 'A German Perspective', *Seek and Sink, Symposium on Battle of the Atlantic, October 1991.*
8. Bolitho, *Command Performance.*
9. Pitchfork, *Beaufighter Boys.*

10. Coastal Command paper, 14 November 1944, National Archives AIR 20/1320.
11. *Coastal Command Review* (December 1944), National Archives AIR 15/475.
12. Nesbit, *The Strike Wings.*
13. Figures from Ashworth, *Coastal Command 1936–1969.*
14. Goulter, 'The Role of Intelligence in Coastal Command's Anti-Shipping Campaign'.
15. Sanders, *Of Wind and Water.*
16. Dönitz, *Memoirs.*
17. Paper by Richard Raikes, 7 December 1944, National Archives AIR 15/55.
18. Douglas to Portal, 16 January 1945, Portal papers.
19. Admiralty memorandum, January 1945, AIR 2/8439.
20. Bergström, *The Ardennes.*
21. Minutes of Chiefs of Staff Meeting, 16 March 1945, National Archives CAB 79/30/17.
22. Douglas, *Years of Command.*
23. *Coastal Command Review* (May 1945), National Archives AIR 15/475
24. Pitchfork, *Beaufighter Boys.*
25. Ibid.
26. Douglas to Portal, 27 March 1945, Portal papers.
27. *Coastal Command Review* (May 1945), National Archives AIR 15/475.
28. Churchill, *The Second World War*, vol. 6, *Triumph and Tragedy.*
29. Douglas, *Years of Command.*
30. *Northern Whig*, 4 June 1945.
31. Speech by Harold Balfour, 19 June 1943, quoted in *Coastal Command Review* (July 1943).

Epilogue: Exodus

1. *Coastal Command Review* (June 1945), National Archives AIR 15/474.
2. Goulter, 'The Role of Intelligence in Coastal Command's Anti-Shipping Campaign'.
3. Nesbit, *The Strike Wings.*
4. *Coastal Command Review* (June 1945), National Archives AIR 15/474.
5. Figures from Hendrie, *The Cinderella Service.*
6. Macintyre, *The Battle of the Atlantic.*

7. Slessor, *The Central Blue*.
8. Roskill, *Churchill and the Admirals*.
9. Roskill, *The War at Sea*, vol. 2.
10. *Seek and Sink, Symposium on Battle of the Atlantic, October 1991*.
11. Ibid.
12. Ibid.
13. Report of conversation between Slessor and Philip Noel-Baker, 18 March 1947, National Archives AIR 19/554.
14. Slessor to Noel-Baker, 20 March 1947, National Archives AIR 75/17.
15. Evill to Churchill, 9 June 1945, National Archives AIR 15/303.

Bibliography

Books

The Air Ministry Account of the Part Played by Coastal Command in the Battle of the Seas, 1939–1945 (HMSO, 1943)

Ashworth, Chris, *RAF Coastal Command 1939–1969* (1992)

Baveystock, Leslie, *Wavetops at My Wingtips* (2001)

Baxter, Colin, *The Secret History of RDX* (2018)

Beevor, Antony, *The Second World War* (2012)

Bennett, John (ed.), *Hitchcock's Partner in Suspense: The Life of Screenwriter Charles Bennett* (2014)

Bergström, Christer, *The Ardennes 1944–1945: Hitler's Winter Offensive* (2014)

Bird, Andrew, *Heroes of Coastal Command: The RAF's Maritime War, 1939–1945* (2019)

——, *A Separate Little War* (2003)

Bishop, Patrick, *Wings: The RAF at War, 1912–2012* (2013)

Blair, Clay, *Hitler's U-boat War: The Hunters 1939–1942* (1996)

——, *Hitler's U-boat War: The Hunted 1942–1945* (1998)

Bodle, Peter, *Liberators in England in World War II*, Images of War series (2009)

Bolitho, Hector, *The Task for Coastal Command: The Story of the Battle of the South-West Approaches* (1944)

——, *Command Performance: The Coastal Command at War* (1946)

——, *A Penguin in the Eyrie: An RAF Diary, 1939–1945* (1955)

Bond, Brian (ed.), *Chief of Staff: The Diaries of Sir Henry Pownall* (2 vols, 1972–4)

Bowman, Martin, *Deep Sea Hunters: RAF Coastal Command and the War Against the U-boats and the German Navy, 1939–1945* (2020)

Bowyer, Chaz, *Coastal Command at War* (1979)

——, *Men of Coastal Command 1939–1945* (1985)

Broadhurst, Robin, *Churchill's Anchor: The Biography of Sir Dudley Pound* (2000)

Buckley, John, *RAF and Trade Defence 1919–1945* (1995)

Budiansky, Stephen, *Blackett's War: The Men Who Defeated the Nazi U-boats and Brought Science to the Art of Warfare* (2013)

Buell, Thomas, *Master of Seapower: A Biography of Fleet Admiral Ernest J. King* (2012)

Campbell, John, *RAF Coastal Command* (2013)

Campbell, Katharine, *Behold the Dark Gray Man* (2021)

Chisholm, Anne and Michael Davie, *Beaverbrook: A Life* (1992)

Churchill, Winston, *The Second World War* (6 vols, 1948–53)

Cole, Margaret, *Beatrice Webb's Diaries, 1924–1932* (1956)

Colman, Jack, *Liberators Over the Atlantic*, ed. Richard Colman (2017)

Cooper, Anthony, *Sub Hunters: Australian Sunderland Squadrons in the Defeat of Hitler's U-boat Menace, 1942–43* (2020)

Cowling, Ted, *The Journey: Per Ardua Ad Astra, Through Hardship to the Stars* (2005)

Dancey, Peter, *Coastal Command v. the U-boat: A Complete World War II Coastal Command Review* (2003)

Danchev, Alex and Daniel Todman (eds), *Alanbrooke: War Diaries 1939–1945* (2002)

Dimbleby, Jonathan, *The Battle of the Atlantic: How the Allies Won the War* (2015)

Dönitz, Karl, *Memoirs: Ten Years and Twenty Days* (1958)

Donnelly, Larry, *The Other Few: Bomber and Coastal Command Operations in the Battle of Britain* (2004)

Douglas, Sholto, *Years of Command* (1966)

Dudley-Gordon, Tom, *I Seek My Prey in the Waters: The Coastal Command at War* (1943)

Edwards, Bernard, *Dönitz and the Wolf Packs* (2020)

Faulkner, Marcus and Christopher Bell (eds), *Decision in the Atlantic: The Allies and the Longest Campaign of the Second World War – New Perspectives* (2019)

Franks, Norman, *Search, Find and Kill: Coastal Command's U-boat Successes in World War II* (1990)

——, *Conflict over the Bay* (1999)

Fraser, Donald, *Live to Look Again* (1984)

Gartner, Scott Sigmund, *Strategic Assessment in War* (1997)

Gibbs, Patrick, *Not Peace But a Sword* (1943)

——, *Torpedo Leader* (1992)

Gilbert, Martin, *Winston S. Churchill* (the official biography; 6 vols, 1971–88)

——, *The Churchill Documents*, vol. 15, *Never Surrender, May 1940–December 1940* (2011)

Goebeler, Hans, *Steel Boats and Iron Hearts: A U-boat Crewman's Life Aboard U-505* (2008)

Goulter, Christina, *A Forgotten Offensive: Royal Air Force Coastal Command's Anti-Shipping Campaign, 1940–1945* (1995)

Greenhous, Brereton, Stephen Harris, William Johnston and William Rawling, *The Crucible of War 1939–1945: The Official History of the Royal Canadian Air Force, Volume III* (1994)

Harrison, Graham, *Ops in a Wimpy: Memoirs of a Sub-Hunting Pilot* (2017)

Hendrie, Andrew, *The Cinderella Service: RAF Coastal Command 1939–1945* (2006)

——, *Short Sunderland: The 'Flying Porcupines' in the Second World War* (2012)

Hunter, Allan, *From Coastal Command to Captivity* (the war memoirs of Jim Hunter; 2003)

Ireland, Bernard, *The Battle of the Atlantic* (2003)

Jaworzyn, J. F., *No Place to Land: A Pilot in Coastal Command* (1984)

Joubert de la Ferté, Sir Philip, *The Fated Sky* (1952)

——, *Birds and Fishes: The Story of the Coastal Command* (1960)

Keegan, John, *The Second World War* (1989)

Kimball, Warren (ed.), *Churchill and Roosevelt: The Complete Correspondence* (3 vols, 2016)

Konarski, Mariusz, *304 Squadron* (2005)

Lardas, Mark, *The Battle of the Atlantic* (2 vols, 2020–1)

Lovell, Bernard, *Echoes of War: The Story of H2S Radar* (1991)

Macintyre, Donald, *The Battle of the Atlantic* (1961)

Macmillan, Harold, *War Diaries: The Mediterranean, 1943–1945* (1984)

McKinstry, Leo, *Lancaster: The Second World War's Greatest Bomber* (2009)

——, *Churchill and Attlee: Allies in War, Adversaries in Peace* (2019)

Nesbit, Roy Conyers, *Coastal Command in Action, 1939–1945* (2000)

——, *Ultra Versus the U-boats: Enigma Decrypts in The National Archives* (2008)

——, *The Strike Wings: Special Anti-Shipping Squadrons 1942–45* (2013)

——, *The Expendable Squadron: The Story of 217 Squadron Coastal Command, 1939–1945* (2014)

Nichols, Edward, *We Held the Key* (1996)

Orange, Vincent, *Ensor's Endeavour* (1994)

——, *Slessor: Bomber Champion* (2006)

Padfield, Peter, *Dönitz: The Last Führer* (1984)

Panton, Alastair, *Six Weeks of Blenheim Summer* (2018)

Pitchfork, Graham, *Beaufighter Boys: True Tales from those who Flew Bristol's Mighty Twin* (2019)

Polmar, Norman and John Bessette, *Spyplanes: The Illustrated Guide to Manned Reconnaisance and Surveillance Aircraft from World War I to Today* (2017)

Potter, John Deane, *Fiasco: The Breakout of the German Battleships* (1970)

Price, Alfred, *Aircraft versus Submarine: The Evolution of Anti-Submarine Aircraft, 1942–1945* (1973)

Probert, Henry, *Bomber Harris: His Life and Times* (2001)

Rayner, Denys, *Escort: The Battle of the Atlantic* (1955)

Rayner, Ted, *Coastal Command Pilot* (1994)

Richards, Denis, *Portal of Hungerford* (1978)

——, and Hilary St George Saunders, *The Royal Air Force 1939–1945* (3 vols, 1975)

Roberts, Andrew, *The Storm of War: A New History of the Second World War* (2009)

Roskill, Stephen, *The War at Sea, 1939–1945* (3 vols, 1956–61)

——, *Churchill and the Admirals* (1977)

Sanders, James, *Of Wind and Water: A Kiwi Pilot in Coastal Command* (1989)

Sebag-Montefiore, Hugh, *Enigma: The Battle for the Code* (2000)

Seek and Sink: Bracknell Paper No. 2, A Symposium on the Battle of the Atlantic, 21 October 1991 (RAF Historical Society, 1992)

Simons, Graham, *Consolidated B-24 Liberator* (2012)

Simpson, Geoff, *A Dictionary of Coastal Command, 1939–1945* (2016)

Slessor, Sir John, *The Central Blue* (1956)

Spooner, Tony, *Coastal Ace* (1986)

Stitt, Robert, *Boeing B17 Fortress in RAF Coastal Command Service* (2019)

Suhren, Teddy, *Ace of Aces: Memoirs of a U-boat Rebel* (2006)

Terraine, John, *The Right of the Line: The Royal Air Force, 1939–1945* (1985)

——, *Business in Great Waters: The U-boat Wars, 1916–1945* (1989)

van der Vat, Dan, *The Atlantic Campaign: The Great Struggle at Sea 1939–1945* (1988)

Williams, Charles, *Max Beaverbrook* (2019)

Wilson, Keith, *RAF Coastal Command: A Pictorial History* (2020)

Wilson, Michael and A. S. L. Robinson, *Coastal Command Leads the Invasion* (1945)

Articles

Barnett, Corelli, 'Engage the Enemy More Closely' (*RUSI Journal*, 1991)

Buckley, John 'Atlantic Airpower Co-operation, 1941–1943' (*Journal of Strategic Studies*, 1995)

——, 'Coastal Command in the Second World War' (*Air Power Review*, 2018)

Byford, Alastair, 'Executive Fuller' (*Journal of the RAF Historical Society*, 2011)

Gardner, Jock, 'The Battle of the Atlantic, 1941 – The First Turning Point?' (*Journal of Strategic Studies*, 1994)

Goulter, Christina, 'The Role of Intelligence in Coastal Command's Anti-Shipping Campaign 1940–45 (*Intelligence and National Security*, 1990)

Greswell, Air Commodore Jeffrey, 'Leigh Light Wellingtons of Coastal Command' (*RUSI Journal*, 1995)

Hendrie, Andrew, 'A Converted Airliner at War: The Lockheed Hudson Aircraft as Operated by Coastal Command, RAF' (*Aerospace Historian*, December 1984)

McGowan, Joe, 'The Donegal Corridor' (*History Ireland*, Summer 2003)

Milner, Marc, 'The Dawn of Anti-Submarine Warfare: Allied Responses to the U-boats, 1944–45' (*RUSI Journal*, 1989)

——, 'The Battle of the Atlantic' (*Journal of Strategic Studies*, 1990)

Pattenden, Hugh, 'Forgotten Memoirs: The Second World War as Remembered by the Aircrews of Coastal Command' (*Mariner's Mirror*, 2020)

Redford, Duncan, 'The March 1943 Crisis in the Battle of the Atlantic: Myth and Reality' (*History*, January 2007)

——, 'Inter- and Intra-Service Rivalries in the Battle of the Atlantic' (*Journal of Strategic Studies*, December 2009)

Schuster, Carl O., 'Aerial Minesweeping: Ingenious Solution to a Hidden Undersea Menace' (*Aviation History*, May 2021)

Terraine, John, 'Atlantic Victory: 50 Years On' (*RUSI Journal*, 1993)

Index

Index